DAILY LIFE IN

THE HELLENISTIC AGE

D0146897

DAILY LIFE IN

THE HELLENISTIC AGE

From Alexander to Cleopatra

JAMES ALLAN EVANS

The Greenwood Press "Daily Life through History" Series

GREENWOOD PRESS
Westport, Connecticut • London

To the memory of C. Bradford Welles.

Library of Congress Cataloging-in-Publication Data

Evans, J. A. S. (James Allan Stewart), 1931–
    Daily life in the Hellenistic Age : from Alexander
to Cleopatra / James Allan Evans.
            p. cm. — ("Daily life through history" series, ISSN 1080–4749)
    Includes bibliographical references and index.
    ISBN 978–0–313–33812–0 (alk. paper)
    1. Mediterranean Region—Social life and customs.   2. Greece—Social
life and customs.   3. Hellenism.   I. Title.
    DE71.E98 2008
    938'.08—dc22   2008001138

British Library Cataloguing in Publication Data is available.

Library of Congress Catalog Card Number: 2008001138
ISBN: 978–0–313–33812–0
ISSN: 1080–4749

First published in 2008

Greenwood Press, 88 Post Road West, Westport, CT 06881
An imprint of Greenwood Publishing Group, Inc.
www.greenwood.com

Printed in the United States of America

The paper used in this book complies with the
Permanent Paper Standard issued by the National
Information Standards Organization (Z39.48–1984).

10   9   8   7   6   5   4   3   2   1

Contents

An unnumbered photo essay follows page 74.

Introduction: The Conquests of Alexander

In the years 1977 and 1978, the Greek archaeologist Manolis Andronikos excavated a great tumulus in northern Greece at Vergina, ancient Aegae, which served as the capital of the Macedonian kingdom until late in the fifth century B.C.E., when a Macedonian king moved his court to Pella, closer to the sea. There Andronikos uncovered four tombs dating to the late fourth and early third centuries. Two were intact, and in one of them, Tomb II, were found the remains of a man and a woman, whom Andronikos identified as Philip II, king of Macedon and father of Alexander the Great, and his new wife Cleopatra. Philip was assassinated in 336 B.C.E., and in the aftermath of the murder Cleopatra was killed by Philip's chief wife, Olympias, for the Macedonian kings were polygamous. Tomb III held the remains of a teenager, buried with a rich collection of offerings, including fine silver vessels. The identification of the remains in Tomb II may be doubted, but we can be sure about the identity of the youth buried in Tomb III. He was Alexander IV, the son of Alexander the Great and his Iranian wife, Roxane, born after his father's death and murdered at the age of 12. He was the last member of the Argeads, the ancient royal house of Macedon, which died out with him. Alexander the Great's conquests were divided among his generals, and each took the title of king once Alexander IV

All dates are B.C.E. unless otherwise noted.

had been eliminated, ruling from capitals such as Antioch in Syria, Alexandria in Egypt, and Pella in Macedon, They did not let Alexander's little son stand in their way.

Alexander the Great, who became king in 336 and died not quite 13 years later, changed the political landscape of the whole eastern Mediterranean world. The Greeks had always called themselves "Hellenes"—*Graeci*, from which we derive the word *Greek*, is a label that the Romans gave them—and the word *hellenizein* meant "to speak Greek," and along with the Greek language, to adapt to the norms of Greek civilization. In the centuries following Alexander, large numbers of non-Greeks in what are now Syria, Turkey, Palestine, Israel, Egypt, Iraq, and Iran *hellenized*, that is, they adopted the Greek language and to some extent the Greek way of life. Modern historians of the ancient world have invented the label "Hellenistic" for this multicultural Greek society, which saw recognizably Greek cities founded all over Asia Minor and the Middle East; in these cities, Greek culture flourished. Touring companies of Greek actors and musicians brought the latest dramas to the city theaters. Urban youths went to Greek gymnasiums for their education. But the majority of the people lived in the countryside, worked the soil and spoke their native languages, and for many in the Middle East and much of Asia Minor, life went on much as it had before Alexander the Great's conquering armies arrived.

In the west, from the third century, the power of Rome was increasing. By the first half of the first century, Rome was supreme in the western Mediterranean. The last surviving Hellenistic kingdom was Egypt, where Cleopatra VII continued to rule until the year 30. The Roman republic had collapsed into civil war, and the Mediterranean world was divided between Julius Caesar's heir and adopted son, who held the west, and Mark Antony, who held the east. Cleopatra cast her lot with Mark Antony—she had little choice—and when Antony lost, she killed herself with a snakebite, and Egypt became a possession of the Roman empire. Daily life in the Hellenistic east went on much as before, except that now Rome did the governing, but the year 30 is the accepted date for the end of the Hellenistic age. For its beginning, most historians give the date 323, when Alexander the Great died in Babylon, not yet 33 years old. However, the great nineteenth-century British historian of the ancient world, George Grote, dated its beginning to 334, when Alexander began his conquest of the Persian empire. For the purposes of this book, exact dates for the beginning and end of the Hellenistic age have limited relevance, for much as Alexander changed the political and economic landscape, no great revolution in everyday life affected the common man either when the Hellenistic age began or when it ended.

THE BACKGROUND

Alexander the Great's father, Philip II, took over a disunited and defeated kingdom in the year 360. His brother, Perdiccas III, had died in battle with the Illyrians, Macedon's bitter enemies on her western border, and since Perdiccas's son Amyntas was still a young boy, Philip took over as king. It was a peaceful succession; Amyntas suffered no harm. But the kingdom was beset by enemies: to the west there were the fierce Illyrians, to the north, another hostile Balkan tribe, the Paeonians, and there were pretenders to the throne who had to be dealt with. Philip began by reforming the Macedonian army, and along with his army reforms, he stimulated social and economic development. Macedonian shepherds and herdsmen were encouraged to become farmers and build their homes in cities. Philip acquired seven wives in all, for polygamy was an accepted custom in Macedon and marriage was a diplomatic weapon. One wedding, to an Illyrian princess, brought him a brief peace with the Illyrian kingdom. Another wife, from his southern neighbor, Thessaly, bore him a mentally challenged son named Arrhidaeus, and in 357 he marked an alliance with the Molossian kingdom on his western border by marrying a Molossian princess, Olympias, who bore him Alexander a year later. Philip was soon strong enough to defeat the Paeonians and then the Illyrians, and by 357 he was expanding into areas of northern Greece that Athens considered within her sphere of influence.

Athens had been the overlord of an empire stretching over the Aegean Sea in the fifth century, and the tribute from this empire had allowed it to maintain the most powerful navy in the Greek world. It had lost it all in a war with Sparta that lasted from 431 to 404, with one short break. But it was still the cultural center of Greece, and long after it was no longer a military power, Athens continued to set the tone of Greek civilization. In the years after its devastating defeat in 404, Athens recovered; democracy was restored at home, and soon it was strong enough to revive its fleet and become the chief naval power in the Aegean Sea once again. Philip was watched with apprehension, however, and in late summer of 348, Athens's interests suffered a major blow: Philip captured the city of Olynthus in northern Greece before an expedition from Athens could arrive to help, enslaving the inhabitants and destroying the city. It was a tragedy that has added to our knowledge of domestic life in the contemporary city, for the remains of Olynthus have provided archaeologists with a Greek community that came to an end at a precise date, just as the age of Alexander was about to begin. None of the houses found at Olynthus are later than its destruction in 348, and they furnish a mute record of city life in northern Greece at a precise point in time, just before the conventional date of the start of the Hellenistic age.

Two years later, in early August 346, Philip's fortune reached its high point. He defeated a citizen army from Athens and Thebes at Chaeronea. Philip commanded the right wing of his battle line while his 18-year-old son Alexander commanded the left. The Macedonian victory was complete. In the winter following the victory at Chaeronea, Philip convened a meeting of the Greek states at Corinth and imposed on them a common peace treaty, thus creating the League of Corinth, as modern scholars call it—what Philip called it, we do not know. The members swore allegiance to Macedon and pledged never to overthrow the monarchy of Philip or his descendants. Then the League resolved on a war of revenge against the Persian empire, which had a long history of hostility with the Greek city-states since their first encounter 200 years earlier. In 480, Persia had invaded Greece, and it was this attack that the League proposed to avenge.

THE PERSIAN EMPIRE

The Persian empire, centered in modern Iran, was founded by Cyrus the Great of the Achaemenid royal house in 550, and at its height stretched from India in the east to Egypt in the west. In 546, Persia captured the Lydian empire, which ruled all Asia Minor east of the Halys River (modern Kizlirimak River in Turkey), and once Lydia fell, the Greek cities along the coastline of Asia Minor that had been subject to Lydia found themselves with a new master, the Persian king. His empire spread west into the Dodecanese Islands, and across the Dardanelles into Thrace in present-day northern Greece and Bulgaria. Then, at the start of the fifth century, the Greek cities under Persian rule revolted. These cities were Ionian, Dorian, or Aeolian, depending upon what dialect of Greek they spoke, but the leaders of the uprising were Ionian, and so the rebellion is known as the Ionian Revolt. The rebel cities asked mainland Greece for help, and Athens sent a small naval force of 20 warships, which helped them in the first year of the revolt, but then withdrew. The little city of Eretria on the island of Euboea followed the example of Athens. Persia took note, and planned retaliation.

In 490, Darius I, king of Persia, sent an expeditionary force against Eretria and Athens. Eretria fell and its chief citizens were deported, but the Athenians met the Persian army on the plain of Marathon and trounced it thoroughly. It was a blow to Persian prestige that the Persians could not overlook. Ten years later, a vast Persian army and navy, led in person by Darius's son and successor, Xerxes, invaded Greece, but at the island of Salamis the united Greek fleet defeated the Persian navy within eyeshot of Athens; without control of the sea, Xerxes's situation became too precarious for him to maintain. He and some of his troops retreated to Asia, leaving behind a smaller but effective army to winter in northern Greece and consolidate Persia's conquests the next year. But the Greeks, led by Sparta, annihilated it at the Battle of Plataea. It was this invasion by Xerxes that Philip planned to avenge.

The real reason for the war of revenge, however, was that the Persian empire in the fourth century showed every sign of weakness. Its provinces, or satrapies as they were called, in Asia Minor were in revolt in the 360s, and Egypt threw off the Persian yoke at the start of the fourth century B.C.E. But all that changed when a vigorous new king, Artaxerxes Ochus, took over in 358, brought the satrapies under control, and recovered Egypt. Had Ochus lived, Alexander the Great might have found it a more difficult task to overthrow the Persian empire. But about the same time that Philip won the battle of Chaeronea, Ochus was assassinated by his grand vizier, Bagoas, who chose Ochus's youngest son, Arses, to succeed his father, and then killed him too after a brief reign, when he became too independent for the vizier's liking. Arses's murder ended the direct line of the Achaemenid royal house of Persia, and Bagoas's next choice, Codoman, belonged to a collateral line. He took the name Darius III, which recalled Persia's great king, Darius I, the monarch who had dispatched the army to Greece that was defeated at the Battle of Marathon in 490. Darius III was no puppet, as Bagoas soon discovered, for the vizier was quickly eliminated and Darius took firm control. By that time, Philip of Macedon's invasion of Persia had already begun; early in 336, his general Parmenio crossed the Hellespont and was taking the cities along the Aegean coast. Then, in June, Philip was assassinated, and his young son Alexander grasped his father's throne with a ruthless grip.

PHILIP'S DEATH AND ALEXANDER'S ACCESSION

The year before, in 337, Philip had divorced Alexander's mother, Olympias, charging her with adultery, and had taken another wife— Cleopatra, the niece of one of Philip's generals, Attalus. Alexander could no longer be certain that he was his father's heir—not if Philip's new wife produced a son, which may have been what some of Philip's most powerful generals, and even Philip himself, wished for. No one expected Philip to die soon. At his wedding ceremony to Cleopatra, where wine flowed freely, Attalus, who was too inebriated to be discreet, offered a prayer for a legitimate heir to the Macedonian throne, and Alexander reacted by emptying his goblet in Attalus's face. Philip, more drunk than either of them, drew his sword and made to attack Alexander, but instead stumbled and fell. "There," said Alexander with contempt, pointing to Philip lying prone on the floor, "is the man who would conquer Asia, and he cannot walk from one couch to the next." By morning, Alexander and his mother Olympias had fled to Molossis, where Olympias's brother was king.

The rift between father and son did not last. Philip's new wife produced a girl, not a son to succeed him. Philip needed Alexander as an ally, not plotting against him. A mutual friend served as a go-between and Alexander returned to court, though Olympias was left in exile. When Philip learned that Olympias was pushing her brother to declare war in Macedon, he countered by offering him his daughter Cleopatra as his wife.

The wedding was held at Aegae, modern Vergina in northern Greece. On the second day of the celebrations, Philip entered the theater in a solemn procession. Before him were carried images not only of the 12 gods of Olympus, but of a 13th as well, that of Philip himself, costumed like a god. Beside him on one side was his son, Alexander, and on the other, the bridegroom, whose name was also Alexander. As Philip paused at the theater entrance, a bodyguard leaped forward and thrust his sword into Philip's side, killing him instantly. The assassin held a grudge against Philip, but was that motive enough for an assassination? Was he acting for someone else? Olympias made no effort to conceal her satisfaction at Philip's death. And what of Alexander? Some Macedonians were suspicious, but no one wanted to investigate Alexander's complicity too closely, for once Philip's body was removed from the theater, Philip's senior general, Antipater, presented Alexander to the Macedonian army, which hailed him as king. Alexander was not yet 20 years old; by the time he died in 323, at age 32, he would have changed the face of the Greek world.

He moved swiftly. Philip's new wife Cleopatra and her infant daughter were killed. Then he marched south to receive the allegiance of Greece, and at Corinth, the League of Corinth elected him to lead the war of revenge against Persia in his father's place. Then he dealt with hostile neighbors in Thrace and Illyria to the north. But a false rumor that he had been killed in Illyria was enough to arouse Greece, and the city of Thebes broke into open insurrection. Thebes had her supporters in Athens, notably the greatest orator of the day, Demosthenes, but the city was not yet in open revolt when Alexander arrived outside Thebes, captured it, and made an example of it. The city was destroyed, except for one house that had belonged to Thebes's one great author, the poet Pindar, who had lived a century and a half earlier. Alexander had been carefully educated and gave literature its due; among his teachers had been the philosopher Aristotle and it was said that when Alexander set out on his campaign, he took with him a copy of Homer's *Iliad*, annotated by Aristotle.

The Greek world that Alexander was leaving for the east was a world of *poleis*, (singular *polis*), a word we translate rather inadequately as "city-states." A *polis* was a small unit made up of an urban center, which the Greeks called the *asty*, surrounded by the *chôra*, the countryside, where there were woodlands that provided fuel, pastures where livestock grazed, orchards and arable land where farmers grew grain for the city's bakeries and vegetables and fruit for its market. There were city-states in the Greek homeland, the coastal regions of modern Turkey, and along the shore of the Black Sea, particularly in the Crimean area. In the west, there were important city-states in Libya, Sicily, and southern Italy as far north as Naples, which had been founded as a Greek colony. *Poleis* were independent political units, or at least they sought to be independent, and the cultural, religious, and political life of Greece revolved around them. Now Alexander was poised to invade an empire that stretched across ancient civilizations, but the settlement patterns were unfamiliar, and the Greeks and Macedonians would encounter gods that were unknown to them. Alexander would precipitate a meeting between two ways of life that the Hellenistic world that followed him would have to deal with.

ALEXANDER'S CONQUESTS

In the spring of 334, Alexander crossed the Dardanelles to Asia without the Persian fleet making any attempt to intercept him. His first act was to go to Ilium, which claimed to be on the site of Troy (it was not) and possessed some relics of the Trojan War—bogus, no doubt, but for Alexander's purposes, that did not matter. He sacrificed at the so-called tombs of the heroes Achilles and Ajax, and exchanged his own shield and panoply for what purported to be the armor of Achilles, which was kept in the temple of Athena at Ilium. He wore it in his first encounter with the Persians, who had mustered at the Granicus River, now the *Koçabas*. It was a hard-fought battle where Alexander was almost killed, but his victory was complete, and Darius learned that Alexander was an enemy whom he could not take lightly.

Yet in this first battle, Alexander displayed the qualities that were to mark his leadership for the rest of his short career. He displayed his courage by exposing himself recklessly to danger. One of Philip's two most trusted generals, Parmenio, was Alexander's second in command, and he frequently advised prudence, but Alexander would have none of it. He had set out on his campaign against Persia with a weak navy and few resources compared with his enemy; one defeat would have stopped him. But he took the gamble without hesitation. When he set out, he placed Macedon and Greece in charge of Philip's other most trusted general, Antipater, but he made no arrangement for a successor in case he should die. He disregarded advice that he marry first and beget an heir before he began his campaign. For two generations after his death, the Hellenistic world would pay a bitter price for his irresponsibility.

Darius himself commanded the Persian army at the next encounter, at Issus, some 15 miles (24.14 km) north of modern Alexandretta in the northeast corner of the Mediterranean, where Darius maneuvered Alexander into a battle on a narrow plain between the mountains and the sea. Darius showed himself an able tactician, but the battle was decided by Alexander's charge against the center of the Persian line, where Darius had positioned himself, and when he saw Alexander's Companion cavalry, his elite squadron of mounted troops led by Alexander himself, converging upon him, cutting through his bodyguards, he turned and fled. Alexander captured his treasure chest, as well as the royal household he had brought with him. Alexander now had more wealth than he had ever had in his life.

He continued down along the eastern Mediterranean coast to Egypt, where he founded the first of many cities he would create—Alexandria—which would become one of the great commercial ports of the Hellenistic world and a center of Greek science and literature. Darius, meanwhile, collected a second army, and on

October 1, 331, Alexander met him on the plain of Gaugamela, near modern Mosul in Iraq. Once again Alexander led a charge of his Companions against the Persian center, and once again Darius fled from the battlefield. His flight decided the battle. His Persian subjects began to lose faith in him. When Alexander moved south against the great city of Babylon after his victory, the Persian satrap (governor) of Babylonia, Mazaeus, who had fought bravely for Darius at Gaugamela, came out of the city and surrendered to Alexander, who then reappointed him to his old satrapy, but now as a satrap owing allegiance to Alexander. Mazaeus did not have the full powers of a Persian satrap, for he had to share the rule with two Macedonians, one the commander of the military garrison and the other in charge of collecting the tribute. Yet his appointment demonstrated to the Persian nobility that, if they joined Alexander, they would be accepted and could expect rewards.

From Babylon, Alexander continued to Susa, near the border of modern Iraq and Iran, where the Persian court used to retire in the summer to escape the searing heat of Babylon. The satrap there was a Persian noble named Abulites, who surrendered without a fight. In the royal palace at Susa, the Persian kings had amassed a vast amount of gold and silver bullion, as well as gold coins minted to pay their Greek mercenaries. The luxury of the Persian kings astounded the Macedonians, and Alexander and his Companions began to develop a taste for it themselves. But there was still a war to be fought, and Darius was trying to recruit another army to fight again.

In early 330, Alexander, having reappointed Abulites as satrap at Susa, set out for Persepolis, the ceremonial capital of the Persian empire where the Great King's subjects brought their tribute each year. Persepolis had even more treasure than Susa, and added to it was the treasure from Pasargadae nearby, where the tomb of Cyrus, the founder of the Persian empire, is still to be seen. A train of 7,000 camels and other pack animals set out for Susa with the bulk of it. Then Alexander turned Persepolis over to his men to loot and rape as much as they wished, and the great palace itself was set afire; a recent inspection of the remains leaves little doubt that the fire was set deliberately. Ancient warfare was a brutal affair, and Alexander followed a policy of ruthless brutality mingled with occasional acts of humanity and clemency. But when spring arrived, he was ready to leave in pursuit of Darius, who was at Ecbatana (Hamadan) trying to raise another army.

Darius's call for recruits fell on deaf ears. His satraps looked on him as a loser, and before Alexander could reach Ecbatana he learned from deserters that Darius had fled eastwards into Afghanistan. Alexander changed his plans. Part of his army, under Parmenio, now 70 years old, went on to Ecbatana with the treasure taken from Persepolis, while Alexander with the rest set out in hot pursuit of Darius. He caught up with him in Hyrcania, south of the Caspian Sea, but Darius was already dead when Alexander found him, stabbed by the treacherous satraps who accompanied him and then left him alone to die. Alexander had his corpse buried at Persepolis with the pomp and circumstance that befitted a king, and proclaimed himself Darius's successor and avenger. The soldiers from the League of Corinth were discharged with a donative; those who chose to stay also got a bonus. The war to avenge the Persian invasion of Greece in 480, which the League of Corinth had authorized, was complete.

THE CONSTRUCTION OF AN EMPIRE

But if the soldiers of the League of Corinth could go home, why not Alexander's Macedonians too? At Hecatompylus (modern Qummis), where Alexander paused to regroup, he had to face an outbreak of discontent among his troops. He had to persuade them that they had a new objective to pursue. They had to maintain and expand the empire that they had acquired, and Alexander played down the difficulties. He let his troops believe that the task would soon be over, and perhaps he believed it himself. In fact, a new task had begun, and the end was not near.

Alexander was now in new, unfamiliar territory, where there were no cities of the sort that the Greeks knew. In Egypt, he had already founded one—Alexandria, named after himself—and in 330 he founded a second Alexandria, modern Herat, in the Persian satrapy of Areia. He would found more Alexandrias, probably about 20 of them, stretching as far east as modern Tajikistan, where he founded Alexandria *Eschaté* (the "Farthest Distant"), on the site of modern Khudjand. These cities, not much more than garrison posts to begin with, were settled with mercenary soldiers, but many of them grew into recognizably Greek cities, which, as the years passed, would spread Greek culture into the remote corners of the old Persian empire. They signaled that Alexander's conquests would be permanent.

There would be a reaction. At first, Alexander had not encountered grassroots resistance, but that changed as he advanced into northern Iran and Afghanistan. He discovered insurgency at his rear. Persian nobles whom he had assimilated into his service rose in revolt, and Alexander dealt with them swiftly and ruthlessly. At the same time, he took care to present himself as Darius's legitimate successor. He entrusted the punishment of Darius's murderer to the Persians whom he had brought into his army in an obvious ploy to win their allegiance, He began to dress himself like a Persian noble, to the dismay of his Macedonian officers and troops. Costume was a mark of nationality, and for Alexander to abandon Macedonian dress was to abandon part of his Macedonian heritage.

It took two years of hard campaigning to quell the insurgency in the northern provinces of Bactria and Sogdiana, the first of which occupied the fertile plain south of the Oxus River, the modern Amu Darya, which flows into the Aral Sea, while Sogdiana was located between the Oxus and the other great river flowing into the Aral Sea, the Jaxartes, the modern Syr Darya. It may have been an effort to win native support in Bactria that led Alexander to marry Roxane, the daughter of a Bactrian chieftain, in early 327. India was to be Alexander's next objective, and the last thing he wanted was for insurgency to erupt again at his rear. Roxane was beautiful, and Alexander married for love as well as political calculation, but in addition, her father Oxyartes was a formidable tribal leader, and the marriage brought over the rebel Bactrian leaders to his side. Roxane was pregnant when Alexander died and her son Alexander IV was the last member of the Macedonian royal house.

In the same year, Alexander invaded India. There, in 326, he fought his last great battle, on the Jhelum River, against an Indian rajah whom the Greeks called Porus, whose army included 120 war elephants. Alexander outmaneuvered Porus and defeated him, taking him prisoner, but it was a hard-fought battle, and after it was over, Alexander restored Porus to his kingdom. The Persians had preferred to rule in this area through native rajahs, and Alexander followed the Persian custom. He himself wanted to push on. He had heard of a fabulous kingdom in the Ganges River basin and he wanted to journey there, more so as an explorer than as a conqueror. But his troops had had enough. On the banks of the Beas River, which the Greeks called the Hyphasis, they mutinied, and Alexander was forced to return.

There was still hard fighting ahead as Alexander's army moved down the Indus River. At one point, Alexander himself led a reckless charge against the citadel of the Malli, a warlike tribe in the lower Punjab, and almost lost his life. For the return journey, he divided his forces. He ordered one of his generals, Craterus, to lead part of his army back through Afghanistan and meet Alexander in Carmania, north of the Gulf of Hormuz. His fleet, which he had built on the Jhelum River, was ordered to sail to the Persian Gulf, hugging the coast, and while along the shoreline, Alexander himself was to lead the land army that would provision the fleet. But the plan was a failure. The fleet was delayed by the monsoons and Alexander found that the route along the coastline was so difficult that he had to abandon it. He had to leave the fleet to fend for itself, and he himself led his troops on a terrible march through the Gedrosian Desert, which the women and children, the sick, and the wounded in his train did not survive. The fleet's ordeal was equally grueling; nevertheless, it reached the Persian Gulf with the loss of only two men.

In late March, 324, Alexander reached Susa, the old summer capital of the Persian kings, which he had left six years before. While there, he made a move that indicated dramatically how he planned to administer the vast empire that he had conquered. He ordered a mass marriage. Ninety-one of his general staff and courtiers, and 10,000 of his troops, were married to Asian women. He himself took two new wives from the old Persian royal house: one was the daughter of the last king, Darius III, the other the daughter of Darius's predecessor, Artaxerxes III. He seems to have planned to breed a new ruling elite by mingling the genes of Asians, Macedonians, and Greeks. But Alexander's Macedonians were decidedly unenthusiastic about their king's orientalist sympathies; the past Macedonian kings they had known had been first among equals, not oriental despots. Their simmering discontent boiled over when the army reached Opis, where the Persian Royal Road crossed the Tigris River on the way from Susa to Babylon. After Alexander's death, the great Hellenistic city of Seleucia-on-Tigris would be founded there, on the opposite bank of the river. At Opis, a large contingent of young Persians, whom Alexander had sent to Macedon to be trained to fight in the Macedonian manner, joined the army, and Alexander's troops welcomed them with apprehension and disgust. Then when Alexander called an assembly and announced that his over-age and unfit soldiers were to be honorably discharged, the discontent broke into the open. Alexander faced a mutiny, and his immediate reaction was ruthless. He ordered his guard to seize 13 of the mutiny's leaders and execute them on the spot, but his troops remained unmoved. Alexander waited two days for them to relent; then he began to put a pro-Persian program, which they feared, into action. He began to replace his Macedonians with Persians.

The troops were aghast. They gathered in front of his palace to beg forgiveness, and wept for joy when Alexander forgave them. Then Alexander held a great banquet of reconciliation, to which some 9,000 Macedonians and Persians were invited, and at the banquet, Alexander stood and prayed for a harmonious partnership between Macedonians and Persians as rulers of Asia. There could be little doubt now what his future policy would be.

In early 323, Alexander reached Babylon. He was planning an expedition against Arabia, which had grown rich on the spice trade, and no one, perhaps not even Alexander himself, knew what his ultimate destination might have been. But he took sick after a drinking party virtually on the eve of his departure, and on June 10, 323, he died. It was malaria, perhaps, or acute pancreatitis brought on by excessive drinking, but we cannot diagnose Alexander's last illness. But his short life of 32 years and 8 months had changed the whole Mediterranean world.

What did he achieve? He had conquered a vast empire stretching from Egypt to Afghanistan and India, but there would be no ruling elite based on a Macedonian-Persian alliance, cemented by inter-marriage. Only one of the marriages between Alexander's generals and Asian women survived as far as we know. Seleucus Nicator, founder of the Seleucid royal family, remained faithful to his Bactrian wife, Apame, and the DNA of his dynasty had contributions from Macedon and Bactria. But by and large, a racial divide separated the Greeks and Macedonians from the Asians whom Alexander had conquered. As for Alexander's empire, it was left leaderless. Alexander had a half-brother, Arrhidaeus, who was mentally challenged, and Roxane, who was pregnant when Alexander died, gave birth to a son after his death. But both were only pawns in the struggles that followed Alexander's death, though both were given royal burials at Vergina, the ancient Macedonian capital of Aegae. Alexander's conquests were torn apart by warlords, each determined to carve out a kingdom for themselves.

Yet Alexander had broadened the world of ancient Greece. Before his conquests, Greek cities were to be found only in the Mediterranean and Black Sea regions. They included cities in Sicily, where Syracuse outmatched most cities in Greece itself, and southern France, where modern Marseilles has a Greek foundation. But Alexander thrust Greek power eastward into Asia. He founded cities named Alexandria in Iran, Afghanistan, and India, and many of them survived as outposts of Greek culture. He liberated the vast wealth accumulated by the Persian kings, who had been storing it in their royal treasuries, and put it into circulation—one modern scholar[1] has put the purchasing power of the Persian treasure at US$285 billion (the calculation was made in 1978)— resulting in rapid inflation followed by deflation in the mid-third century. In Egypt and Mesopotamia he introduced a monetary economy where it had not existed before, and along with it the Greek banking system, which was still rudimentary by present-day standards, but which meant that the economy of the ancient world expanded beyond anything that classical Greece had known. The cities of the Hellenistic age that Alexander created could afford temples and public buildings that were far more opulent than anything we find in the cities of classical Greece. Greek culture flowered as it had never done before, and though there was no immediate revolution in Greek everyday life, Greece moved into a new age with broader horizons than it had ever known before. Many of the old city-states of Greece continued to thrive—Athens lost its dominance of the seas after a naval defeat in the year following Alexander's death, but it remained a great cultural center, and Rhodes became an important trading and naval power—but it was the Hellenistic kingdoms, ruled by hereditary monarchies wielding absolute power, that dominated the history of the period. These monarchies were a new political development: Greece had known kings before, but not like these great monarchs, who minted coins bearing their royal portraits and ruled with the pomp and circumstance that was once the reserve of gods.

THE HELLENISTIC KINGDOMS

The half century after Alexander's death was filled with struggles among Alexander's ambitious generals, who fought for their shares of Alexander's conquests. Alexander's posthumous son, Alexander IV, was not allowed to reach adolescence, and with his murder any pretence of unity among the successors evaporated. Eventually three major kingdoms emerged. One was the Ptolemaic kingdom in Egypt, founded by Ptolemy, the son of Lagos, one of Alexander's generals, whose memoirs are one of our best sources about Alexander's career; though the memoirs themselves failed to survive, they were used by later authors, notably Flavius Arrianus, dating to the mid-second century C.E., whose history has survived and can still be read. Unlike some of Alexander's other generals, Ptolemy did not yield to any overblown ambitions after Alexander's death. He simply took the governorship of Egypt, where he made Alexandria his capital, and the dynasty he founded lasted until its last monarch, Cleopatra VII, lost the kingdom to Rome. In the civil war that followed the assassination of Julius Caesar in 44, she had supported the losing side and paid for it with her life.

The kingdom that made the best attempt to carry on Alexander's legacy was the Seleucid monarchy, founded by Seleucus Nicator, "the Victor." At its height, the Seleucid kingdom, with a western capital at Antioch on the Orontes River in Syria, and an eastern capital at Seleucia-on-the-Tigris, stretched from Iran to Asia Minor. The Seleucid kings, like Alexander himself, were founders of cities that were centers of Greek culture and spread the Greek way of life over the Middle East, where the native populations were both attracted and repelled by it.

Macedonia itself, the kingdom of Philip and Alexander, went through a difficult period in the years following Alexander's death. When Alexander left on his career of conquest, he left Macedonia under the charge of one of his father's most trusted generals, Antipater, and after Antipater's death, his son, Cassander, made a bid for power in the Greek peninsula. It was Cassander who killed Alexander's son, Alexander IV. But it was not Cassander who founded the line of kings that would rule Hellenistic Macedonia. Instead it was a general named Antigonos Gonatas, whose grandfather, Antigonos the One-Eyed, was a warlord who at one time looked most likely to succeed as the heir of Alexander's world empire. But he was defeated before a coalition of enemies, chief of them Seleucus I, who had acquired a regiment of war elephants from India and learned to use them efficiently. Antigonos's son, Demetrius the Besieger, was a brilliant but unstable military leader, and he would eventually drink himself to death in one of Seleucus's prisons. But his son, Antigonos Gonatas, who inherited from his father only a fleet and a few strongholds in Greece, managed to defeat an incursion of Gauls into Greece; the wild Celtic tribesmen who invaded the Balkan peninsula terrified the Greeks, and the Macedonians gratefully accepted Antigonos as king. He brought them peace, and the Macedonians transferred the loyalty they had once felt for the Argeads, the old royal house to which Philip and Alexander belonged, to a new royal dynasty descended from Antigonos.

The pillar of the Macedonian kingdom was the Macedonian conscript army, made up of many small landholders who remained loyal to the traditions of Philip and Alexander the Great. As time went on, the Macedonian kings hired large numbers of mercenary soldiers; they had the wherewithal to pay for them, for they were the largest property owners in the kingdom, and their holdings included mines, as well as forests that exported timber and pitch for shipbuilding. In peacetime, the mercenaries were used mostly as garrison troops in Greece. Unlike the other Hellenistic kingdoms, Macedonia presented two faces to the world: within her borders, she was a national monarchy with a rural aristocracy that still played a major role in the administration—there were no self-governing cities in Macedonia—but beyond her borders, her neighbors knew her as an imperial power that tried to dominate Greece. Her rule was maintained by force, and the Greeks never accepted it willingly.

There was a fourth, much smaller, Hellenistic kingdom, Pergamon, which was founded not by one of Alexander the Great's immediate successors, but by the trusted treasurer of one of them, Lysimachus. Lysimachus was one of the first generation of warlords who fought for a share of Alexander's conquests, and Pergamon, situated high on the Pindasus mountain range in northwest Asia Minor, was a secure stronghold where Lysimachus deposited his personal wealth under the watchful eye of a faithful vassal, a eunuch named Philetaerus. Philetaerus ran afoul of Lysimachus's wife, Arsinoe, the daughter of Ptolemy I of Egypt, whom Lysimachus married in his old age, and he switched his allegiance to Seleucus. It was a lucky move, for Seleucus soon defeated and killed Lysimachus, and then, a few months later, was himself assassinated. Philetaerus was too cautious to break away from the Seleucid empire immediately, but his successor Eumenes I did make the break, and Eumenes's successor, Attalus I, took the title of king and gave his name to the dynasty. The Attalids of Pergamon followed a shrewd foreign policy based on friendship with Rome; in fact, the last Pergamene king, Attalus III, left Pergamon in his will to Rome when he died in 133 and thus gave Rome its first province east of the Dardanelles. He was the first, but by no means the last, Hellenistic prince to decide that Roman imperialism was a force that could not be stopped.

Alexander's legacy resulted in other kingdoms as well, which this book will deal with only in passing. One was Bactria, modern Afghanistan, in the northeast corner of Alexander's conquests. Sometime in the mid-third century, the satrap of Bactria revolted from Seleucus II and declared himself king, taking advantage of Seleucus's preoccupation on his western frontiers. More than a half century ago, one of the great Hellenistic historians, Michael I. Rostovtzeff, wrote that historians would like to know more about life in the immense and rich kingdom of Bactria but there was practically no evidence. Since then, archaeology had yielded more information, notably the remains of a Hellenistic city at Ai Khanum (see below), but Rostovtzeff's complaint is still well founded. We know even less about a Hellenistic kingdom in India, founded by Greeks from Bactria, except that Buddhist tradition preserves information about one of the Greek adventurers who campaigned in India, Menander, who converted to Buddhism. The Bactrian kingdom was overrun by nomadic Scythian tribes about 135.

In Asia Minor, bordering the Black Sea to the north and the Sea of Marmora to the west was Bithynia, inhabited by the warlike Bithynians who never accepted Macedonian rule, and in the early third century won their independence. The kings of Bithynia may not have been Greek, but they founded cities and promoted Greek culture as much as any Hellenistic king. The last Bithynian king followed the example of the last king of Pergamon, Bithynia's neighbor to the south, and willed the kingdom to Rome when he died in the year 74. North of the Taurus Mountains in modern Turkey was the kingdom of Cappadocia, which had been a satrapy, or province, of the Persian empire while the Persian empire lasted, and in the late fourth century, while Alexander's generals were fighting over his conquests, a Persian nobleman established himself there as king. North of Cappadocia, by the Black Sea, was the kingdom of Pontus, where another Persian noble made himself king. Asia Minor was a patchwork of kingdoms, but until the early second century, the dominant power there was the Seleucid empire.

These Hellenistic kingdoms were magnets for Greek emigrants. In Egypt Ptolemy I encouraged new settlements in the Nile Valley. The royal government undertook irrigation projects in which new settlers reclaimed land from the desert, which increased Egypt's productivity as well as provided the king with soldiers for his army; for as long as they could, the Ptolemies did not enlist native Egyptians. These soldier-settlers were given parcels of land called *kleroi* (hence their name *kleruchs*) on long-term leases with easy terms. The natives provided the muscle that powered the Egyptian economy, but they were treated as a conquered people, and resented it. Alexandria, the Ptolemaic capital, became a brilliant cultural center, but the culture was Greek, not Egyptian. In the Nile Valley, however, where the rhythm of life was set by the annual Nile river flood that inundated the arable land, the Ptolemaic government did little to disturb the ancient patterns of Egyptian life; it founded only one city, Ptolemais Hormou in the south of the country, but elsewhere the population lived in villages where the gods of Egypt continued to be worshipped with no less devotion than in the time of the pharaohs. In the Middle East, however, Seleucus I and his successors, following Alexander the Great's example, founded many new cities, beginning with Seleucia-on-Tigris, which was close enough to Babylon to drain Babylon of its population, though it continued to be an important religious center with cultural roots going back two millennia. At the height of the Seleucid empire in the third century, Greek settlements spread over all the eastern satrapies of the old Persian empire. The last king of Afghanistan, Zahir Shah, chanced upon the remains of one of them at Ai Khanum on the Oxus River, the modern Amu Darya, while he was out hunting. Excavations revealed a city founded about 300, while the region was still under Seleucid control. Its ancient name is unknown. But it was only one of a number of cities in ancient Bactria, far removed from the Mediterranean home of Hellenistic culture.

Seleucus's new foundations needed settlers, and the immigrants who populated them brought with them their Greek way of life, their language, their art, architecture, and city planning. Ai Khanum, for instance, had a Greek temple, a theater seating 5,000 spectators, a public library, and a gymnasium sprawling over nearly 100 square yards. Outside the city walls there was found a villa built for a Greek settler, evidently a landowner who lived on his estate and used the locals as farm hands. Ai Khanum, whatever its ancient name, was an enclave of Greek culture in what was, in Greek eyes, a barbarian world.

What did the local population think of these intruders? The lingua franca of the old Persian empire had been Aramaic, and Greek replaced it only among a minority. Alexander may have hoped that the barriers between Greek and non-Greek would dissolve as Greeks and Asians intermarried and learned to honor each other's traditions, but his policy of promoting a synthesis of cultures died with him. His son in his person represented his father's policy, for he was half-oriental, but the ruthless generals who divided up Alexander's conquests did not allow him to reach adulthood. Few, Greek or non-Greek, felt any enthusiasm for crossing the cultural divide. Yet the natives, as we can call the non-Greeks, could not escape the allure of Greek culture. Natives who wanted to "get ahead" in the Hellenistic world acquired a working knowledge of the Greek language and a Greek cultural veneer. They might resent the Greek immigrants and their foreign ways—some resented them bitterly—but the rulers of the Hellenistic kingdoms encountered surprisingly little outright insurgency.

THE DECLINE AND FALL OF
THE HELLENISTIC KINGDOMS

If asked to define a period when the Hellenistic world reached its height, the best choice would be the last years of the third century. The Ptolemaic kings ruled not only Egypt but also southern Syria and Palestine, as well as Cyprus. The Seleucid empire, ruled by a vigorous young king, Antiochus III, stretched from Afghanistan in the east—where Antiochus restored Seleucid rule by making the king of Bactria accept Seleucid suzerainty, though he wisely did not suppress the Bactrian kingdom, and renewed Seleucid links with India—to the west, where Antiochus's empire in Asia Minor supplied him with some of the best recruits for his army. In 217, he had tried to wrest southern Syria from Palestine, which appeared easy prey, for Ptolemy III had allowed the Egyptian military to decay and his young successor Ptolemy IV had just come to the throne. But the Ptolemaic government coped with the desperate situation by recruiting native Egyptians and training them to fight Macedonian-style in a phalanx, and at the battle of Raphia, it was the Egyptian phalanx that won the day. Henceforth it was no longer so easy to treat the Egyptians as an underclass. They had a new sense of their own worth, and they, too, could become *kleruchs* and lease parcels of land from the government. In any case, the battle of Raphia only delayed the fate of southern Syria. Egypt lost it to Antiochus III in 200.

Rome made her presence felt before the end of the third century, during her life-or-death struggle with Carthage, her rival for control of the western Mediterranean. The brilliant Carthaginian general Hannibal invaded Italy and inflicted two stunning defeats on the Romans at Lake Trasimene (216) and at Cannae (215). In the aftermath of Cannae, Hannibal made an alliance with the young king of Macedon, Philip V. Hannibal wanted Macedonian assistance, but he got none, for Rome stirred up enough trouble for Philip in Greece itself to keep him occupied. But Rome did not forget Philip's action. In 197, a Roman army defeated Macedon at the battle of Cynoscephalae, and the next year, the Roman general who had defeated Philip came to the Isthmian Games, one of the four great athletic festivals of Greece, and proclaimed to everyone present that all the Greek cities should be free. The cheers were deafening, and in 194, the Roman army *did* evacuate Greece. But the liberty that Rome was willing to grant to Greece was always qualified, and though the kingdom of Macedon survived a little longer, Rome regarded Philip V and his son and successor Perseus with suspicion. In 168, a Roman army destroyed the Macedonian army of Perseus at the Battle of Pydna; the royal dynasty of Macedon came to an end, and after a brief experiment at republican government—Rome divided Macedon into four republics—the Macedonian kingdom became a Roman province in 146. In the same year, Greece became Achaea, a protectorate of the Roman empire. It enjoyed only the shadow of independence.

The death throes of the Seleucid empire were much longer. Antiochus III aroused Rome's apprehensions, and when diplomacy failed to resolve their differences, the so-called First Syrian War (192–188) broke out. Antiochus dispatched an army into Greece, but in 191 it was routed at Thermopylae, and in 189, at Magnesia in Asia Minor, Rome overwhelmed the best military force that Antiochus could muster. It was clear to all that no Hellenistic kingdom could stand up to the Roman juggernaut. The peace that ended the Syrian War shut the Seleucid empire out of Asia Minor, which had always been a good recruiting ground for the Seleucid army. Meanwhile in the east, the Seleucid empire faced a new enemy. About 250, the Parni, a semi-nomadic people from the Russian steppe, invaded the old Persian province of Parthia and took their name from it, for it was their first conquest in what used to be the old Persian empire. The Seleucids, fatally weakened as they were by their defeat at the hands of Rome, could not stop the Parthians from expanding; by about 140, the Parthian king, Mithridates, had ended Seleucid rule over much of Iran. Mithridates's son, Phraates II, dealt the fatal blow by defeating and killing the last strong Seleucid king, Antiochus VII. The remnant of the Seleucid empire was squeezed between the Euphrates River and the Mediterranean coastline. Even there it faced a challenge, for in Judea, a nationalist movement known as the Maccabaean Revolt resulted in the establishment of an independent Jewish state in territory that the Seleucids had once ruled, and the Seleucids were too weak to suppress it. It must be added that the Seleucid royal family engaged in self-destructive quarrels over the succession. The empire became a shadow of its former self, and when the Roman general Pompey, then at the height of his career, entered Syria he deposed the last Seleucid king. The king's name was Philip II, which recalled Alexander the Great's father, who had laid the foundation for the Hellenistic age which his son would usher in.

Egypt was the last survivor. The native population had looked on the conquering army of Macedon, when it invaded Egypt under Alexander, as liberators from the Persians, but it did not take long before they realized that these newcomers had come to exploit Egypt, and they reacted with sullen resentment. The instrument the Ptolemaic kings used to conciliate the Egyptians was the immensely powerful Egyptian priesthood. The pharaohs of ancient Egypt had all been gods, worshipped in life and death, and the Ptolemies stepped into their role, adopting the royal regalia of the pharaohs, including the red crown of Lower Egypt and the white crown of Upper Egypt, and on the walls of the many temples they built, sculptures of the Ptolemaic kings depicted them as pharaohs, and heirs to Egypt's ancient past. Thus the Ptolemaic kings assumed a double role: to the native Egyptians they were divine–gods on earth like the pharaohs; to their Greek, Jewish, and Macedonian subjects they were Macedonian kings. Yet only one of the Ptolemaic monarchs, the last of them, Cleopatra VII, took the trouble to learn the language of their native subjects and could speak to them without an interpreter. No matter how much they might try to present themselves as pharaohs, and heirs of the ancient traditions of Egypt, they remained a Macedonian family with roots in Greek culture.

The need to appease native discontent increased sharply after the Battle of Raphia (217), which was an ambiguous victory for the young king Ptolemy IV. It was his native Egyptian troops belonging to the Egyptian warrior class that defeated the Seleucid army at Raphia, and as soldiers, they were eligible for land grants as *kleruchs*, though the grants were small compared with those that Greeks received. The cost of the war had left the royal treasury very needy, and taxation was already a heavy burden on the Egyptian natives. Not only the native soldiers, but the Egyptian priesthood saw an opportunity to increase its influence. It was a hereditary caste of priests whom the kings offended at their peril. They knew that the kings needed them as their allies, and as the Ptolemaic regime grew weaker, they pushed their advantage.

As native self-confidence grew, so did discontent with Ptolemaic rule. Ten years after the victory at Raphia, civil war broke out, and until 186, Upper Egypt in the southern Nile Valley was ruled by black-skinned Nubian pharaohs. In the north, in the region of the Nile Delta, brigandage became common. The flow of immigrants to Egypt on which the Ptolemaic government had once relied had dried up, and it had little choice but to conciliate the Egyptian priesthood, who emerged as representatives of Egyptian nationalism. At the same time, there was a steady trickle of Egyptians who mastered Greek language, acquired a Greek education, and obtained posts in the Ptolemaic civil service. How far this process of mutual assimilation would have gone we cannot say, for Rome ended Egyptian independence in the year 30.

In the year 80, the last legitimate king of the Ptolemaic dynasty, Ptolemy XI, died without an heir, and the Romans chose to believe he had left his kingdom to Rome in his last will and testament. It had happened before: When the last legitimate king of Pergamon, Attalus III, died in 133, he left his kingdom to Rome and it became the Roman province of Asia. Ptolemy XI's will, however, was probably wishful thinking on the part of the Romans, but in Alexandria, the Greek ruling moved quickly to avert a Roman takeover, and crowned an illegitimate member of the royal house as Ptolemy XII Neos Dionysos ("the New Dionysos"). An enormous bribe to Julius Caesar won him belated recognition from Rome as king of Egypt, but his attempts to find the wherewithal to pay the bribe led to a rebellion that ousted him from the throne for almost three years until Rome reinstated him. He died in 55, and his three young children succeeded him—Cleopatra VII, and her younger brothers, Ptolemy XII and Ptolemy XIII. The survivor was Cleopatra, one of the most brilliant queens in history, and one of the most ruthless.

Cleopatra lived at a time when the Roman republic dissolved into civil war. Julius Caesar defeated the defenders of the Roman republic led by his rival, Pompey, who fled to Egypt, where Caesar followed him, only to find that Pompey had been killed as soon as he reached Alexandria. But the young Cleopatra became Caesar's mistress, and before he left Egypt, he had established her on the throne with her brother, and she was pregnant with Caesar's son. She followed Caesar to Rome and was there when he was assassinated by a cabal of senators led by the diehard republicans, Marcus Brutus and Quintus Cassius. She fled with her son to Egypt, but the war followed her. Caesar's assassins, Brutus and Cassius, were defeated by Mark Antony, an officer of Julius Caesar who tried to take over his legacy, and Caesar's great-nephew, Octavian, whom Caesar had adopted in his will and named his heir. After the defeat of Brutus and Cassius, Mark Antony took over responsibility for the eastern half of the empire, and along with it, Cleopatra. The two became lovers, but Cleopatra was a foreigner and Rome did not recognize a marriage to a non-Roman citizen. Octavian's propaganda machine demonized her as little better than a louche oriental despot and a seducer who had Mark Antony in her thrall. Cleopatra's hope that her son by Julius Caesar might be recognized as Caesar's heir never had any chance of fulfillment.

The struggle between Mark Antony and Octavian for supremacy ended with a naval battle off the coast of northwest Greece at Actium. Mark Antony and Cleopatra returned to Alexandria, defeated, and both committed suicide. Rome annexed Egypt, but it did not become an ordinary province; instead, the royal palace became the residence of a prefect appointed by Octavian, or the emperor Augustus, as he was soon known, and Egypt's wheat, which had made the Ptolemaic kings wealthy, now flowed to Rome. Historians have chosen the date of 30, when Rome annexed Egypt, as the final chapter of the Hellenistic world. The great temple that Cleopatra had built for the worship of Julius Caesar and the son he had fathered was dedicated to Augustus, and eventually, when the Roman empire became Christian more than three centuries later, it became the Alexandrian cathedral, the seat of the Christian patriarch of Alexandria.

Yet, while Rome brought a change of governance to the Hellenistic world, and the ruling elite had to make their accommodations with the new ruling power, life for the ordinary people went on much as usual. Rome was a stern ruler. With Roman legions to back them, the Roman governors did not have to take popular opinion into account as much as the Hellenistic kings did. Roman tax collectors were more exacting. But the people on the streets continued to attend the theater and watch spectacles in the amphitheaters. People still filled the markets to buy and sell everything from food to fine cloths imported from India and China. Trading vessels continued to ply the trade routes more than ever, and shipping no longer closed down completely in the winter to avoid winter storms. In the Greek homeland, the propertied classes felt secure under Roman rule; they had lost their political importance but in return Rome protected them against any threat of revolution by the have-nots, and there was always the possibility that a Greek might acquire Roman citizenship and with it the rights of a Roman citizen. The society and economy of the world that Alexander the Great had brought into being was continued by Rome, which became heir to Alexander's empire in the Near East. It is the social, cultural, and economic life that the man on the street experienced in this age, created by Alexander, that this book aims to describe.

NOTE

1. Green, *Alexander to Actium*, p. 366.

Chronology: The March of History in the Hellenistic Age

All dates are B.C.E.

408   The city-state of Rhodes is formed by the union of three small city-states on the island and a new urban center is built to serve as its capital.

404   The Peloponnesian War between Athens and Sparta comes to an end with the surrender of Athens. Sparta and Persia share the Athenian empire between them, with Persia taking the Greek cities in Asia Minor as her portion.

371   Sparta loses the battle of Leuctra to Thebes, and along with the defeat, she loses her dominance in Greece.

369   A Theban army led by a general of genius, Epaminondas, invades the Peloponnesus and sets Messenia free from Spartan domination. For a brief period until Epaminondas's death, Thebes is the chief power in Greece. For a couple years, Philip II, Alexander the Great's father, is a hostage at Thebes, where he has the opportunity to observe the greatest general of his day.

359   Philip II becomes king of Macedon.

356   Alexander the Great is born. His mother, Olympias, is a princess of the royal house of the kingdom of Epirus, west of Macedon, which claimed descent from the hero Achilles.

348   Philip takes the city of Olynthus and destroys it. The ruins of Olynthus thus serve to provide evidence for domestic life in northern Greece in the mid-fourth century.

338   (August 2) The fate of Greece is decided at the battle of Chaeronea where Philip defeats the combined armies of Thebes and Athens. Philip's 18-year-old son, Alexander, commands the left wing of the Macedonian army.

338   (winter) Philip summons delegates from all the Greek cities to Corinth to create a common peace and set up a league of cities with a "United Nations" assembly called a *Synhedrion*, where Philip does not have a seat. This pan-Hellenic league then makes a perpetual alliance with Macedon.

337   (spring) The *Synhedrion* meets with Philip at Corinth to proclaim a war of revenge against Persia, which had invaded Greece in 480 and destroyed Greek temples.

336   Philip is assassinated and his son Alexander succeeds him.

334   (spring) Alexander leads his army across the Hellespont and begins his campaign against the Persian empire, begun by his father.

334   (May–June) Alexander wins his first victory over a Persian army at the Granicus River.

333   (November) Alexander defeats a Persian army led by the Persian king, Darius III, at Issus near modern Alexandretta on the Syrian coastal plain. Alexander continues his advance through Phoenicia, modern Lebanon, where the Phoenician cities surrender except for Tyre, which resists stubbornly.

332   (August) Alexander takes Tyre, and continues south to Egypt, meeting stiff resistance only at Gaza.

331   (January?) In Egypt, Alexander lays the corner stone of Alexandria on the western estuary of the Nile River.

331   (October 1) Alexander's army defeats the Persian army under Darius near the village of Gaugamela. Darius flees from the battlefield.

331   (end of October) Babylon surrenders to Alexander.

331   (December 15) Alexander reaches Susa and captures the Persian treasury kept there.

330   (January 30) Alexander enters Persepolis, the ceremonial capital of the Persian empire, and captures enormous wealth there. The great Achaemenid palace is burned.

330   (midsummer) Darius is mortally wounded and deserted by his followers. Alexander orders his corpse to be taken to Persepolis and buried there with honor.

330   (autumn) The so-called Pages' Plot against Alexander occurs. Philotas, the son of Parmenio, the old general whom Alexander had inherited from Philip's army, is judged guilty by the Macedonia army and is put to death. His father is also executed.

330–28   Alexander suppresses insurgency in northern Iran and Afghanistan.

327   Alexander marries Roxane, the daughter of a Sogdian chieftain. Roxane will bear Alexander's posthumous son. In the summer of the same year, Alexander leads an army of Macedonian and Iranian troops into northern India.

326   (May/June) Alexander defeats the Indian rajah Porus, who surrenders and is reappointed to his throne as a vassal prince. Alexander reaches the Beas River, where his army refuses to advance further.

325   Alexander subdues the Punjab.

324   A Macedonian-Persian mass wedding is held at Susa. Alexander takes two princesses of the Persian royal family as new wives, and 80 of his officers also take Asian wives. Ten thousand Macedonian soldiers marry Asian women.

324   Alexander demands that the Greek cities recognize him as a god. The next year, at Babylon, sacred envoys from Greece come to meet Alexander, crowned with wreaths, as before a god. Alexander prepares for a new expedition.

323   (June 13) Alexander the Great dies in Babylon. The cavalry and the infantry sections of Alexander's army nearly come to blows over the succession. Perdiccas, the senior cavalry officer, emerges as leader, with Meleager, the leader of the infantry, as second in command. Perdiccas proposes waiting for the birth of Alexander's child by Roxane and Meleager backs Alexander's half brother, Philip Arrhidaeus. Roxane gives birth to a boy who is recognized as king jointly with Arrhidaeus.

     Perdiccas has Meleager murdered and becomes regent for the kings. Ptolemy becomes satrap of Egypt. Antigonos the One-Eyed, the satrap of Phrygia, gets all of western Asia Minor. Lysimachus gets Thrace as his portion. Antipater is left in control of Macedon.

323–22   Rebellion in Greece against Macedonian rule (the so-called Lamian War) is suppressed by Antipater. Athens is badly defeated at sea, and ceases to be a naval power.

India asserts its independence under an anti-Macedonian leader, Chandragupta.

322   Aristotle dies. Theophrastus becomes head of the Lyceum, the school that Aristotle founded.

320   Perdiccas is murdered after having made a disastrous effort to invade Egypt to drive out Ptolemy I. The successors meet at Triparadeisus in northern Syria and decide that Antipater, now an old man, will control Europe and be guardian of the kings, and Antigonos the One-Eyed will be general of Asia. Seleucus, commander of the hypaspists (an elite guards regiment) is assigned the satrapy of Babylonia. Lysimachus retains Thrace.

321   Menander, the greatest playwright of the New Comedy (a comedy of manners), produces his first play in Athens.

319   Antipater dies and, passing over his son Cassander, names Polyperchon, a former officer of Alexander the Great's father, as his successor. Cassander joins Lysimachus and Ptolemy against Polyperchon. In the ensuing struggle, Polyperchon allows Olympias, Alexander's mother, who had taken refuge in Epirus, to invade Macedon. Once in charge there, she eliminates Philip Arrhidaeus and his wife.

317   Cassander garrisons Piraeus, the port of Athens, and makes Demetrius of Phalerum, a protégé of Aristotle, the ruler of Athens. Meanwhile, Olympias's misrule has alienated all support, and Cassander invades Macedonia, captures Olympias, and tries and executes her. Cassander is now guardian of the boy king, Alexander IV.

315   Antigonos, who has by now made himself master of Central Asia and Iran, drives Seleucus from Babylon, who takes refuge with Ptolemy of Egypt.

315   Antigonos seizes Syria and lays siege to Tyre, which falls the following year. Ptolemy puts down a revolt in Syria. He also moves his capital from Memphis, the old capital dating from the time of the pharaohs, to Alexandria. Alexander's corpse is moved there and a great mausoleum is built for him.

313   Zeno of Citium on Cyprus, founder of the Stoic School of philosophy, comes to Athens to study and attend lectures by the leading philosophers of the day. Later he began himself to give lectures at the 'Painted Stoa' in the Athenian agora—hence the name 'Stoics' for his followers.

312   Seleucus returns to Babylon with the help of Ptolemy of Egypt and grasps the right hand of the god Bel-Marduk at the New Year's Festival, thereby receiving Bel-Marduk's recognition as the Lord of Asia. This ceremony marks the beginning of the Seleucid empire, and year one of the Seleucid era.

311   Ptolemy I creates the cult of Alexander the Great, who is placed on the same level as the Olympian gods. Members of prominent Macedonian families and even, upon occasion, Ptolemaic kings serve as high priests of the cult. Thus Alexander becomes the patron god of the Ptolemaic royal family.

310 (?)   Alexander IV, Alexander the Great's son, and his mother, Roxane, are murdered by Cassander.

308–06   Seleucus wins control of Iran and Central Asia. He then tries to reassert control of the Punjab where he battles with Chandragupta, the founder of the Mauryan empire in India.

307   Demetrius, son of Antigonos the One-Eyed, liberates Athens from Cassander, and is welcomed warmly by the Athenians, who hail him as a god. Cassander's governor of Athens, Demetrius of Phalerum, flees to Ptolemy of Egypt, where he may have acted as an advisor for the building of the Great Library of Alexandria.

306   Antigonos the One-Eyed assumes the title of king. In the following year, Ptolemy, Lysimachus, and Seleucus all give themselves the title of king. The emblem of kingship, worn by the kings, was the diadem, a headband encrusted with pearls. In same year, too, in Athens, Epicurus opens his philosophic school—the first organized philosophic school to admit women.

305   Seleucus makes peace with Chandragupta and evacuates India. Chandragupta gives him a force of trained war elephants.

305   Cassander becomes king of Macedon.

305–04   Antigonos's son, Demetrius, besieges Rhodes but fails to take it after a yearlong siege. This siege gives him the sobriquet Poliorcetes, meaning "the Besieger."

301   Antigonos the One-Eyed is defeated by a coalition of Lysimachus, Cassander, and Seleucus at the Battle of Ipsos. His son, Demetrius Poliorcetes, flees, and spends the following years trying to restore his fortunes; for a brief period after 294 he is

king of Macedon. After the Battle of Ipsos, Lysimachus takes over most of Asia Minor as far west as the Taurus mountain range. Ptolemy seizes Coele Syria (Hollow Syria). Seleucus takes northern Syria, and founds 10 cities, including Antioch-on-the-Orontes, between the Mediterranean coast and the upper Euphrates.

298–297   Cassander dies. His son Philip V dies soon afterwards and Macedon is divided between Cassander's two younger sons. Perhaps it was in this year the Museum and Library of Alexandria is founded.

285   Seleucus captures Demetrius Poliorcetes, who dies in prison two years later.

280   Pyrrhus, king of Epirus, invited by the Greek city of Taras (in Latin, *Tarentum*), lands in Italy and defeats the Romans at Heracleia. Next year he defeats them again at Asculum.

279   A horde of Gauls invades Macedon and penetrates Greece as far south as Delphi, where the Gauls are defeated by the Aetolians.

278   Gauls, invited by the king of Bithynia, invade Asia Minor.

277   Antigonos Gonatas, son of Demetrius Poliorcetes, inflicts a defeat on the Gauls.

276   Antigonos Gonatas establishes himself firmly on the throne of Macedon and founds a royal line that continues until Rome defeats and captures the last king, Perseus, in 167.

276   Ptolemy II Philadelphus marries his sister, Arsinoe II. Arsinoe dies at some point before 270.

275   Pyrrhus, defeated by the Romans at Beneventum in southern Italy, returns to Epirus. The following year he invades Macedon and forces Antigonos Gonatas to flee.

272   Pyrrhus dies in a street battle in the city of Argos, and by the next year Antigonos recovers his throne of Macedon.

250   Bactria and Sogdiana break away from the Seleucid empire.

248   The semi-nomadic Parni under Arsaces invade the old Persian satrapy of Parthia.

239   Antigonos Gonatas, king of Macedonia, dies. He is succeeded by his son, Demetrius II Aetolicus (reigned 239–229).

223   Antiochus III ("the Great") comes to the Seleucid throne. Antiochus is the first Seleucid king to institute state-sponsored worship of himself and all his ancestors.

215	Philip V of Macedonia makes an alliance with Hannibal. Rome reacts by making an alliance with Philip's enemies, the Aetolians. The so-called First Macedonian War between Rome and Philip begins in 211.
212–205	Antiochus III makes an expedition to the eastern provinces of his empire and restores Seleucid rule there.
206	Philip V makes a separate peace with Aetolia and her allies. Rome makes peace in the next year—the so-called Peace of Phoenice—and withdraws its forces from Greece.
204	Ptolemy IV dies and is succeeded by a boy king, Ptolemy V.
203–202	Philip V and Antiochus III make a compact to take over Ptolemy V's possessions outside Egypt. War breaks out between Antiochus III and Ptolemy V. In 200, Egypt is driven out of Coele Syria. Judea comes under Seleucid rule.
200–197	The so-called Second Macedonian War. Philip is defeated by Rome at the Battle of Cynoscephalae (197).
197	Eumenes II becomes king of Pergamon.
196	The royal library at Pergamon is founded. At the Isthmian Games held this year, Rome proclaims the "Freedom of the Greeks"—all the Greek cities are to be free.
194	Roman forces leave Greece.
192	War breaks out between Rome and Antiochus III. The next year, Antiochus's army invades Greece and is defeated at Thermopylae.
189	Antiochus III is soundly defeated at Magnesia in Asia Minor by a Roman army led by Lucius Scipio. Pergamene forces under Eumenes II play a key role in the defeat of Antiochus.
189	Rome imposes a peace treaty (Peace of Apamea) on Antiochus III, forcing him to abandon all of Asia Minor, pay a huge indemnity, and give up all his fleet except for 10 ships. Pergamon and Rhodes are the chief beneficiaries of Antiochus's defeat. Pergamon takes over the Seleucid possessions in Asia Minor.
187	Antiochus III dies, and is succeeded by Seleucus IV.
179	Philip V of Macedon dies and is succeeded by the last Macedonian king, Perseus.
175	Antiochus IV Epiphanes ("God Manifest") succeeds to the Seleucid throne, shoving aside Seleucus IV's eldest son. A rift results in the Seleucid royal house which hastens its decline.

172   War breaks out between Rome and king Perseus of Macedon.

169   Antiochus IV Epiphanes launches an attack on Egypt. He reaches Alexandria but is forced by a Roman envoy to withdraw to Antioch. As he passes through Jerusalem, he raids the Temple.

168   Rome defeats Perseus, king of Macedon, at Pydna in northern Greece. Rome abolishes the Macedonian monarchy and breaks Macedon up into four republics. In Greece, Rome takes stern action against Greeks who helped Perseus, even those who helped only by their good wishes. One thousand prominent Achaeans belonging to the Achaean League are taken as hostages to Rome and held there without trial, among them the historian Polybius of Megalopolis, who used his time to write *Universal History*, part of which survives and serves as an important source for the Hellenistic period.

167   Delos becomes a free port under Athenian control. Delos becomes an international trading center. In December, the Seleucid king Antiochus IV attempts to impose Hellenism in Jerusalem by abolishing the Yahweh cult and all Jewish rites. An altar to Olympian Zeus is erected in the Temple, and a statue of Antiochus set up beside it.

166   The devout Jews (the Chasidim), who oppose Hellenization in Judea, rise in rebellion against Antiochus. The so-called Maccabaean Revolt breaks out, led Judas Maccabaeus, whose father, before his death, had struck the first blow.

164   In Jerusalem, Judas Maccabaeus captures the Temple and purifies it, restoring the worship of Yahweh. A thanksgiving festival is held in December, which continues to be commemorated by the festival of Hanukkah.

163   Antiochus IV dies while leading an expedition against the Parthians.

148   Rome suppresses a revolt in Macedon led by a man named Andriscus who claimed to be the son of Perseus, the last king. Macedon becomes a province of the Roman empire.

146   In Greece, the Achaean League makes a bid for independence from Rome and is defeated. Rome takes Corinth, kills the men, sells the women and children into slavery, and destroys the city. Greece becomes a Roman protectorate.

145   By 145 or shortly thereafter, the Seleucid empire has lost both eastern and western Iran to the Parthian king, Mithridates I,

who takes the title "King of Kings," which once belonged to the Achaemenid kings of Persia.

133 The last king of Pergamon, Attalus III, dies and leaves his kingdom to Rome. It is reorganized as the province of Asia.

129 The Seleucid king, Antiochus VII Sidetes, is defeated and killed by the Parthian king, Phraates II, son of Mithridates I. The Seleucid empire is now confined to north Syria and eastern Cilicia.

117 About this time, it was discovered how to sail directly from Egyptian ports to India with the aid of the monsoons.

89 Mithridates VI Eupator, King of Pontus, challenges Roman rule in Asia Minor.

88 The Greeks in western Asia Minor, embittered by 40 years of Roman exploitation, massacre 80,000 Italian residents there. Mithridates sends an army into Greece and Athens sides with him.

86 The Roman general Sulla defeats Mithridates's army in Greece led by his general Archelaus, and in the same year, Sulla takes Athens by storm and plunders it. The port of Piraeus is set ablaze.

85 Sulla makes peace with Mithridates.

80 The legitimate line of the Ptolemaic royal house in Egypt dies out, and the Alexandrians make the illegitimate son of Ptolemy IX Soter ("Savior") II, king. He calls himself the "New Dionysos" but is popularly known as Ptolemy Auletes ("the *aulos*-player"). Rome refuses to recognize him.

74 Nicomedes IV, the last king of Bithynia, dies and leaves his kingdom to Rome in his will.

74 War with Mithridates breaks out again. Pompey has suppressed the pirates who infested the eastern Mediterranean in 68, and now he takes command of the Mithridatic War in 67 and defeats Mithridates, who commits suicide in 63.

63 Pompey dethrones the last Seleucid king, thus terminating the Seleucid empire. Pompey creates the Roman provinces of Syria stretching from Mount Amanus in the north to Mount Carmel in the south.

62 Pompey returns to Italy after his successful campaign, which brought all the Hellenistic East, except the Ptolemaic kingdom of Egypt, under Roman rule. On the eastern borders, however, the Parthians remain a threat.

59   In Rome, Julius Caesar, having won the support of two power-
             ful allies—the successful general Pompey, and the immensely
             rich Marcus Crassus—is elected one of the two consuls for the
             year in spite of the stubborn opposition of a conservative faction
             in the Roman senate led by Cato the Younger, who considered
             themselves the defenders of Rome's ancient republican consti-
             tution. Caesar extends Rome's recognition to Ptolemy Auletes
             in return for an enormous bribe. Yet Caesar also dispatches Cato
             to annex Cyprus, which was still part of the Ptolemaic realm.
             Ptolemy Auletes spends the years 58–55 in Rome, bribing and
             petitioning to return to Egypt.

58   Caesar becomes governor of Gaul. His campaigns over the
             next 10 years will add all the territory of modern France to the
             Roman empire, and make him a very rich man. He also builds
             up a battle-hardened army that is intensely loyal to him.

55   Ptolemy Auletes is finally installed as king in Alexandria.

53   Marcus Crassus is defeated and killed by the Parthians at
             Carrhae in northern Mesopotamia and the Parthians capture
             the standards of the vanquished Roman legions. Thus one of
             Caesar's political allies is eliminated.

52   Cleopatra VII and her brother Ptolemy XIII are associated with
             Ptolemy Auletes as rulers of Egypt. Auletes dies the next year
             and they rule independently.

49   Julius Caesar crosses the Rubicon River dividing Italy from the
             province of Cisalpine Gaul (the Po River valley) and the civil
             war begins that will destroy the Roman Republic.

48   Caesar defeats the senatorial army led by Pompey on a battle-
             field near the city of Pharsalus in Thessaly, in northern Greece.
             Pompey flees to Egypt where he is assassinated, and when Cae-
             sar arrives there in hot pursuit, he is presented with Pompey's
             mummified head.

48–47   Caesar, who had come to Egypt with only a small force, finds
             himself marooned in the royal palace in Alexandria along with
             the queen Cleopatra, facing an insurgency led by Cleopatra's
             brother and coruler, Ptolemy XIII and her sister Arsinoe. The
             Great Library in Alexandria may have been a casualty of these
             street battles, but it is more likely that it suffered damage rather
             than complete destruction. Caesar leaves Egypt in 47, having
             placed Cleopatra securely on the Egyptian throne along with
             her remaining brother, Ptolemy XIV, and goes on to fight three
             more battles before he is supreme.

45 Julius Caesar returns to Rome, where Cleopatra has joined him with a son who she claims is Caesar's. The Roman ruling elite suspect that Cleopatra is advising Caesar to establish a monarchy of the Hellenistic type in Rome.

44 (March 15) Julius Caesar is assassinated. Cleopatra flees to Alexandria, where she eliminates her last brother, Ptolemy XIV.

42 Caesar's assassins, Brutus and Cassius, are defeated at Philippi in northern Greece. In the division of the spoils that follows the victory, Mark Antony is assigned the eastern Mediterranean, including Egypt, and soon makes contact with Cleopatra.

31 The fleets of Mark Antony and Cleopatra are defeated at Actium on the coast of northwest Greece. Antony and Cleopatra flee to Egypt.

30 A Roman army led by Octavian, the future emperor Augustus, enters Egypt. Antony and Cleopatra both commit suicide. Egypt becomes a Roman possession ruled by a prefect appointed by the emperor, who moves into the palace of the Ptolemies in Alexandria.

27 The emperor Augustus makes Greece the province of Achaea. Some prosperity returns, but Greece as a whole fails to recover from the devastations inflicted on it by Rome's civil wars.

1

The Landscape of the Hellenistic World: The Geographical Background

MEDITERRANEAN GREECE

History is played out against a landscape, the Hellenistic age no less than any other period, and the geography of the Greek world after Alexander is important for our understanding of the age. Before Alexander, Greek cities were to be found spread across the Mediterranean world, clinging generally to the coastline, but often penetrating into the interior, where the contact with the indigenous peoples was not always friendly. Even in Egypt there was a Greek colony—at Naucratis on one of the mouths of the Nile—though it was more a trading post than a true colony, and it was founded with the permission of the last dynasty of independent pharaohs before the Persian empire occupied the country. In Italy and Sicily, Greek cities were founding other colonies as early as the mid-eighth century. They called them *apoikiai*, "homes away from home," but they rapidly became independent cities themselves, without any political linkage to their mother cities. The earliest Greek colony in Italy was on the offshore island of Ischia in the Bay of Naples and it was soon followed by colonies on the Italian mainland and in Sicily. Sicily and the southern Italian coastline were filled with prosperous Greek cities in the classical period, but even before Hellenistic age the cities in Italy were feeling the pressure of Italic tribes in the interior: Samnites, who spoke an Italian dialect called Oscan, or their cousins, the Lucanians, whose expansion seems to have been fueled by a high birthrate. In Sicily, the native tribes, the Sicels and the Sicans, were pushed into the interior of the island and assimilated into Greek culture, but on Sicily's western tip the Carthaginians, who had been Phoenician colonists from Tyre, maintained a foothold and in the fourth century moved aggressively against the Greeks. In the Hellenistic age, Sicily was a battleground between Greek and Carthaginian until the Romans intervened and Sicily became Rome's first province overseas. Yet the modern traveler to Sicily is taken aback by the Greek remains in Sicily and southern Italy: Some of the largest temples in the Greek world were built there.

Greek colonization also crept along the coasts of southern France and Spain, though Carthaginian pressure had pushed the Greeks out of southern Spain by the Hellenistic period. In France they founded one great city, Massilia, the ancestor of modern Marseilles, which was greatly admired for its constitution that placed political power in the hands of a council of 600 men, all of them well-to-do. It was a type of government known as an oligarchy, or "rule by the few." No family was to have more than one member in the council, a rule that was later relaxed, and the council had the good sense to open its ranks to outsiders, which contributed to the stability of Massilia's government. Massilia produced one famous explorer, Pytheas, who made a voyage into the North Sea and circumnavigated Great Britain. His reports were generally disbelieved, but modern scholars are more impressed by his achievement.

Then there was the Greek homeland, the peninsula of Greece and the Greek islands. This was the center of Greek culture and the region of the world that the Greeks overseas considered home. Greece is a land filled with mountains and beautiful scenery, but only one-fifth of the land is fit for growing crops. The forests that were once found in the Greek peninsula had largely disappeared by the Hellenistic period; some were cleared to make room for farms, others to provide fuel for cooking or manufacturing—potteries had an enormous appetite for fuel to heat their kilns, and smelting iron ore demanded a large supply of charcoal. Cities had public woodlands of their own, and took measures to maintain them as best they could, but by the Hellenistic period, wood for shipbuilding had to be imported from mountainous regions such as Macedonia with more-than-average rainfall. Land that was deforested had little chance to recover, for uncultivated fields, as well as fallow lands, were used for pasture. Cattle, sheep, pigs, and goats grazing the land were all destructive, each in its own way—goats did the most damage, for they will eat anything, though they prefer young bushes and trees. Summers are hot and parched; the rivers run dry for lack of rainfall. Rain does come in the fall, sometimes as early as the first week in September but usually later, and the total amount of rainfall is about the same as in Paris, but the gentle showers of central France and England are not to be found in Greece. Rainfall there comes in cloudbursts that are often destructive. It is little wonder that large numbers of emigrants left to look for better opportunities elsewhere, leaving Hellenistic Greece with a declining population.

The peninsula of southern Greece is split almost in two by the Gulf of Corinth, and the region to the south of the gulf would have been an island—in fact, its name, the Peloponnesus, means "the island of Pelops"—except for the Isthmus of Corinth, a narrow ridge of land that connects the Peloponnesus with central Greece. Nowadays a canal cuts through this rocky neck of land, but the ancient world lacked the technological expertise for excavation on that scale, though the city-state of Corinth did the next best thing: it built a slipway that allowed small ships to be dragged across the isthmus. Arcadia, the central core of the Peloponnesus, is rough and mountainous but around the fringes of the core there are fertile regions. Sparta in the southeast occupies one of them, and west of Sparta, across the Taygetus mountain range, was Messenia, which occupied the lush Stenyclarus plain. In the classical period, Sparta dominated Messenia and the Messenians worked as serfs, or helots,[1] for their Spartan overlords until it was liberated after Sparta lost the Battle of Leuctra in 371, and along with it, her status as a great power in the Greek world of the fourth century.

North of the Isthmus of Corinth was Athens, the urban center of the state of Attica. The countryside of Athens was poor land for growing wheat, though barley grew well enough, but the olive tree thrived there, and Athenian olive oil was a prized export commodity. Press further to the north, or more accurately, the northeast, and across the Mount Cithaeron range is the Boeotian plain, another fertile region. Unlike Athens, which was a unitary state, Boeotia was a federation, but its dominant city, Thebes, had been for nine years (371–362) the strongest power in Greece, and it did not forget it. Alexander the Great razed it to the ground but it was rebuilt with donations from the rest of Greece, and Hellenistic Thebes was a model of up-to-date city planning that people compared favorably with Athens.

The Pindus mountain range forms the spine of the Greek peninsula, and on the west, the cliffs press close to the coast of the Ionian Sea, so close that there are no useful harbors. The Acarnanians who lived there eked a poor living out of the few pockets of arable land, and not surprisingly, Acarnania produced a large number of the brigands who preyed on travelers in the Hellenistic period. The Aetolians to the east of the Acarnanians were no better off. For them, transhumance was a way of life: that is, they drove their flocks of goats and sheep into the mountains for the upland pastures in the summer and brought them down into the valleys in the winter. Settlements were small and sparse, and the Greeks of the classical period considered Aetolia barely civilized. But in the late fifth century, Aetolia organized itself into a federation, and in the Hellenistic period it was the Aetolians who defeated a horde of Gauls who overran Macedonia in 279 and got as far south as Delphi, the site of the god Apollo's oracle. They remained a power to be reckoned with in Greece.

Further north were the plains of Thessaly, not a land that was notably hospitable to olive orchards or vineyards, but well-known for its cattle, horses, and grain fields. Still further north was the kingdom of Macedonia, with Thrace to the east of it and Epirus to the west. At this latitude, the climate is closer to the central European type than to the Mediterranean; winters are cold and summers hot, deciduous trees flourish, and the rivers flow year round. Macedonia was a good land for cattle and sheep; understandably, a Macedonian was likely to have more meat in his diet than a Greek to the south.

Nowadays the republic of Turkey occupies Anatolia, otherwise known as Asia Minor, which stretches from the east coast of the Aegean Sea to the headwaters of the Euphrates River. The eastern coastal territory and the Dodecanese Islands were settled by Ionians in the Bronze Age; technically the settlers in the north were Aeolian Greeks from central Greece, Dorian Greeks from the Peloponnesus settled in the southwest, and the Ionian cities were in between, but the label "Ionian" was applied to them all. Ionia was famous for its pleasant climate—the sort of climate that, according to Greek geographers, bred soft men. However, the central plateau of Anatolia gets plenty of snow in the winter, particularly in Cappadocia on the high upland in the east. Beyond Anatolia is the great landmass of the Middle East, which had been dominated by great empires: the Assyrians, then the Medes and the Babylonians, and finally Persia, which conquered Babylon in 539. Before Alexander's expedition, conquering armies had advanced from east to west—from Iraq and Iran to the Mediterranean coast. Alexander reversed the process.

THE NEW LANDS WON BY ALEXANDER

The Arabian desert thrusts north, reaching towards the boundary of modern Turkey, and pushing the strip of arable land against the coast of the Mediterranean. A fertile crescent, starting at the Sinai Peninsula, swings north through Judea, paralleling the shoreline of the Levant. Judea was part of Coele Syria (Hollow Syria), for the Great Rift Valley between two of the earth's tectonic plates runs through it, stretching from the Bekaa Valley some 19 miles east of modern Beirut, south to the Dead Sea, then continuing to the Gulf of Aqaba and under the Red Sea into Africa. Along the coastline of Coele Syria were the little Phoenician kingdoms of Tyre, Sidon, Aradus, Byblos, modern Jubayl, and Berytus, modern Beirut. The Phoenicians were famous for their export of purple dye—in fact, their name means the "purple-dye people"—and they roamed the Mediterranean in search of the shellfish from which they extracted their dye. Rainfall in Coele Syria is fairly abundant, though most of it falls between November and May, and there is no frost in the winter, but push further to the east and the land grows arid. This land was disputed territory between the Seleucid and Ptolemaic kingdoms. The Ptolemies, who wanted it because it provided commodities that Egypt lacked, held on to it until the year 200, when the Seleucids drove them out and Judea was taken over by the Seleucid empire. Judea itself was a small state centered around Jerusalem when Alexander the Great passed by, on his way to conquer Egypt. There was a Jewish legend that he stopped to visit the Temple of Yahweh in Jerusalem and pay his respects, but it is almost certain that a visit to Jerusalem was not on his agenda.

Further north, in the northeast corner of the Mediterranean, a wide area of fertility stretches east from the Orontes River valley to the upper reaches of the Euphrates River. Seleucus I Nikator won this region in 301 and immediately founded 10 cities in it, one of which, Antioch, near the mouth of the Orontes, would develop by the mid-second century into the capital of the Seleucid empire and rival Alexandria. But that was in the future. When Seleucus founded these cities, he seems to have chosen their sites for their strategic value. All of them had strong walls, and they seem to have been islands of Greek and Macedonian settlers in a region populated with Aramaic-speaking farmers, who must have resented these newcomers who simply appropriated whatever land they needed for their own use. Seleucus did not intend these cities as centers of Greek culture. Their purpose was to secure a vital route between Mesopotamia and the Mediterranean.

The name Mesopotamia, the "land between the rivers," was coined in the Hellenistic period to refer to the region of modern Iraq. West and southwest of it was desert, and to the north and northeast were the Zagros Mountains. Between the rivers, the Euphrates to the west and the Tigris to the east, there were rolling uplands in the north and the alluvial plains of Babylonia in the central and southeast regions. The Greek historian Herodotus, who visited Babylonia in the fifth century while it was still part of the Persian empire, marveled at its fertility. Grain fields normally produced crops 200 fold, he reported, which was almost unbelievable to the Greeks of his day, who got yields of 8 or 10 fold. This was already a land of ancient civilizations when Alexander the Great reached it; the Sumerians, and after them the Akkadians, had been living in city-states there and irrigating the land long before Greek-speaking people even arrived in Greece. The ancestors of the Sumerians were there 7,000 years ago; their farming villages grew into towns, and by 5,000 years ago, the Sumerians had set the pattern for the Mesopotamian city-state in that each city acknowledged a god as its overlord whose temple was built on an artificial mound called a ziggurat. The ziggurat at Babylon was the Esagila, and on its summit was the holy of holies of Babylon's god, Marduk, the overlord of southern Mesopotamia in the worldview of the Babylonians; the king of Babylonia cemented his relationship as Marduk's representative each year at the New Year's Festival by grasping the right hand of Marduk's image in his temple. The Persians had been Zoroastrians, and Zoroastrianism, like all non-pagan religions, had scant tolerance for pagan gods. It was once thought that King Xerxes of Persia, who was a devout Zoroastrian, had destroyed the Esagila as punishment for a revolt in Babylon, and Alexander found it in ruins. The story is not true; the Persians did not destroy the Esagila, but they did neglect Marduk and his temple, and Alexander ordered that matters be set right. But not much was done and king Antiochus I (281–261) undertook the task again[2] and still—apparently—left it unfinished.

The Royal Road, which Darius I of Persia built to bind his empire together, ran from Sardis, 60 miles (96.5 km) east of Izmir in modern Turkey, to Nineveh, the old capital of the Assyrian empire, and from there south to Babylon. From there one branch of the Royal Road continued to Opis on the Tigris River—Seleucus I built his city of Seleucia-on-Tigris on the west bank opposite Opis, some 22 miles (35 km) south of modern Baghdad—and from there it went on to the old capital of the Medes, Ecbatana, and connected with the Silk Road along which the caravans carrying silk trudged from China. A southern branch went directly east from Babylon to Susa, one of the capitals of the Persian empire. It, too, would have a Hellenistic city built beside it, Seleucia ad Eulaeum—Seleucia on the Eulaeus River—which flowed out of the homeland of the Persians, Persis, as the Greeks called it, or Fars, according to the Persians themselves. Persepolis in Fars was the ceremonial capital of the Persian empire, where every March 21 the kings of Persia celebrated the New Year's Festival, and the provinces of their empire, or satrapies as they were called, brought them their tribute. Alexander's troops had set fire to the palace there, and it must have burned well, for the columns were made of wood. But the destruction eliminated the possibility of Alexander's successors ever assuming the role of a Persian king, for no Macedonian king could ever celebrate the New Year's Festival at Persepolis, and Persian nationalism smoldered in Fars.

East of Fars and Media, the country of the Medes who, like the Persians, were Iranians (or *Aryas,* as they called themselves), were the satrapies of Parthia, Bactria, and Sogdiana, nowadays part of Iran, northern Afghanistan, and Tajikistan. Bactria would have a history of its own in the Hellenistic period. About 245, the satrap of Bactria, Diodotus, revolted from the Seleucid king Antiochus II at a time when he was embroiled in war with Ptolemy III of Egypt. Bactria became an oasis of Hellenistic culture, and about 180, Greeks from Bactria expanded into northern India and founded an Indo-Greek kingdom there that lasted until 10 C.E. But Bactria was out of the mainstream of the Hellenistic world, even though it served as a conduit for Hellenistic cultural influences that reached not only northern India but China as well.

Egypt

Egypt was a world unto itself. The Nile flowed north from central Africa through a country where rain fell so rarely that Egypt would have been desert without the river. Egyptian agriculture depended on the Nile flood. Every year about mid-summer, the river flooded and covered the fields with water and silt. The land that the water inundated was fantastically fertile by the standards of ancient Greece, for in Egypt crops could be grown every year, whereas the usual pattern in Greece was to let the fields lie fallow every second year, though crop rotation was known and practiced. In Egypt, no crop rotation was necessary; the silt that the Nile deposited on the land served as fertilizer. Unlike Babylonia, where the land had to be irrigated, the Nile Valley was self-irrigating.

Yet the Egyptians did irrigate, for they soon learned to increase the arable area by digging irrigation canals to carry the water further into the desert and control its flow with dykes and sluices. Compared with the Tigris and the Euphrates, the Nile was a benevolent river, but it had to be monitored carefully. The farmers on its banks had to be warned when the flood was about to begin—it generally coincided with the heliacal rising of Sirius, the Dog Star—so that they could move to higher ground in time. Egyptian villages were usually sited on the edge of the desert. The dykes and sluices had to be ready, and once the floodwaters receded, the fields had to be planted according to plan.

If the flood was too small, Egypt went hungry, and a decree dating to 237 which lists the benefactions of king Ptolemy III, tells how his government once bought grain in Syria, Phoenicia, Cyprus and elsewhere to make up for a shortfall when the crops failed.[3] To run all this, a bureaucracy was necessary; all the Macedonians had to do was to take it over, make Greek the working language, and put immigrants in charge. The native Egyptians resented it, but fortunately for the Macedonians, the rule of the Persian empire had been hated in Egypt, and at first, at least, Alexander and his conquering army were seen as liberators. But the initial goodwill of the Egyptians soon faded.

In Middle Egypt, in the desert west of the Nile, there is a natural depression called the Fayum that is fed by water carried by a long canal called *Bahr Yusuf* (The Canal of Joseph), which connects with the Nile in Upper Egypt far to the south, and then follows the Nile along its western bank until it pours its water into the Fayum. When Herodotus visited Egypt in the mid-fifth century, he saw a lake in the Fayum called the Lake of Moeris. In fact, the pharaohs of the Middle Kingdom had already started to reclaim the lake, and as soon as Ptolemy I took control, the reclamation project went on apace. The lake shrank; all that is left today is a small saltwater lake called the *Birket el-Qarun* in the northwest corner of the Fayum, well below sea level. This area was made to order for the Macedonian and Greek settlers coming to Egypt. It is also rich in finds of papyri, for after the Roman empire fell the irrigated area shrank, and villages dating to the Hellenistic period were left high and dry. The arid desert is a great preservative.

Some of these papyri are fragments of Greek authors, and they give us some idea of what the Greeks in Egypt read. The majority, however, deal with everyday life: private letters, petitions, complaints, real estate transactions, trade and commerce, and the like. Nowhere else in the Hellenistic world do we get so intimate a look at everyday life.

In the north, before the Nile reaches the Mediterranean it flows through a delta where it splits into several branches. The Nile has built up the delta with layer upon layer of silt that it washed down from the interior of Africa. Archaeologists can expect to find little or nothing there, for ancient remains are buried too deep for them. But on the westernmost mouth of the Nile was the Egyptian village of Rhakotis, and it was there, cheek-by-jowl with the village, that Alexander founded Alexandria. Alexandria ad Aegyptum, it was called: Alexandria beside Egypt. It was Alexander's last resting place, for Ptolemy I managed to hijack the cortege that was taking Alexander's corpse from Babylon to Macedonia, where he was to be buried in the tomb of the Macedonian kings at Aegae in Greece, and brought it instead to Alexandria. Alexandria was intended as a Greek city, and it did become a center of Greek culture, with Rhakotis as its Egyptian quarter. But the Egyptians always regarded Alexandria as alien.

Nowhere else in the Hellenistic world was organized religion as important as it was in Egypt. It was a country of vast temples with throngs of priests. They possessed a generous portion of the arable land, which they leased to Egyptian farmers. The priesthood had loathed the Persians; there was even a tradition that king Cambyses II of Persia, who had conquered Egypt in 525, had killed the sacred Apis bull that incarnated the spirit of Osiris, god of the Underworld. The story is probably not true; it was born out of the hatred that the priests felt for their Persian masters. The Ptolemaic kings were careful to be generous to the temples, and for the most part the priesthood repaid them with loyalty. But the temples were the guardians of Egyptian customs and laws, and as the Ptolemaic monarchy grew weaker, they became centers of unrest.

The landscape of the Hellenistic world was diverse, but some features were shared by most regions. Summers were hot and dry and winters wet and cool but rarely extremely cold. Prolonged freezing temperatures were uncommon. Agriculture was primitive and labor-intensive by twenty-first century standards, though not by the standards of the early modern era, and crop yields were small. Egypt and Babylonia were exceptions. Travel was slow whether by land or sea, in spite of which the roads were full of travelers compared with the classical period that preceded it. Transportation overland was expensive: if crops failed in one region, its inhabitants faced starvation unless a king or a wealthy private individual intervened to subsidize the cost of transporting supplies from a region where the harvest had been good. Fuel was always scarce; without oil, natural gas or coal, the Hellenistic world may do with wood, shrubs, even dry grass or desiccated dung. Without an adequate supply of fuel, the steps that the early modern era took towards an industrial revolution were not possible. Nonetheless, the Hellenistic world was a brilliant period of western civilization.

NOTES

1. The probable meaning of *helot* is "captive."
2. Austin, no. 222.
3. For the Canopus decree, which is cited here, see Bagnall and Derow, no. 136; Austin, no. 222.

2

The Features of the Hellenistic City–State

ECONOMIC REALITIES

There is a story that Deinocrates, the city planner who designed the layout of Alexandria, once approached Alexander the Great with a proposal to found a city on Mount Athos, the easternmost of the three promontories that thrust down into the northern Aegean Sea. Alexander liked the plan. But, he asked, were there fertile farms in the region? Was there sufficient arable land to supply the food-stuffs that a city needed? For if there was not, a city on Mount Athos could not thrive. The story is a reminder of the economic realities of the Greek city. However attractive the site of the urban center, if the farms and orchards in the land round about—the *chôra*, as the Greeks called it—could not yield enough produce to supply the city, then it had to import.

Cities tried to feed themselves from the produce grown on their own farmland. Lucky the city that could do so reliably every year! The economics of transportation for bulky merchandise were quite different from what is familiar to us in the twenty-first century. The produce from the gardens in the *chôra* was brought to market-place in the urban center on the backs of patient donkeys. But wheat for bread, which was the staff of life in Greece, was another matter. If a city-state could not produce enough grain for its own needs, then it had to import it, often from a considerable distance: Egypt and the Ukraine were the breadbaskets of the Hellenistic world. Athens, for instance, had been importing grain from the Ukraine as early as the beginning of the classical period, if not earlier.

Transportation by sea was cheap; sailing ships needed no fuel, and the sailors, even the captain himself, were frequently slaves. Merchantmen, however, were slow and small, capable of carrying on average about 80 tons, with steering oars rather than rudders, and like all sailing ships, they were dependent on the weather. The navigation season closed for the winter. Some trading vessels in the Hellenistic period did brave winter storms, but it was a risky business. Overland transportation, by contrast, was expensive. The cost of carrying a wagonload of grain 200 miles could double its price. For luxury items such as silk that came by caravan from China, the market could bear the cost, for only the well-to-do bought silk. But bread was a necessity in Greece, for the poor as well as rich.

The Greeks knew several varieties of bread wheat, but all of them needed good soil and water. Marginal land could grow the second-most popular cereal crop of Greece, barley, which could be made into a porridge or polenta, and in years when the rains failed, polenta made from barley saved many poor families from starvation. But it was not a preferred food. It is ironic that the soil in Attica, the land of the Athenians, who considered barley fit to feed slaves and livestock but not free citizens, was far more suitable for growing barley than wheat. But wheat and barley were not the only grains. There were others as well, such as spelt and millet, both the common and the Italian varieties. In Egypt, a type of grain called *olyra* was used for baking bread. However, rye was probably unknown.

Food storage was a problem, for the ancient world had no refrigeration. Yet food had to be stored, otherwise a family would have little to eat in the winter and early spring. Olive trees could not be expected to produce bountiful crops every year, and so olive oil had to be stored when it was plentiful and cheap so that there would be a good supply in a year when there was a poor harvest. Olive oil was stored in large storage jars, whereas grain was stored in granaries, though a small farmer might keep a supply in a silo. Our best evidence for granaries comes from Hellenistic and Roman Egypt, where large houses might have had bins in their basements, and the state built large structures with rows of bins to store the grain collected as tax payments. Granaries were found everywhere. Cities had public granaries where they stored grain to release into the market when there was a local shortage, or if the city found itself under siege by an enemy. Wheat did not store as well as other grains such as millet, sesame, chickpeas, and the bean-like seeds of lupines, which are still used in parts of Europe as a cereal crop. Some fruits and vegetables could be pickled or dried; figs and grapes, for instance, were particularly valued because they were well suited for drying. Dates were an exotic fruit; the date palm grew well in Syria, and Babylonian dates were famous, but the date palm would not bear fruit in Greece.

Dried, smoked, or salted fish (*tarichos*) also kept well, and apparently salted fish was cheap, though the quality varied. Salted tuna had its champions and so did salted mackerel. Fresh fish was another matter. It was a favorite food, and there were many varieties of fish available at the market, such as carp, dogfish, skate, sturgeon, pike, sea bass, octopus, anchovies, gray mullet and little red mullets, and various shellfish, among others. Eels were particularly prized, and there were tradesmen called "eel-keepers" whose jobs were to transport eels in tanks to market, alive and healthy, for eels must be eaten absolutely fresh unless they are cooked or cured when they are caught. But the Greeks at dinner are a separate topic. Here our subject is not eating for pleasure, but to sustain life and avoid food shortages. Food supply was an ever-present concern for the government of a *polis.*

Supply shortage translates into inflated prices, and for the fourth century we do have some statistics. By 300, the cost of wheat was five times what it was 100 years earlier, and the price of oil trebled. This was partly because demand outstripped supply, but also partly because once the wealth that the Persian kings had hoarded in their treasuries was put into circulation, gold and silver became cheaper, and the purchasing power of the standard Greek coin, the drachma, dropped. As the economy adjusted to this flood of Persian gold and silver released into the economy, prices leveled out. In the century after 300, the cost of wheat dropped by nearly half. These are sketchy figures, but they show that even though we find much more affluence in the Hellenistic age than in the classical period that preceded it, every city had large numbers of people who lived below the poverty line. We should remember that about the time Alexander was setting out on his war of conquest, one could hire a slave for unskilled labor at three obols, that is, one-half a drachma a day. The troops in Alexander's army were not paid much more, but they lived with the hope of plunder.

THE *POLIS*, AS THE BASIC UNIT
OF GREEK CIVILIZATION

There is a tale told by the Greek historian Herodotus that when Cyrus the Great, the founder of the Persian Empire, overthrew the kingdom of Lydia and was about to send an army to secure the coastline of the Aegean Sea, he received a delegation from Sparta that warned him not to harm the Greek cities of Ionia. Surprised, Cyrus wanted more information about these Greeks, and when they were described to him, he snorted contemptuously. He could never respect men who set up a place in the heart of their city where they bought and sold and cheated each other. The marketplace or agora in the center of a Greek city was the shopping center where people bought and sold, but it was more than that: it was a place where Greek met Greek to converse freely about politics, gossip, or even questions of philosophy. In the heart of an Asian city such as Babylon, there was a ziggurat, and on its summit stood the temple of the city's god. The buying and selling of goods seems to have been done at the city gates.

The story illustrates the difference between a Mesopotamian city and a Greek *polis*, the word that is usually translated, rather inadequately, as the "city-state." The *polis* consisted of an urban center called an *asty*, with a marketplace, public buildings, and temples to the gods, and usually surrounded by a wall for defense, for the threat of enemy attack was a constant of Greek life.[1] The urban center was the hub of the city's trade and commerce, but outside its walls was the *chôra*—the countryside, where the citizens of the *polis* had their farms and orchards. A small farmer who worked his own acreage with the help of a slave or two might live on an isolated farm, but more typically he would live in a country village, where early each morning he would rise and go out to his fields, riding his donkey with a slave, or perhaps his wife, following behind. After a day's work, he would return to his village to eat and sleep and prepare for another day. Villages were more than dormitories, however. They had a social life of their own. The farmer's year was marked by religious festivals where feasting, dancing, choral singing, and dramatic presentations took place, and many villagers rarely left their homes to visit the urban center unless warfare intruded upon their lives. Owners of large land holdings, however, would have houses in the urban center, and their farms were worked by tenant farmers or slaves.

A *polis* aspired to be free and independent. It wanted to pass its own laws, administer justice on its own terms, shape its own foreign policy, and coin its own money, with the result that Greece had no currency that was internationally accepted until Alexander the Great minted his silver tetradrachms.[2] Yet, in reality, even in the classical period before Alexander the Great, few *poleis* were completely independent. The great city-states were anomalies: Athens, which possessed the western peninsula of Greece called Attica; Sparta, which at its height ruled the southern half of the Peloponnesus; Argos, south of the Isthmus of Corinth; and Thebes, which dominated the fertile Boeotian plain north of Attica, could claim to be independent. But there were a great number of smaller *poleis*—Aristotle in his *Politics* puts their number at about 300—and their average size was about 125 square miles. For many of these, freedom was little more than an aspiration, even in the classical period, and in the Hellenistic period few cities could call themselves completely free and able to chart their own course.

However, much as the idea of freedom might tug at the heartstrings, it often meant simply freedom to dominate other cities. In the fifth century, Athens collected tribute from a vast array of city-states on the Greek islands and the lands bordering the Aegean Sea, allowing them limited independence at best. Sparta dominated the *poleis* of the Peloponnesus with a network of alliances, and in central Greece, the *poleis* that shared the Boeotian plain where Thebes was the most powerful city joined in a federation known as the Boeotian League. Yet a Greek's loyalty to the city was strong, and odd as it may seem, he would remain loyal to his native city even if it was destroyed, or forcibly merged with another city, which occasionally happened. A *polis* guarded its citizenship jealously and did not grant it easily to immigrants. Athens in the mid-fifth century passed a law restricting Athenian citizenship to persons whose fathers and mothers were both citizens, and Athens set an unfortunate example to other cities. In the Hellenistic period, there are many instances of cities granting honorary citizenship to aliens who were benefactors, rather like the honorary degrees that universities confer on large donors, but these honorary citizenships did little to mitigate the situation. If a citizen was exiled from his city of birth, he would not find it easy to acquire citizenship in another *polis*, unless as a settler he could join a new city that was being founded;

otherwise he remained a resident alien in a *polis* that was not his own. The *polis* remained the basic unit of Greek social, cultural, and religious life, even after its political importance was diminished in the new world that Alexander created.

It is well to remember this, for Alexander and his successors used the city-state to spread Greek hegemony and culture over the vast area that the Macedonians conquered. Alexander himself founded some 20 cities, the greatest of which was Alexandria in Egypt, and his successor, Seleucus I, who grabbed control of the vast region from Asia Minor to Afghanistan, followed his example. Seleucus founded 16 cities named Antioch after his father, and 5 named Laodicea after his mother. He named 9 Seleucia after himself, 4 he named after his wives, and many others he named after cities in Greece or Macedonia. The public architecture and town planning in these *poleis* was recognizably Greek; in their schools, students followed a Greek curriculum, and in their gymnasiums, their young men exercised naked in the Greek manner, and learned what it was to be an inheritor of the Hellenic cultural tradition. The political freedom of these cities founded in the Seleucid realm was restricted, for the kings knew how to protect their own interests, but in most local matters, they were self-governing. They had the appurtenances of self-government, such as popular assemblies and councils to control their agendas, though it looks as if they spent much of their time passing decrees awarding honors to very important persons, as well as benefactors past, present—and future, if the city's hopes were fulfilled.

The process of founding a city followed by the Seleucid kings—and also by the kings of Pergamon, who were also founders—was first to plant a colony of Macedonian or Greek settlers at a chosen location, which might be near a native city or village. For instance, Seleucia-on-Tigris, which became for practical purposes the Mesopotamian capital of the Seleucid empire, was founded across the Tigris River from the ancient city of Opis. Each settler would be given a parcel of land and a site for a dwelling, and in return he would be expected to belong to the army reserve—in fact, many settlers were former mercenary soldiers. A successful colony quickly evolved into a city, with a marketplace, gymnasium, and a theater. The kings of Ptolemaic Egypt were also founders of cities in their overseas territories, but within Egypt itself, the arable land was a long, narrow strip on either side of the Nile, and native villages were sited on the edge of the desert, out of reach of the Nile flood. The Greek settlers in Egypt lived in the villages, and each was given a *kleros*—that is, a parcel of land, and a house site in a village. In return, the settler owed the king military service. The land continued to belong to the king, as all land in Egypt did, but the settlers had generous leases; in fact, as the royal government became weaker toward the end of the Hellenistic period, the settlers treated their *kleroi* very much as if they were private property.

In the Greek homeland, the old cities that had been important before Alexander the Great changed the Greek world forever lived under the shadow of the Macedonian kingdom. Corinth, Chalcis, and Piraeus, the harbor town of Athens, were garrisoned with Macedonian troops, for their strategic importance was too great for the Macedonian kings to relinquish them. Athens itself was free from 288 onwards, though for a brief period of seven years she had a Macedonian garrison. Sparta, now reduced to the southeast corner of the Peloponnesus peninsula, had its independence finally terminated by Rome in 195. Elsewhere in Greece we find cities experimenting with leagues and federations. Dominating the Peloponnesus was a league known as the Achaean League, which sought to limit Macedonian influence, and in the northwest there was the Aetolian League, a federation that at its height dominated central Greece and controlled Delphi, the site of the god Apollo's oracle as well as the Pythian Games, one of the great festivals of Greece. Most of the cities were—or claimed to be—democracies, but in fact, political power was concentrated in the hands of the well-to-do, who were generally large property owners. For all of these, however, independence would end with the coming of Rome. Greece became a Roman protectorate in 146.

THE APPEARANCE OF A CITY

According to Aristotle—who, among other claims to fame, briefly tutored Alexander the Great, and later in his life founded one of the Hellenistic world's great philosophic schools, the Lyceum, at Athens—the first Greek to design a model city was Hippodamus of Miletus, who lived in the fifth century. His ideal city had an orderly, orthogonal plan, with streets crossing each other at right angles to form a grid. Sometimes, as at Pergamon, which was sited on a hillside, the cross-streets followed the contours of the slope, but if the site allowed it, the streets were straight even if they had to climb a steep slope with staircases. There was always an agora or marketplace in the Hellenistic city, and town planners liked to define the agora with porticoes, called stoas by the Greeks, around its perimeter. Stoas were expensive to build, of course, and many cities owed theirs to kind benefactors who donated the money. Hellenistic Athens had a good example: a marble stoa built with funds given by the king of Pergamon, Attalus II (159–138), which defined one side of the Athenian agora. In the 1950s, the Stoa of Attalus was rebuilt to serve as a museum, and it gives the modern tourist a vivid impression of what an ancient stoa looked like. Merchants hawking their wares could set up their stalls between the columns, where they would be protected in the summer from the heat of the sun, and from the rain in the winter. The *bouleuterion*, or council house where the city council met to deliberate, would also be in or close to the agora: At the city of Priene on the slopes of Mount Mycale, for instance, the little rectangular council chamber with tiers of seats along three sides opened on to the agora. Nearby there might be other public buildings, such as a fountain-house, an open-air theater, public baths, and perhaps an *odeion* or roofed music hall, where audiences could gather for musical performances or poetry recitations. There might be a gymnasium where young Greeks went to school; in classical cities gymnasiums were generally found in the suburbs, but in the Hellenistic period they tended to move closer to the city center, which is a sign of their increased importance. Athens, for instance, had three gymnasiums in the classical period, all built in the suburbs, but in the Hellenistic period king Ptolemy VI of Egypt (181–145) provided the funds for an urban gymnasium called the Ptolemaion in the heart of the city. There would be temples to the gods. A temple to the city's patron deity would probably be near the city center; in Athens the temple to Athena *Polias* ("Guardian of the City") was on the acropolis, which towered above the agora. A defensive wall surrounded the city, and outside the city gates the main roads leading into the city would be lined with tombs, for burial of the dead within the urban space that the walls defined was forbidden.

In fact, orthogonal city plans did not begin with Hippodamus, nor were they a Greek invention: ancient Babylon, for instance, had one. Yet Hippodamus's name became synonymous with town plans where streets crossed each other at right angles. He laid out the design for Piraeus, the harbor town of Athens, and he was associated with the planning for Rhodes, for in 408, the three *poleis* on the island of Rhodes joined to form a single *polis*, with a new urban center that was laid out following Hippodamian principles. Priene, about 30 km south of Ephesus, is another well-preserved example of Hippodamian planning. Priene was moved from its previous location and rebuilt about 350, while the Persian empire still ruled the region, but Alexander the Great's army liberated it in 334: One house found at Priene has been named the House of Alexander and it is at least possible that Alexander stayed there briefly. The city faced south: It was important to take advantage of the winter sun, for the houses had no central heating, nor, for that matter, any efficient method of heating them at all. There were six major east-west streets; one, the main thoroughfare, was about 8 yards wide, and the others slightly less than 5 yards. Intersecting them were streets 3.8 yards wide, and since they ran north-south (that is, up the side of the hill), they were built with steps to allow pedestrians to climb the slope. The streets divided the city into standard blocks, and in the quarters reserved for public buildings, each building took up a full block, whereas in the domestic quarters where the private houses were built, a block generally accommodated four houses. The typical house was small, with an open court and rooms surrounding it, and with some exceptions the houses had only a single story.

In the city center was a temple of Athena, the city's patron goddess. According to an inscription found on the site, it was dedicated in 334 in the name of Alexander the Great, who gave Priene the funds to complete its construction. Inside the temple stood a cult statue of Athena, which was a replica of the gold and ivory statue of Athena Parthenos ("the Virgin") in the Parthenon at Athens. East of the temple was the agora, the city's marketplace, surrounded by stoas, and opening on to it on the north and south sides were pubic buildings: a *bouleuterion* where the city council met, a *prytaneion* or town hall, a gymnasium, a stadium, various temples, and a theater. If we had a census of Priene we would probably discover that it had a population of between four and five thousand. Plato, who outlined an ideal foundation to be built on Crete in his last major work, the *Laws,* put the population of his model city at 5,040 souls, and Priene was close to Plato's ideal. It was a homogeneous community, where religion and state were intimately connected, persons wearing foreign dress rarely walked the streets, and everyone took part in the religious festivals and sacrifices that honored the gods, particularly the patron goddess of the city.

A small, homogeneous city like Priene contrasts with the large multicultural cities of the Hellenistic world, such as Alexandria in Egypt, Antioch in Syria, or Seleucia-on-Tigris. Alexandria was the first city that Alexander the Great founded, and even though he never visited it during his lifetime, he came there in death, for

Ptolemy I, who founded the Ptolemaic dynasty that ruled Egypt, saw to it that the cortege bearing Alexander's body to Macedonia for burial was diverted, first to Memphis, the old dynastic capital of Egypt, and then to Alexandria, where a magnificent tomb was built for him, near the royal palace, and there his body was laid in a golden casket. The city planner was Alexander's favorite architect, Deinocrates. Most of ancient Alexandria has now subsided beneath the sea, but underwater archaeology, along with the surviving descriptions of it, allows us to reconstruct what Deinocrates's vision was. He laid out a rectangular city with city blocks measuring 300 by 150 feet. Adjoining the city center to the northeast were the royal palaces and gardens, and on the southwest side was the Sarapeion, the temple of the god Sarapis, a god that was promoted by the Ptolemaic kings who imagined that his worship would attract both their Greek and Egyptian subjects. The main east-west avenue, the Canopic Way, 100 feet wide, cut through the city center, where we would have found the agora, and probably the law courts, a gymnasium, and the Mouseion with its great library, founded by Ptolemy I. Alexandria became the most populous city in the Hellenistic world, attracting immigrants both Greek and non-Greek, including a Jewish community that took over one of the five quarters of the city. With its orderly plan, it was almost an aggressive symbol of Hellenistic culture attached to Egypt, which the Greeks and Macedonians had acquired by conquest, and which had its own ancient civilization and its own religious cults that owed nothing to Greece.

Only a small portion of Seleucia-on-Tigris has been excavated, but there is enough to show that it must have been one of the largest cities of the Hellenistic world, and laid out according to a gridiron plan. Antioch, on the Orontes River in northern Syria, has been extensively explored, but most of the remains found there are Roman—it has some splendid examples of late Roman houses. It was one of 10 cities founded by Seleucus I Nikator after 301, when he added northern Syria to his empire after the defeat and death of Antigonos the One-Eyed at the Battle of Ipsos. Antioch was not built as the capital city of an empire, for Seleucus I and his immediate successors had various major cities in their vast empire where the royal court might reside for extended periods, such as: at Babylon; Seleucia-on-Tigris, or the old Persian capital of Susa; and in the west, Ephesus was a favorite residence until the early second century, when the Seleucids were forced out of Anatolia by the

Romans. Antioch came into its own in the late Hellenistic period, when its population soared to over 400,000. The original city that Seleucus founded on the north fringes of the Orontes River imitated the gridiron plan of Alexandria, and over it arose Mount Silpius, which served as its citadel.

From the beginning, Antioch was multicultural. Greeks, Macedonians, and Jews made up its original settlers. Seleucus's son, Antiochus I, added a native quarter. As the city grew, a third quarter was built on an island in the Orontes River, and finally, king Antiochus IV (175–164) added a fourth quarter. Antioch acquired the appearance of a Hellenistic city, but Hellenistic culture there was never more than skin-deep. The common language of the streets was Aramaic, the native tongue of the Syrians, and the gods that attracted Antiochene worshipers were Syrian, not Greek. However, a few miles outside the city Seleucus built the park of Daphne, a "paradise," as the Greeks called it, borrowing the word from the Persians, who loved to built parks with trees and flowering plants where a person could find relaxation. A great temple of Apollo stood in the park of Daphne, with a cult statue by the sculptor Bryaxis, who also sculpted the cult statue for the great temple of Sarapis in Alexandria. Apollo, the god of music and poetry, and of the physical perfection of the naked body, whether male or female, was the emblem of Greek culture, where as among cultures of the orient, nakedness was a mark of immodesty.

City bylaws were enforced by officials known as *astynomoi*. Athens had ten of them, five for Athens itself and five for Piraeus, the city's port. An inscription[3] survives from Pergamon which illuminates the situation there. Main streets were to be at least 30 feet wide, and secondary streets no less that 8 feet, and owners of property along the streets were to keep them neat. Drains were to be underground; digging open drains was forbidden. The *astynomoi* see to it that the cost of garbage collection was shared among the property owners, and if an owner failed to pay his share, the *astynomoi* could seize goods belonging to him and sell them. Other regulations dealt with building permits and water supply. Washing clothes at public fountains was forbidden and so was watering animals there. Pergamon was the royal city of the Attalid kings and was better off than the average city where unpaved streets and open drains were the norm. Yet all Hellenistic cities were high-density centers of population where everyday life produced garbage, sewage, street litter and quarrels between home owners whose houses shared party walls.

NOTES

1. *Polis* is a somewhat slippery word. In the Hellenistic period it can refer to the city itself, or to the city plus the countryside and its villages that made up a political unity. Modern students of the ancient world have coined the word *city-state* to refer to the latter.

2. A tetradrachm was a coin worth four drachmas. A drachma was worth six obols.

3. Austin, no. 216.

3

Dwelling Houses

The Roman architect and engineer Vitruvius Pollio, who lived in the reign of the emperor Augustus, wrote an influential handbook on architecture and design that we still have, and in it he devoted one chapter to the Greek house and how it differed from the contemporary Roman house. He explains the features of a grand Hellenistic house, and by now we can supplement it with a great deal of new information from archaeological excavations that graphically illustrate how people lived. The finds range widely. At Pella, the capital of Macedonia, there are splendid houses, and at Aegae, modern Vergina, which was the Macedonian capital before Pella, there is a palace dating to the reign of the king Antigonos II Gonatas (283–239). The Vergina palace had magnificent mosaics on its floors and splendid paintings decorating its walls. On the island of Delos, where there were also fine houses, we have found humble rental properties for the working poor. New cities founded in the Hellenistic age typically had palaces, and they were a far cry from the crowded one- or two-story shops where poor tradesmen lived— some free, others slaves.

Archaeologists have also found the remains of farmhouses, some isolated in the countryside and others built in country villages. Their architecture varied, but one feature they shared was a courtyard of generous size that could shelter the family's livestock. Another feature was a tower, which some archaeologists think was slaves' quarters, for the towers could be locked. Other scholars speculate that these towers were the women's quarters in the farmhouse, where the women of the household could seek shelter from intruders. But cities were the centers of commercial and cultural life, and urban sites provide the most abundant evidence.

The city of Olynthus in northern Greece was destroyed by Alexander's father, Philip II, in 348, and its remains have provided archaeologists with information about how the Greeks in a north Aegean town lived at the start of the Hellenistic age. Houses, which at Olynthus were roughly square and averaged about 56.4 feet across, presented a blank wall to the street like most houses in the eastern Mediterranean, and there were no windows on the first floor, though in two-story houses small windows may have been found on the second floor. From the Acts of the Apostles[1] we learn that when Paul the Apostle was in the city of Troas near ancient Troy, a young man was sitting in a window on a third floor when sleep overcame him while Paul was speaking, and he fell to the ground. So some houses did have upper floors with windows large enough for a man to fall through, but on excavation sites, upper floors are rarely well preserved enough for archaeologists to draw plans of them. From the front door, a hallway led into an open courtyard that supplied the rooms off it with air and light. House walls at Olynthus were constructed of mud brick on stone socles, for if the mud brick walls were in direct contact with the earth they would have been easily damaged by winter downpours, when rainwater ran down the streets.

Greek master builders sought, if possible, to orient their houses towards the south and even build the north wall of the courtyard higher than the south wall, so that it would protect the courtyard from the north winds and at the same time catch the winter sun, for these houses must have been chilly in the winter. The *oikos*, or main living room, may have been heated—very inadequately from a modern viewpoint—by an earthenware brazier that burned charcoal, though in northwest Greece at Leucas, a house type has been found where there is a large inside room with a hearth in the center. At Olynthus, the typical house often had a portico built along the north wall of the courtyard, sometimes with enclosed rooms at both ends, which served to keep the rooms that opened on to the courtyard cool in the summer when the sun was overhead, while in winter, when the sun was low in the southern sky, light would shine into the portico and keep the rooms warm. This architectural feature was evidently called a *pastas*. At Priene we find a variation of the type, the *prostas* house. The *prostas* was a narrow porch without enclosed rooms at either end, projecting on to the courtyard in front of the main group of rooms. There was another, grander type of dwelling, too, the peristyle house, which was a house with colonnades surrounding three or four sides of the courtyard. There were a few examples at Olynthus, but many of the best examples are found on the island of Delos, where most of them date to the island's great period of prosperity in the second half of the second century and the early first century.

Courtyards regularly had earth floors, but some might be paved with cobblestones, pebbles, or even mosaics, if the owner could afford them—Delos had some splendid examples of the mosaicist's art. The courtyard was the only area in the house that was well lit, and it was there that much of the everyday work of the household must have been done.

What sort of life went on in these rooms? One room in Greek houses that archaeologists have unearthed can be recognized with certainty—the *andron,* or men's room—for the entrance is always off center, and a slightly raised platform usually runs along all four sides. It was at the front of the house and was clearly the room where the master of the house entertained his guests, who reclined on couches resting upon the low platform around the room's perimeter. The doorway had to be off center to accommodate the couches, for if there were 7 couches, or 11, which was a more common number in the Hellenistic period, 3 could be placed along each of three sides, but there was space for the other 2 along the entrance wall only if the doorway was off center. This was a purpose-built room where the master of the house could share a meal with a few friends, and as the name, *andron* indicates, it was a meal for men only. Once the meal was done, a symposium—a drinking party—might follow, where a large mixing bowl for the wine, called a *krater,* was brought in; once the wine was mixed with water, the guests drank deep and made merry.

Other rooms are more difficult to identify. At Olynthus a number of the houses had rooms with earth floors that were clearly kitchens, and used for cooking, but at other sites, kitchens are often not easy to identify. One of the rooms off the courtyard would be a living room, and it might have several small rooms opening off it. Ancient authors such as Vitruvius also refer to women's quarters, which has led students of ancient Greece to believe that women were secluded from the outside world in a set of rooms within the house. Yet, archaeology has revealed no evidence for any group of rooms in Greek houses that were clearly intended as women's quarters. However, archaeologists rarely come across second floors of houses that are well preserved, and according to ancient authors, women's quarters were often on the second floor. The archaeological evidence for women's quarters is somewhat ambiguous. However, weaving and sewing were women's tasks, and both need rooms that are well lit, which would be the rooms around the courtyard; in fact, one ancient author refers to the women's quarters simply as the rooms for everyday living that surrounded the courtyard. Greek women used an upright loom with the warp threads held taut with loom weights, and though the loom could be dismantled and stored when it was not in use, once a weaver began to produce a textile, the loom could not be moved until the textile was finished. Thus we could expect to find a purpose-built weaving room in a Greek house, where a weaver might set up her loom and leave it undisturbed until the textile was finished. But we do not. In fact, finds that we would associate with women's activities, such as loom weights, to say nothing of cooking pots, are discovered everywhere in the excavated remains of ancient houses. Loom weights are not confined to any single area. So the women's quarters that ancient authors mention may simply be the rooms that women occupied most frequently as they carried on their household chores, and we cannot expect to find separate apartments in Greek houses where women could be sequestered away from male eyes.

THE HOUSE AT LEUCAS: AN EXAMPLE
OF MIDDLE-CLASS LIVING IN A COLD CLIMATE

The remains of one house on the island of Leucas in northwest Greece are instructive, for it was built as a seven-room house at the end of the third century or the beginning of the second, and then later, three more rooms were added. The *polis* of Leucas was moderately prosperous until it was suddenly abandoned about the year 30. We can guess what happened. Leucas was close by Actium, where the fleets of Mark Antony and Cleopatra were defeated by Julius Caesar's heir, Octavian, in the year 31, and to commemorate his victory, Octavian founded a city on the Ambracian Gulf named Nicopolis, the City of Victory. To provide Nicopolis with an instant population, the people dwelling in the cities nearby were moved there whether they wanted to go or not, and Leucas was largely abandoned. The misfortune of the Leucadians was a lucky break for modern archaeologists who excavated Leucas in the 1990s, for city life there ended at the same time as the Hellenistic age came to a close, and what its population left behind when they left the city are valuable clues for the life that went on there.

The house in question had 10 rooms after it was enlarged, and two courtyards, one behind the other, which divided the house into two sets of rooms. A visitor would enter from the street through the front door and find himself in the smaller of the two courtyards, which took the place of a hallway. The *andron* was on his right and on his left was the main living room—the *oikos*. The floors were of earth, but both the *andron* and the living room had walls of painted plaster. These were the public rooms of the house; the visitor might go no further unless he was a special friend. The living room had a fireplace to heat it, for Leucas is far enough north to have chilly winters. This home at Leucas is not a peristyle house, nor a *prostas* or *pastas* type, but a new type of house that has been encountered in northern Greece, where there is a large interior living room with a hearth for heat when it was cold outside. Two rooms opened off this living room, and one of them must have been a bathroom, for it had a small drain and a floor plastered with mortar that, if not completely waterproof, was at least water resistant. The family members who lived in this house at Leucas did not have to go to the public bath to bathe themselves. A small door connected the front courtyard with the rear courtyard, which was evidently not a place that a stranger would penetrate. As in most Greek houses, the layout leaves us with the strong impression that the people who lived here placed a high value on privacy.

The kitchen at the back of the house was easy to identify, for it had a hearth and a large number of vessels for cooking, and between it and the rear courtyard was a storeroom—at least a large storage jar called a *pithos* was found there. This second courtyard had a well, and a little room close by it with a waterproof floor was perhaps a laundry room; perhaps, too, there was a wooden stairway off this courtyard to an upper story, though no trace of it was found. Two rooms tucked in behind the *andron* were intriguing. One of them, a small room with a latrine en suite, seems to have been the antechamber for a windowless room with painted walls where a good deal of pottery was found, both fine and plain ware, but no cooking pots. Can this have been the private chamber of the master of the house and his wife, where they slept and kept their valuables?

UPSCALE HOMES

This house at Leucas must have belonged to a family that cannot be described as rich, but they were comfortably above the poverty line. The house was spacious, but not by any means deluxe. For more luxurious houses, we must look elsewhere. Large houses had peristyle colonnades surrounding a central quadrangle with a mosaic pavement. At Pella, the capital of Macedonia, some large houses of this type were built at the end of the fourth century, and the examples that have been partially restored demonstrate how spacious and airy this type of house must have been. On the island of Delos, archaeologists have also found lavish peristyle-type houses of a later date, whose owners must have been wealthy merchants or traders who migrated there after 167, when Rome made Delos a free port and it became a great marketplace especially for wheat and slaves. But in addition to the upscale houses with fine wall paintings and mosaics on the floors of their peristyle courtyards, there were also more modest dwellings with a vestibule leading to a courtyard and two or three rooms that provided living space at the back. Instead of an *andron* or a living room in the front of the house, there would be space for a shop that might be rented out. Or it might be a work space for the tradesman owner of the house. Besides these, the excavations at Delos, which have gone on since 1873, have revealed a whole range of shops and humble living units that allow us to imagine how the working poor existed.

LIVING CONDITIONS OF THE WORKING POOR

The shops on Delos, or *tabernae* as the archaeologists designate them, numbered more than 500 and were scattered over the city, perhaps as rental units in houses or as part of larger building complexes. They can be identified by their separate entrances on to the street, and many were rented out to poor tenants. The numerous inscriptions found on the island tell us, among other things, that the temple of Apollo was a large-scale landlord, for Delos was Apollo's birthplace; like temples elsewhere, Apollo's temple was a property owner, and it was in the business of leasing and banking. A *taberna* might have a second floor or a mezzanine where the tenant might sleep, though in many cases the second floor would be rented out separately, and the first-floor tenant would live and work in his little shop. Water, which is scarce on Delos, was available from communal wells or cisterns. It was in dwellings like these that laborers in the Hellenistic world lived and worked; some of them were free persons, many of them, no doubt, slaves.

HELLENISTIC HOMES IN EGYPT

So much for old Greece—that is, the Greek world as it was before Alexander. What of Hellenistic Egypt? Egypt was not a country of *poleis*, but it was divided into nomes, which predated the arrival of its Macedonian conquerors, and the nomes had nome capitals, usually the largest village in the nome. Let us look at one of them: Oxyrhynchus, which took its name from the sharp-nosed oxyrhynchus fish, which was sacred in Egypt, and especially at Oxyrhynchus. Excavations at Oxyrhynchus between 1897 and 1906 have yielded an enormous harvest of documents written on papyri, ranging from private letters to tax registers, but including important fragments of documents by ancient authors that were discarded and preserved for modern scholars by the dry climate. Oxyrhynchus is on the *Bahr Yusuf*, the channel west of the Nile that carries water to the depression in the desert known now as the Fayum. Oxyrhynchus had a wall for protection, with five entry gates. The town inside the walls had no systematic plan, but it did have some impressive public buildings built of stone. There was a gymnasium, a record office, a theater, public baths, and many temples: old shrines belonging to the native gods, and more recent constructions built by the Ptolemaic kings. The largest of them all was the temple of Sarapis, whose cult the Ptolemaic kings favored. Egyptian temples were a complex of buildings: workshops, small housing units for workmen connected with the cult, a market for traders who rented space in the temple complex to hawk their wares, and money changers who carried on their activities in the shadow of the temple.

Most of the population in Hellenistic Oxyrhynchus lived in very unpretentious accommodations. The evidence is far better for the Roman period or later, in the Byzantine period, but we can make some inferences about what life was like for a native Egyptian or a Greek settler who dwelt in Oxyrhynchus in the Hellenistic age. He might live in a housing complex with apartments that housed a number of families. A moderately well-to-do Oxyrhynchite might own apartments or rooms in several such dwellings, which he could rent out or use as surety for loans. There were individual houses, too, usually very modest, built of mud brick with two floors, containing courtyards where there were clay ovens for baking and millstones for grinding grain into flour; there might also be pens in the courtyard where pigs, goats, geese, or chickens were kept. Pigeons were also kept to supply both food for eating and guano for the fields, and were fattened on the grain that was wasted in the harvest. In one village in Egypt, there was found a communal dovecote.

One would not mistake Oxyrhynchus for a Greek city. Troupes of actors on tour no doubt visited its theater—a contract with a troupe has survived, though it dates from the Roman period. In the Oxyrhynchus gymnasium, the village youth received a Greek education. Hellenistic culture pervaded public life. Yet the temples of the Egyptian gods remained strongholds of pharaonic traditions dating into the distant past. Egypt was full of monuments that must have reminded both the Egyptians themselves and their Macedonian conquerors of Egypt's long history. There were the pyramids built in the Old Kingdom period, tombs of divine pharaohs already more than 2,000 years old when the Macedonians arrived. There were the great temples with their multitudes of priests, who preserved Egypt's traditions and regarded the Macedonians as interlopers who had to be tolerated so long as they respected the ancient gods of Egypt and the priests. Yet Greek settlers and Egyptians lived side by side, and inevitably crossover between the two cultures took place, particularly after Egypt became part of the Roman empire and Greeks and Egyptians found themselves with one thing in common: they were both subjects of Rome.

NOTE

1. Acts 20:9–10.

4

Clothing and Fashion

GREEK STYLE

The clothes that people wear make a statement, and the statement that Greek fashion made was that the wearer was a Greek by ancestry or by assimilation to Greek culture. He was not a Persian or Egyptian or a Scythian. Greek fashion remained remarkably stable over the years, perhaps because it signaled participation in Hellenistic civilization. The Hellenistic Greeks wore the same types of clothing as the Greeks in the classical period, before 323. The sleeveless tunic called the *chiton* was the basic item of men's clothing. Adding sleeves to the tunic was considered a mark of oriental luxury, and the Greeks had a lively prejudice against orientalism, but in fact sleeved tunics were worn when the temperature dropped. So was a woolen cloak known as a *chlaina* or a *himation,* an outer garment that both men and women wore wrapped around their shoulders and falling in graceful folds over their body. A woman might draw it over her head to form a cowl. The *himation* was not a practical garment for the working man, for it confined his arms too much, and in fact, the *himation* signaled that its wearer did not have to do physical labor.

The cloak known as the *chlamys* was a swatch of cloth, more or less rectangular, with three straight sides and the fourth side concave, that was draped around the shoulders, straight edge up, and pinned at the base of the neck so that the folds fell down as far as the knees. It was the favorite costume for horsemen in Greece. In Sparta, the military elite called the Spartiates, who trained from an early age to be effective infantry troops, wore the *chlamys* as their customary dress. The Spartiate *chlamys* was red; long before the British army adopted red uniforms and formed a thin red line on many battlefields, the Spartiates also had their own thin red line, and perhaps for the same reasons: red was a cheap dye, and it hid blood stains. In Sparta, the military elite that ruled the state made the *chlamys* their customary dress. The *chlamys* was also the favorite dress of horsemen in Greece, and it became virtually the national costume of the Macedonians, along with a hat with a brim called the *petasos* or *causia*. Macedonian nobles wore a purple *chlamys*. It was Alexander the Great's favorite costume.

For women the standard dress was the *peplos,* a sheet of woolen cloth, oblong in shape, that was first folded horizontally so that the top quarter was turned back, and then folded from top to bottom to make a double sheet, shaped to form a square with an overfold along its upper edge. This folded sheet was then draped over the body and fastened at the shoulders with safety pins or brooches. The right side was pinned shut; otherwise, one might glimpse the wearer's body as she moved, though apparently the emancipated women of Sparta, who used to exercise naked in the gymnasium with their men, preferred an open *peplos*. For most Greek women, however, the open *peplos* was immodest. The overfold of the *peplos* could hang down freely over the breasts, or be gathered at the waist with a girdle.

Fabric and Adornments

The most common fabrics were wool and linen. Wool was easier to dye than linen, and skilful weavers could weave it into a very fine, light textile. Linen, which was found in the Mediterranean as early as the Bronze Age, was made from domesticated flax that produced the fiber used to make linen thread and also the seeds that produced linseed oil. The finest linen came from Egypt, where the Egyptian priests wore white linen garments, and those who could afford it wore linen that was so fine it was semitransparent. Hemp was used for cloth in Thrace on the northern fringe of the Aegean world, and cotton fabric was imported from India late in the Hellenistic period. Silk, however, another imported fabric, was a different matter. It was the epitome of luxury dress. There was domestic silk fabric produced on Cos, the second largest of the Dodecanese Islands after Rhodes. It was made from thread extracted from the cocoon of a moth native to the island, and the silk of Cos was much prized. But the best silk came from China over a long caravan route across the continent of Asia. The volume was small until after 100, and it was not until the period of the Roman empire that large amounts of silk were imported.

Silk was not the only sign of status and wealth. Hellenistic graves have yielded examples of gold jewelry that are splendid examples of the goldsmith's craft. A wealthy woman in the Hellenistic period might wear an exquisite golden wreath of laurel or oak leaves to her grave. The wafer-thin leaves copied nature in beaten gold. Perfumes and unguents were in demand, too, and little flasks used to hold perfumes have been found in tombs that date as early as the Bronze Age, long before the Hellenistic period. Egypt's exports included perfumes, which were an important item of trade that was encouraged by the government. Roses were grown commercially in Egypt for making attar of roses, and frankincense and myrrh were imported from Arabia and East Africa for making ointments and salves. The scents that little perfume and unguent containers in graves once held vanished long ago, but many examples of the containers themselves have survived as mute evidence of the popularity of perfumes.

Greek garments were often woven in intricate patterns using dyed yarn, and the weavers had various dyes that they could use. The most expensive was the purple dye with a hint of crimson that was made from a shellfish found in the Mediterranean. Purple garments signaled high office; they were worn by kings and princes, and important city magistrates. The cheapest dye was a red pigment extracted from the root of the madder plant, and a cut-rate purple dye could be made by combining madder red with indigo. The stamen of the safflower provided a bright orange dye, and from the leaves of the henna shrub came a reddish orange pigment. From India came a much-prized violet blue dye made from the indigo plant, though a dye almost as good could be made from an indigo plant native to Egypt. There was also a bright scarlet dye, made from a scale insect called the *kermes* that was found in India. For mordants to fix the colors, the cloth industry used human urine, alum from wood ashes, or natron from Egypt—that is, sodium carbonate or washing soda. Until the discovery of chemical dyes in the nineteenth century, dyers in the modern period used methods little more advanced than the Greeks.

STYLES OF THE "OTHER"

Clothing was a mark of nationality, and in the Hellenistic world there were many different ethnic groups that rubbed shoulders on the streets. Some adopted Greek-style clothing. The book of Second Maccabees[1] describes how Judea adopted Greek ways under the high priest Jason—his Jewish name was Joshua—in the reign of Antiochus IV Epiphanes ("God Manifest"). He built a gymnasium in Jerusalem where Jewish youth belonging to the leading families exercised naked, Greek style, wrestling and throwing the discus, and he induced them to wear the "Greek hat." The Greek hat was the broad-brimmed hat called the *petasos,* which the god Hermes wore; it was also the style in Macedonia. In Judea and elsewhere it was a symbol of the Greek way of life. Wearing the Greek hat was the first step in the process of Hellenizing the Jews, encouraged by the Seleucid kings, particularly Antiochus IV. It triggered a revolt that led to the purification of the Temple in Jerusalem, an event still celebrated as the festival of Hanukkah in the Jewish calendar.

The Babylonians wore a linen tunic like the Greek *chiton,* reaching to their ankles, and over it they wore a shorter tunic made of wool, and over their shoulders they might wear a little white shawl. On their heads they wore a kind of turban over their hair, which they allowed to grow long. Phrygia, in central Anatolia, was the home of the Phrygian cap, which was a soft, red conical cap with the top pulled forward. It was charged with meaning. In Greek art it was worn by non-Greeks; the Trojan hero Paris, who abducted Helen of Troy, was shown wearing it in Greek art. It was a marker of "otherness," of the alien world beyond Hellenistic civilization. Later, it acquired another symbolism: it became the cap of freedom, for in Rome it was worn by slaves who had been freed, and it was taken over as a symbol of liberty in both the American and French revolutions. But for the Greeks of the Hellenistic world, it symbolized an alien culture. The Persian cap, known as a tiara, was similar; it was a conical cap with the peak bent forward, though the Persian king wore his tiara upright. The Persians also wore another marker of otherness: trousers.

Adopting Greek clothing styles was a means of signaling that the wearer was a Greek by culture, whether or not by ethnic origin. The opposite was also true: There must have been many who felt the same as the conservative Jews in Jerusalem who objected to their youths wearing the Greek hat.

NOTE

1. 2 Maccabees 4:12.

5

Education

A child in a Hellenistic city started school at the age of seven. Until then, children were reared at home by their mothers, though in well-to-do families a nurse, who was usually a slave, would take over the actual care and feeding of the young child. Slave or not, however, the nurse became a member of the family and stayed with it until she died, and the children whom she reared looked on her as a foster mother. The Roman poet Vergil, in his epic poem, the *Aeneid*, tells the story of how Aeneas fled from Troy after its destruction and made his way to Italy, bringing with him his nurse Gaeta. She died in Italy and was buried there, where today a pleasant little Italian town between Terracina and Naples bears her name. Gaeta was a beloved nurse and she was not left behind when Troy burned.

These early years were not wasted, however. From his mother and his nurse a child got his first introduction to the Greek cultural heritage. They introduced their children to the vast store of Greek mythology. Mythology surrounded them; paintings showing scenes from myths decorated the rooms of the houses where they lived, and statues of gods and heroes graced the public spaces of their city. Children were taken to religious festivals and became familiar with the hymns that were sung in honor of the gods. An alert child must have had many questions for his nurse. But at seven years of age, he was ready for serious learning.

Before sunrise the young student set out for school attended by his pedagogue—a family servant, usually a slave, who took his charge to school and brought him home again, carrying his belongings and guarding him from any dangers lurking in the streets, for policing in the cities was always a little haphazard. He waited for classes to be finished, socializing with other pedagogues or sitting inside the classroom itself to observe the lessons. As a slave, his social status was low—for that matter, so was the status of the teacher—but it was from the pedagogue that a boy learned his standards of behavior. Daughters of free citizens went to school, too, and their classes followed the same curriculum as boys; in some cities, there were also secondary schools for girls. But schooling varied from city to city. We know of two *poleis* on the west coast of Asia Minor, Miletus and Teos, where the schools were owned by the city, which guaranteed the teachers' salaries, but as a general rule schools were likely to be private ventures, and schoolmasters collected fees from the parents of their pupils, who tended to consider school fees among their less urgent debts. At Miletus and Teos, the schools had private endowments. They were not funded by taxpayers.

Papyrus finds from Egypt have produced enough discarded school books and other educational material to give some idea of what education in the Hellenistic classroom was like, and its techniques did not resemble what is prescribed in the faculties of education in modern universities. As far as we can see, Hellenistic teachers did not try to make learning fun. However, the year was punctuated by holidays for religious festivals: the schools in Alexandria, for instance, had two holidays each month in honor of Apollo. Choirs of singing boys were expected to perform at the great public ceremonies on holy days, and many of them must have been youngsters from the local schools. Then there were civic festivals and special family occasions that merited holidays, such as birthdays or weddings.

But when the student was in the classroom, he worked hard. Discipline was strict and schoolmasters did not spare the rod. First, there was the alphabet to be mastered: the "elements," as the letters of the alphabet were called, were used not only as a means of writing, but as numbers (alpha = one, beta = two, gamma = three, and so on) and as musical notation as well. First students learned the names of the letters. Then they were introduced to the alphabetical signs themselves, uppercase letters first. They committed them to memory by chanting them in chorus: alpha, beta, gamma, delta, epsilon, and so on until they knew them. Then they learned the syllables, and finally they progressed to sounding out words. Then they began to read selected passages from Greek authors such as Homer, who was a favorite, or the great tragic poets of the fifth century. They read aloud; silent reading was not the rule in ancient Greece. Recitation from memory was also an important part of the educational process.

For girls, schooling generally stopped at the primary level, but once a boy could read and write he went on to secondary school in the gymnasium, provided his parents could afford the fees. There he was taught by a *grammatikos*—the English word *grammarian* does not translate the term adequately, for the *grammatikos* taught the literary masterpieces of the past. Homer, particularly his *Iliad*, Euripides, and Menander were the pillars of Greek literary achievement, though the list was more extensive than that. The Greek orators, particularly Demosthenes, were also important, though students encountered them at the senior level. Mathematics was also part of the curriculum, but the Greek method of writing numbers, using letters of the alphabet, lacked the flexibility of the Arabic system that we use. Multiplication and division were best done using an abacus. However, the science where the Hellenistic world excelled was geometry, and the great master was Euclid (about 330–275). His textbook, the *Elements*, was used in schools from the Hellenistic period up until the twentieth century.

THE EPHEBIA

Once a young man of good family reached the age of about 18, he became an *ephebe* and entered upon his *ephebate*, or *ephebia*, a period of military service. We are best informed about the *ephebia* of Athens, which dated back to the classical period, though we cannot assign an exact date to its creation. The evidence for the *ephebate* does not extend earlier than the fourth century, when, in the aftermath of the battle of Chaeronea in 338—which made Alexander the Great's father, Philip, master of Greece—Athens reformed her *ephebia* and made it into a compulsory period of military service, lasting two years, the first of which was spent in the barracks. By 267, the *ephebia* had been reduced to one year, and it was voluntary. The enrollment had fallen from 600 to 700 a year in the late fourth century to between 20 and 40, and in practice only the sons of wealthy fathers attended. The ephebate evolved into a sort of finishing school, and in 119, it began to accept non-Athenians.

For the ephebe, athletic and philosophical pursuits went hand in hand. Physical exercise was important, particularly wrestling and track; so also was taking part in religious processions and attending lectures in philosophy at centers of learning such as the Lyceum, the school founded by Aristotle, and the Academy, founded by Plato. By the time the *ephebe* graduated, he had a sound mind in a sound body, or at least he had both a smattering of philosophy and well-developed muscles and he belonged to the circle of elites in his city.

Other cities in the Hellenistic world also developed their own *ephebates*; they were to be found in cities as far afield as Massilia (that is, modern Marseilles on the south coast of France), the cities in Sicily, and in the Greek colonies on the Black Sea, and all of them shared some features with the Athenian *ephebate*. The products of the program were the Ivy League alumni of the Hellenistic world, and they formed associations much like their modern counterparts. They maintained contact with the old school, and with each other.

THE GYMNASIUM, AN EDUCATIONAL AND CULTURAL CENTER

The building or complex of buildings where young Greeks were schooled was the gymnasium, which became the chief center of the educational and cultural life in the Hellenistic city. In the classical period, we find them built in the suburbs. In the Hellenistic city, they are closer to the urban center, and their architecture becomes more impressive. Athens, for instance, had three old gymnasiums in the suburbs, but in the Hellenistic period, two were built close to the city center, one of them with funds donated by a king of Egypt, probably Ptolemy IV. It was named the Ptolemaion after him. Priene had two gymnasiums: one higher up the hillside on which the city was built for boys and youths, and a lower gymnasium for young men about 65 yards down the hillside from the city center. At Delphi, the site of Apollo's most important oracle, the gymnasium had a track sheltered by the roof of a colonnade, which allowed students to practice running even when it rained, and there was an open-air track as well for use in good weather. The gymnasium had a pentagonal courtyard where there were showers for bathing after exercise; lion-head spouts served as showerheads, and the water drained into a circular pool that served as a plunge bath. This was a real luxury; water was too scarce for pools in most gymnasiums. Off the bath courtyard was a *palaestra*: a "wrestling school," though it was actually a general-purpose gymnastic building. It was a square court surfaced with fine sand and surrounded by a colonnade. Behind the colonnade were rooms for storage or for classrooms, though classroom activity did not leave a lot of evidence at the Delphi gymnasium. Not so at Priene's gymnasiums. There the *ephebes* left evidence of their presence, for they covered the walls of their rooms with graffiti.

The gymnasium was the center of higher education. At Pergamon in modern Turkey, the gymnasium, which was built on a hillside, had three sections. The upper gymnasium was for young men, the middle one for teenagers, and the lower one for young boys, for all three age groups attended the gymnasium. The man in charge of education in a city was the *gymnasiarch,* and he became one of the city's most important officials. The *gymnasiarch* had to be a public-spirited citizen with deep pockets, for he regularly found that he had to dip into his own private funds to pay for the gymnasium's cost overruns. But a well-regulated gymnasium was a source of great pride for the city. In the newly founded towns of Asia and in Egyptian villages with a substantial Greek population, the gymnasium was the flagship of Hellenic culture. There were waiting lists of students seeking admission, and their alumni formed an elite group.

Physical education in the gymnasium was thorough, but apart from it, what did the curriculum emphasize? Poetry, grammar, and public speaking certainly, along with music and dancing. Plato[1] stated baldly that a man who could not dance and sing was a man without education. There was a good deal of time spent marching in processions in the religious festivals, or parading when visited by a king or a wealthy benefactor, for gymnasiums were heavily dependent on donations. They had libraries; when *ephebes* graduated from the Ptolemaion, they would donate books to it as gifts to their alma mater, and the Ptolemaion library seems to have become the unofficial Athens public library, for Athens did not get a purpose-built library until the Roman emperor Hadrian gave her one in the second century c.e. But most of all, the gymnasium taught a way of life. Its graduates were men who carried on the Greek cultural traditions.

A detailed inscription[2] commemorating a donation made by a wealthy citizen named Polythroos earmarked for education has survived from the city of Teos, and it allows us to see what sort of curriculum a typical Greek school might have had. The school at Teos was to have three instructors called *grammatikoi* to train the students in literature, two physical education trainers, and a music teacher who taught the lyre or the harp to talented young children, as well as well as tutored the *ephebes* in music and no doubt dancing as well. The *ephebes* also had an instructor in archery and spear throwing, and another instructor in arms and armor. No mention was made of mathematics. But probably most gymnasiums did teach mathematics, for we have a second-century inscription from Magnesia on the Maeander River in Anatolia that records the names of victors from the local gymnasium in contests on Sports Day, which doubled as the Examinations Day, and two lads won prizes in arithmetic. The decree from Teos also laid down ferocious penalties for anyone who tried to subvert the intention of Polythroos's donation or use it for other purposes. Apparently the misuse of school endowments was by no means unknown.

In the far-flung colonies of the Seleucid empire, stretching from Asia Minor as far east as Afghanistan, the gymnasium took on a special importance, for these were settlements where the Greeks were surrounded by a much larger indigenous population of non-Greeks with ancient cultures of their own. The gymnasiums became both educational and cultural centers: Not only did they offer instruction, but they also had libraries, presented exhibitions, and entertained visiting lecturers. The royal cult was celebrated there, for the Seleucid kings claimed to be gods, and were venerated by religious ceremonies in their honor; in some gymnasiums, games with athletic contests were held in their honor. The gymnasium separated Greek from non-Greek, though once the latter acquired the Greek language they might be admitted, and in some places the non-Greeks founded their own Greek-style gymnasiums. This happened in Jerusalem, where Jews who wanted to participate in the dominant culture of the Hellenistic world sent their youth to a gymnasium founded by the high priest of the Temple. Even Babylon, the center of Mesopotamian cultural traditions—which was dominated by the great temple of Marduk-Bel, the paramount god of ancient Iraq—had a gymnasium, and after the Seleucid empire lost Babylon to new invaders called the Parthians, the gymnasium continued to offer Greek education. In Egypt under the Ptolemaic kings, the gymnasium was a bastion of Greek culture even more than in the Seleucid empire. We find them in Egyptian villages in the Nile valley: Oxyrhynchus, for example, had one. Waiting lists for enrollment in these Egyptian village gymnasiums were long, and children from unsuitable families, that is, non-Greeks, or Egyptians who were insufficiently assimilated to Greek culture, were not included.

Higher Education

A few might seek higher education by attaching themselves to a well-known teacher who rented space at a gymnasium for his lectures. Plato established his school at the Academy park, which was sacred to the hero Academus (hence the name), where there was already a gymnasium. Plato's school took over the name of the park and became known as the Academy, which about 385 was established as a corporation and hence could own property. Aristotle rented space at the Lyceum gymnasium, for he was an alien in Athens with residence rights, and hence could not own property. Both founded organized institutions that charged fees for instruction, and their schools continued after their founders' deaths. At Pergamon, the gymnasium on the upper level was clearly a cultural center, for it had an auditorium with seating for 1,000, and it cannot have been for the exclusive use of the *ephebes*. Visiting intellectuals would have given lectures there as well.

On the island of Cos, where the great physician Hippocrates was born about 460, there was a medical school dedicated to Asclepius that was founded in the mid-fourth century, and its priests, the Asclepiads, honed their skills at diagnosis by observing the progress of a disease through its various stages and writing them down for future study, case by case. The Asclepium itself, with its complex of buildings, developed into a school for medical doctors in the Hellenistic period, and it continued to flourish under the Roman empire, though it was Alexandria that attracted the stars of the medical profession, and students who apprenticed there got the best training in anatomy and surgery that the Hellenistic world had to offer.

Doctors were the only learned profession. When a city hired a doctor to oversee public medical services, the city council would check the applicant's references and educational background with great care, for disease was the major cause of death, and a city's physician was not only its medical officer of health, but he was also expected to give public lectures on how to avoid illness. Law schools had to await the coming of Rome, for every city had its own laws and legal system, and it was not until two and a half centuries after the end of the Hellenistic era that a Roman emperor, Caracalla, made almost everyone in the Roman empire a Roman citizen and thus brought them all under one set of laws. As for the teaching profession, it was considered a trade, and traders were held in contempt. There were no teachers' colleges or normal schools, and philosophers dealt with the grand ideas of education and not with classroom teaching techniques.

NOTES

1. Plato, *Laws*, II, 654a–b.
2. Austin, no. 120; Bagnall and Derow, no. 65.

6

Social Life

The glimpses that we get of social life in the Hellenistic cities are few and far between. The scanty remains of the situation comedies that were produced in the theaters give us a picture of life among the middle-income group in the cities. Young men drank too much at festivals. Fathers were anxious to find suitable mates for their sons and daughters. Slaves could be clever rascals, but they were never rebellious. In the background there might be disorder; pirates, for instance, might make travel by sea hazardous. These were the equivalent of today's television situation comedies. They did not deal with the great crises of life. The humor was gentle and the audience came to the theater to be amused.

CITIZENSHIP STATUS

In the classical period, cities had been exclusive. A citizen was a citizen by right of birth, and only citizens were entitled to own property in a city. The Romans developed the concept of a citizenship that could be acquired by non-citizens—for instance, slaves in Rome who were manumitted became citizens—but the idea was foreign to the Greek *polis*. Nonetheless the old exclusiveness began to break down in the Hellenistic period. For one thing, cities would bestow honorary citizenship on aliens; thus, if a citizen of Thebes was granted honorary citizenship in Corinth, he had the right to settle in Corinth and exercise citizenship rights there. However, if he chose not to make his home in Corinth, his Corinthian citizenship would remain only potential. Philosophers who traveled from city to city to give public lectures, as well as poets, playwrights, and actors, must have found honorary citizenships useful; for others, an honorary citizenship must have been like one of the honorary degrees conferred by universities nowadays that expects recipients to be generous whenever there is a fund-raising campaign. Some cities even negotiated treaties with other cities, exchanging citizenship rights, a process that was called *ispoliteia* (equal citizenship rights) or sometimes *sympoliteia* (joint citizenship). Athens and Priene, for instance, exchanged citizenship, and there are other examples of this process: a third-century inscription[1] survives from Pergamon that records a treaty of *isopoliteia* between Pergamon and its little neighbor Temnus, which sets forth a treaty of *isopoliteia* between the two. Everything is shared, including the right to own property and the requirement to pay taxes.

Along with honorary citizenships, the institution of *proxeny* became widespread. There were no diplomatic representatives in Greek cities, but they did have what might be called honorary consuls. If an Athenian went to Thebes and was involved in some incident or business deal where he needed someone to represent his interests, or even to offer him hospitality, he would seek out a Theban citizen who was a *proxenos* of Athens. The *proxenos* would give him what help he could. A *proxenos* of a city could expect favors from the foreign city he served, such as good seats in the front rows of its theater whenever he visited it. He might also get free meals in the town hall, which was a signal honor. In the Hellenistic period, cities handed out *proxenies* generously; for instance, Delphi made all the citizens of the *polis* of Messenia in the Peloponnesus *proxenoi*. A citizen who went to the theater in his home city must often have seen representatives from abroad sitting in the front rows among the very distinguished persons who had the right to sit there.

EVIDENCE OF SOCIAL RELATIONSHIPS
IN HERONDAS'S POEMS AND OTHER WRITINGS

The Greek-language papyri that have been found in Egypt give us some very intimate glimpses of ordinary life. We have marriage contracts and divorce agreements. A slave girl was mugged on her way to her music lesson, and her owner, a lonely old woman who was clearly very fond of this slave girl, petitions for redress. A Greek woman resident in an Egyptian village complained that the male attendant at a public bath—an Egyptian—had brought her jugs of hot water to rinse herself off after she had soaped herself, and poured one over her that was far too hot, scalding her and giving her severe burns. Life-threatening ones, she claimed. She had already had the attendant arrested but also wants him suitably punished. She, a working woman, should not be subjected to this unlawful treatment. But the finds of papyri produced one gem in 1891: a papyrus roll that contained seven poems by the Hellenistic writer of mimes, Herondas, plus an eighth poem in poor condition and other detached fragments. Herondas had been known earlier by name and a few quotations from his mimes, but here were some examples of his work that modern scholars could read for the first time. The mimes were little dialogues that could be read, or produced on stage, and they portrayed a slice of life, sometimes with brutal realism.

The first mime presents a scene, probably on the island of Cos, while Ptolemy II Philadelphus (285–246) ruled Egypt. An old woman named Gyllis visits a young wife name Metriche, whose husband had gone to Egypt several months ago to seek his fortune. Gyllis soon makes her business clear. She is a matchmaker; she reminds Metriche that she has had no letter from her husband, and Egypt is a fine place where there are many beautiful women, as many as the stars in the sky. It is a land of wealth and fame, with wrestling grounds for young men to exercise, philosophers who gave lectures, and many shows, all of which are, no doubt, distracting Metriche's husband. Gyllis wants Metriche to know that a young man—an athlete, and Gyllis claims, a virgin— has seen Metriche at a festival and fallen desperately in love. Metriche rejects the offer. She is a virtuous young woman. However, she tells her slave to give Gyllis a drink of wine. Evidently she does not want to make an enemy of Gyllis, and she refuses the offer, while at the same time offering a hint of encouragement. In the Hellenistic world, emigration to the new lands that Alexander's conquests had opened up for Greek settlement tore families apart, and letters moved slowly between absent husbands and their families left at home, and sometimes not at all.

The second mime in the collection introduces us to the seamy side of life at Cos. A procurer complains that a man of higher status in the city has broken into his house where he kept his girls and has seized one, a girl named Myrtale, and kidnapped her. The reader is left to fill in the details from his imagination. Was Myrtale a baby whom the procurer found abandoned and raised himself to become a member of his stable of dancers and courtesans, and did the kidnapper see her and fall in love with her? In the third mime, a naughty schoolboy is brought to his schoolmaster to be flogged. The schoolmaster first agrees and then changes his mind. In the next mime, two women in Cos, Kynno and her slave Kokkale, arrive at the temple of Asclepius at sunrise, prepared to sacrifice a cock to the god. The temple was a magnificent building, and Kokkale, who apparently had not seen it before, prattles on about it while Kynno grows impatient.

The next mime presents an unexpected domestic drama. A respectable woman is jealous: her slave was her lover, and now she finds that he has had an affair with another woman, probably, though Herondas does not say so, a woman who was younger and more attractive than the slave's mistress. She is furious and orders the unfortunate slave to be flogged. Then she changes her mind and decides to have him branded on the face instead. But then her favorite slave girl intervenes; there is a festival in the offing, she reminds the mistress, and the punishment will be suspended until it is past. In Athens, in the days preceding and immediately following a religious festival, it was forbidden to punish prisoners and slaves: in one famous case, Socrates, who had been condemned to die in 399, had his execution postponed for this reason.

The final mime preserved whole on the papyrus presents a glimpse of commercial life. A woman named Metro brings a group of friends to a cobbler's shop, where Kerdon, the cobbler, makes and sells shoes. He has a great variety of shoes on display, which should remind us that, though sandals were the most popular footwear and some Greeks simply went barefoot, there were many styles of shoes, named after their places of origin. There were Boeotian shoes from Boeotia, northwest of Attica, and Ambraciot shoes and Babylonian shoes, and so on. There is much haggling over the price, but in the end the ladies make their purchases, and Kerdon offers Metro a commission for bringing him customers.

Life in Hellenistic cities was not always lighthearted. There were wars, shortages of food that weighed heavily on the poor, and diseases. Malaria attacked both adults and children every summer and autumn, and tuberculosis preyed on young adults. The Hellenistic world knew measles, chicken pox, diphtheria, mumps, whooping cough, and conjunctivitis, which could cause blindness. Then too, there were always taxes to be paid. The theater presented situation comedies, but it might also present revivals of the great classical tragedies, and audiences could weep over the fates of Oedipus, who killed his own father and married his own mother, thus fulfilling the fate that an oracle had prophesied, and of Antigone, who buried her brother because carrying out the rites of religion was more important to her than obeying the law of the state. But periodically evidence surfaces that reveals an everyday life in the cities where people shop for shoes, have love affairs, and long for absent husbands.

CLUBS AND ASSOCIATIONS

Polybius,[2] a historian who lived in the second century, described what he considered a disgusting situation in Boeotia, Athens's neighbor to the northwest, near the start of his own century. Life there had become chaotic, he complained, and one symptom of the disorder that was prevalent there was that childless men did not leave their property to their next of kin but rather to their clubs; indeed even men with families might leave a large share of their fortunes to their clubs to hold banquets in their memory. Consequently many Boeotians did not have enough days in the calendar for all the banquets they were expected to attend.

Clubs were a feature of the social life of the Hellenistic cities. The Greeks called them *koina* (the singular, *koinon*, is an association). The same word was used to describe a state, and in fact, the clubs governed themselves rather like little city-states, except that citizenship was not a criterion for joining, and women could become members. There is a good deal of evidence for how they functioned, most of it in the form of inscriptions of one sort or another. In some instances, archaeologists have found burial plots within an ancient necropolis that are identified by inscriptions as the property of a club. There is a nice example at Rhodes, where a burial plot belonging to the *Sabaziastai* (the worshipers of the Phrygian god, Sabazios) has been discovered in the Rhodian necropolis. On the island of Delos, which was particularly fertile ground for clubs, the merchants and traders from Berytus, modern Beirut, had a club for the worshipers of the Ba'al (Lord) of Berytus, whom was identified with the Greek god of the sea, Poseidon, and hence these club members were known as the *Poseidoniats*. The *Poseidoniast* clubhouse, which has been excavated, had four chapels, one of which was a later addition: it was dedicated to the goddess Rome. The clubhouse also had a meeting room and reception rooms, and on the basement floor, shops for rent. The businessmen from Tyre also had a club on Delos, dedicated to Heracles, who was equated with Melqart, the Ba'al of Tyre. There might be what we would recognize as Old Boys' clubs: alumni from one gymnasium or another, or military clubs for soldiers, sailors, or veterans of the armed services. There was even a club for the poets who lived in Athens. In the Hellenistic cities in Asia, we find clubs of ex-mercenary soldiers. The doctors who had trained at Cos had a club. Women founded clubs; in Athens and at Alexandria, we find clubs for women only. Some clubs were family associations, and others seem to be simply clubs of persons who shared a common interest. Late in the Hellenistic period we even find a slaves' club in Egypt.

The Greeks labeled them *thiasoi* or *eranoi*, and they were not quite the same. The *thiasos* was a religious association, whereas the *eranos* was a club where the members paid membership fees. The *eranos* was built around the ideas of mutual aid, reciprocity, and equal contributions from its members, who ate meals together and sometimes made loans to each other. The synods or troupes of Dionysiac artists—that is, the performers that toured from city to city or from one festival to another to present their shows—qualified as *thiasoi*: religious associations, for their patron was the god Dionysos. The worshipers of the god Sabazios, who had a burial plot on Rhodes, were a *thiasos*. Clubs had temples and clubhouses where the members met; one club on Rhodes even owned a vineyard, perhaps to provide wine for club banquets. Many clubs did not find it easy to balance their budgets. The lucky clubs had a wealthy member or two who could help pay their bills.

Clubs attempted to look after the interests of their members. They might make loans to other club members, and they helped to preserve the memory of members who died, especially if, like the childless men in Boeotia whom Polybius mentions with disgust, the deceased members left legacies to pay for banquets in their honor. If a club passed a resolution declaring that a deceased member was a hero, then he was owed the honors of a hero, chief of which were a sacrifice and a banquet each year in his honor. In Egypt we find Egyptian women forming *thiasoi* to defray the costs of taking part in women's festivals and paying for mummification of their members. But the chief role of the clubs was social; their clubhouses and temples were places within a city where like-minded people could meet, citizens and aliens alike. Their members were often multi-ethnic, and for a non-Greek immigrant who settled in a Greek city, the clubs must have provided a pathway allowing him to find a niche in its social and religious life. It is probable that at least some of the clubs helped to break down racial prejudices and integrate newcomers into city life. Society had become increasingly mobile; men, separated by distance from their extended families and the cities to which they belonged as citizens, felt the danger of becoming anonymous units. For them, the clubs filled a void and gave them a sense of belonging.

NOTES

1. Rhodes, p. 228(j).
2. Polybius, *Universal History*, 20.6–7. See Austin, no. 84.

7

City and Country Living

INDUSTRY AND COMMERCE: THE AGORA

The Hellenistic city was a hive of industry. The city dwellers worked at a variety of specialized occupations: we can recognize at least 170 of them, ranging from retail sales to transportation. The center of commerce was the agora—the marketplace, the economic heart of the city. Respectable citizens might look down on tradesmen—in one city,[1] tradesmen along with slaves, pederasts, drunks, and madmen were barred from working out in the gymnasium—but a city could not do without a market. There is a quotation from a writer of comedies in the fourth century who describes what the agora of Athens looked like in the time of Alexander the Great. Everything could be found for sale there—figs, bunches of grapes, turnips, pears, apples, roses, medlars, haggis, honeycombs, chickpeas, beestings pudding, myrtle berries, irises, and slaves, who could be hired by the day, or perhaps bought outright. One might find a slave seeking to hire a professional cook—a *mageiros*—for his master who was planning a dinner, for the expertise of a *mageiros* was necessary if meals were to be catered properly. The agora of Athens even had a section for selling books, called the "orchestra" or dancing-place, for in the very early days of Greek drama that was the spot where the audience sat on wooden bleachers during performances, and the name survived even after the theater moved to a new location after a catastrophe when the bleachers collapsed during a performance. There was a market area called the "rings" where utensils were sold, and perhaps slaves, too. The agora was a great, colorful bazaar.

What is surprising about Hellenistic marketplaces is the degree to which the peddlers specialized. There was no equivalent of the department store. In Greek marketplaces, we find one group of vendors peddling olive oil, another garlic, perfume, or onions, and so on. The fish market was particularly popular. There would be shops selling wine, though not all of them would be in the agora. A wine shop would not only sell wine in bulk, by the amphora—an earthenware vessel, pointed at the bottom, that was the standard container for ancient trade—but also by the cup. Before pouring it into the cup, the barista would strain the wine to remove impurities and then mix it with water, for drinking wine straight was considered barbaric. There was a clothes market, where we might have found shops specializing in sleeveless tunics and others in the outer cloak called the *himation,* and so on. There was a women's agora where women bought and sold what they needed for running their households, such as yarn, wool to be spun into yarn, or cloth. Shops overflowed the Athenian agora proper and lined the street leading northwest to the Dipylon Gate, and there might be shops as well in the front rooms of private houses. We cannot tell if the marketplace of every Hellenistic city had the degree of specialization that Athens did, for Athens was, by the standards of the time, a large city. But the general store was not a Greek concept, nor was the supermarket.

The connotation of the Greek word for market, *agora,* had undergone a change by the Hellenistic period. Originally it meant a "gathering place," but then it became a place where people bought and sold, setting up tents as booths or tables where business deals were transacted. The Greek word for *table* also means "bank," as it still does in modern Greek, and no doubt the ancient agora was a place where bankers met their clients. Permanent buildings for trade and commerce appeared in agoras by the beginning of the fourth century; Athens, we know, had one by 391, and in the Hellenistic city, the marketplace had developed into a space defined by colonnades, or stoas, where buying and selling took place and customers could seek shelter from the rain or the searing heat. An up-to-date marketplace in a well-planned Hellenistic city had stoas around its perimeter. Hellenistic Athens was in sharp contrast with its neighbor, Thebes, for Thebes had been destroyed by Alexander the Great and rebuilt as a well-planned city, whereas Athens, with its old winding streets, acquired a stoa to define its west side only when Attalus II, king of Pergamon (159–138), built the Stoa of Attalus, which has now been reconstructed.

But what went on in the agora was not all commerce. Customers came not only to buy and sell, or to deposit a sum of money with a banker, but they also chatted with friends, traded gossip, and discussed politics or the ideas that occupied the thinkers of the day. Socrates, who was put to death in Athens in 399, had loved the cut and thrust of debate in the Athenian agora, and a century later, one might have heard Zeno of Citium, the founder of the Stoic school of philosophy, lecturing in the Painted Stoa on the south side of the agora. More than three centuries later, when Saint Paul visited Athens, he went to the agora every day to talk and argue with the people he encountered there.[2]

Some of the people who crowded the agora would be well-to-do landowners, for the soundest investment was land. Some could be slaves with a list of errands for their masters. Others would be small farmers and traders, and in Athens, which ceased to be a great power in the Hellenistic world and instead became a center for higher education, there would be students who came to attend the lectures in her philosophic schools, such as the Academy, founded by Plato, or the Lyceum founded by Aristotle. Athens attracted students came from all over the Greek world, and increasingly, after the mid-second century, from Rome. Another type of professional who might rub shoulders with the regular shoppers was the mercenary soldier. Employment as mercenaries helped to absorb surplus labor in the Hellenistic world, and serving in the army of a king could be a profitable occupation for some men, though there must have been many who returned home maimed, without an eye or a limb, and with little to show for their efforts except a host of stories. The "boastful soldier," that is, the mercenary who talked incessantly about his exploits as a prodigious warrior in far-off places, became a stock figure of fun on the Hellenistic stage. There must also have been some men who lived by their wits, for another stock figure on the stage was the "parasite," a person who made himself useful to a man of means, and whose chief aim in life was a free meal.

NEW COMEDY: A REPRESENTATION OF THE MIDDLE CLASS

There was a middle class in the Hellenistic cities, meaning a class of people who were neither very rich nor very poor, and we get a glimpse of what their lives were like from the comedy of manners discussed earlier. New Comedy is the name given to the genre, to distinguish it from the earthy song and dance of Old Comedy and the Middle Comedy that was popular in the first half of the fourth century. It drew crowds to the theaters in the Hellenistic period. Menander, the greatest playwright of these situation comedies, produced his first drama in Athens only two years after Alexander the Great died, and thanks to recent discoveries of papyrus documents from Egypt, we now have one complete play of his and substantial fragments of several others. They reveal the comfortable life lived by city dwellers who owned farms that they leased to tenants or worked with slave labor, and which were probably their chief source of income, though they might often be absent on long trips for business purposes. In one play, the protagonist has just returned to Athens from a trip to the Black Sea, and the purpose of the trip was not simply to see the sights. In these dramas, young men drink too much at religious festivals and rape girls who then get pregnant, or fall in love with courtesans or other unsuitable marriage partners who have no dowries. They get themselves into awkward situations, and extricate themselves only with the help of their resourceful slaves. Unwanted children are exposed and left to die, sometimes for no better reason than that their fathers are going through a patch of bad luck and are financially embarrassed. The courtesan with whom the young man of good family is madly in love may turn out to have a respectable, well-to-do father: she was captured by pirates and sold into slavery, as it turns out in the final act; or she had been an unwanted child exposed as an infant, but rescued by a kindly passer-by who appears with the swaddling clothes or a brooch that was found with her, and the unsuitable courtesan is recognized as the daughter of a reputable citizen, possibly a neighbor and friend of the young man's father. The plays have happy endings. The audience left the theater pleasantly amused.

These people whom the plays depict lived in houses that lined the street, side-by-side, and behind their doors were rooms for weaving and cooking, but we do not see inside. Except for the front door, the house presented a blank wall to street. The cast of characters would include artful household slaves, and generally they used their talents to advance the interests of their dull-witted masters. Yet these middle-income families were only one segment of Hellenistic society. The lives of the poor were very different.

THE UPPER CLASS

The gap between the rich and the poor was wide, and we get the impression that it grew wider as the age progressed. The rich could be amazingly generous: Their donations funded schools, built roads, bridges, and public buildings, and when a city's poor faced starvation because crop failures had inflated the price of grain, a rich citizen might come to the rescue with a gift of food or money. The city might repay the generous donor with an honorary decree, which would be inscribed on stone and set up in a public place. But though the rich made donations, they hated paying direct taxes and cities were reluctant to impose them. Athens was an exception: Necessity forced her to collect a direct tax called the *eisphora,* which was based on an assessment of a citizen's wealth. But the great majority of cities preferred indirect taxes, such as harbor dues, a 2 percent ad valorem duty on imports and exports, or a tax on stalls in the market. Cities invented a great number of indirect taxes that fell on rich and poor alike: modern economists would call them regressive taxes.

JOBS FOR THE LOWER CLASSES

A citizen in the low-income category did not have a wide choice of jobs. Prices rose in the Hellenistic period, and the wages for working men seem not to have kept pace. What wage did the ancient factory worker make? The simple answer is that the industrial revolution had not yet taken pace, nor would it for centuries to come. A great deal of manufacturing, such as spinning and weaving, was done within the household. There was no separate industrial zone for factories—a shop might be side-by-side with a private house; in fact, it might be a rental unit in the house. Yet there were factories in Hellenistic cities that produced a great variety of goods for sale, from musical instruments to arms and armor. They consisted of a craftsman, perhaps a freed slave or a resident alien, working in a shop with a number of assistants, manufacturing a specialized product such as shoes, pottery, swords, or the like. Little production units of this sort were common not only in ancient Greece but in all the pre-industrial world.

We might ask why these factories did not offer more employment to the working poor, and part of the answer must have been the institution of slavery. The fact is that many of the tradesmen who in modern times would hire free labor preferred to use slaves instead. The tradesman himself might be a slave or freedman, and his little establishment might belong to an investor, such as a well-to-do citizen or a temple, for temples invested their deposits and their endowments in shops that they rented to storekeepers and journeymen. The prejudice was not all one-sided: craftsmen may have preferred slave assistants, but free citizens, for their part, did not like to work for hire. But there is no doubt that slavery played a role in the Hellenistic economy that deserves careful consideration.

CITIZENS, RESIDENT ALIENS, AND SLAVES

The concept of citizenship that we find in the Hellenistic world contrasts sharply with the Roman concept, as well as with our own. Rome was a city unlike Athens or Alexandria. A Roman citizen need not necessarily have been born a citizen. Citizenship could be conferred on aliens who would then have the rights of Roman citizens, including the right to vote, though they might vote only rarely if they lived some distance away, for they had to travel to Rome to do it. Yet little by little Rome's citizenship spread throughout Italy until, by the year 88, all Italians from the Rubicon River, which marked the southern boundary of the Po Valley, to the toe of Italy in the south were citizens. The people of the Po Valley, which was the province of Cisalpine Gaul, were given citizenship by Julius Caesar, and citizenship continued to be conferred on aliens until 212 c.e., when the Roman Emperor Caracalla gave citizenship to everyone in the Roman empire. Nothing of the sort happened in the Hellenistic world. Each city guarded its citizenship jealously.

Within a Hellenistic *polis*, citizens made up only a minority of the inhabitants, sometimes only a small minority. Thus when a *polis* called itself a democracy, we should remember that it was always a democracy with a limited franchise. In every *polis*, there were large numbers of aliens. Some were simply visitors from abroad who came for business or to see the sights, and some might take up temporary residence for a while. But some got the status of *metic*, which was a sort of halfway house on the way to citizenship, though a *metic*'s chances of becoming a citizen were always doubtful at best. They always remained citizens of their native *poleis*. *Metics* were found in many city-states, but those in Athens are the best known. There, every *metic* had to have a citizen who acted as his sponsor. He had to be registered in the *deme*,[3] that is, the township where he had his residence, for *demes* kept the citizen lists. He had to pay a head tax (*metoikion*) every year, and he might not own property in Athens unless the right was granted to him as a special privilege. He could not contract a legal marriage with an Athenian citizen. However, *metics* had to serve in the army and were often conscripted to row the warships in the fleet, and needless to say, they paid the taxes that a citizen paid, as well as the *metoikion*. In return, *metics* did have the protection of Athenian law, and they could take an active role in commercial life. Probably in many cities *metics* dominated the trades, though we lack statistics to prove the point. And, it should be added, though they could not invest their savings in property, they could invest in slaves. Slaves were an asset that brought a good return to the investor.

Some *metics* grew wealthy and cities with needy treasuries were not above selling them citizenship. A decree[4] survives from the little city of Dyme on the Gulf of Corinth offering citizenship to resident aliens who are freemen and born of free parents for one talent, which was to be paid in two installments within a year. The price was steep: only rich aliens could afford it.

As the Hellenistic age wore on, there was a subtle change in the status of *metic* in Athens. Evidence from inscriptions indicates that citizenship requirements grew more lax. Persons with only one parent a citizen became acceptable. The *metoikion* disappeared. Athens as not alone: the new internationalism of the Hellenistic age made the old exclusive citizenships increasingly obsolete. Yet citizenship was still valued; it was far more than an empty honor for it conferred on the *metic* a sense of belonging as well as, on the practical level, the right to own property and access to the host city's religious cults.

The Prevalence of Slavery

Slave dealers are not often mentioned in our ancient sources, and one gets the impression that, although all traders were generally held in contempt, special contempt was reserved for the dealers in human bodies. Yet slavery was universally accepted in the world of ancient Greece. It was not an institution that offended anyone's moral code. The Stoic school of philosophy, founded by Zeno of Citium (335–263 B.C.E.), did urge slave owners to treat their slaves humanely, but the Stoics never attacked the institution of slavery itself. Aristotle,[5] in his *Nicomachean Ethics*, defines the slave as a living tool, and the inverse was true as well: a tool was a slave that was not alive. In his *Politics* he examines the nature of slavery again: A slave, he argues, is a "living piece of property," a tool that can perform tasks at its master's bidding. If there were robots that could perform the tasks that slaves do, then the institution of slavery would be unnecessary, but only the divine craftsman, Hephaistus, and not mere mortals, could make robot slaves. The early Christians condemned slavery no more than anyone else. Paul, in his Epistle to Titus,[6] writes, "Bid slaves be obedient to their masters, and give satisfaction in every respect; they are not to be refractory, nor to pilfer...." A good slave should be docile, and loyal, and masters in turn should treat them decently; yet the slave belonged to a class of beings that did not share the norms of humanity.

The manner in which Greek artists depicted slaves is telling: They are shown smaller in stature than their masters. Particularly revealing is a tombstone of a child from Athens with his pedagogue, the slave who escorted him to school. The child has not reached puberty whereas the pedagogue has the physique of a muscular young man, yet the pedagogue is half the size of the boy, who stands with one hand resting on his pedagogue's head. The slave was a lesser being than a free citizen. His welfare did not matter. If he became sick, his owner might abandon him in a temple, and if he died, his owner wasted no money on his funeral.

We have no good evidence for an estimate of the actual number of slaves, or their proportion of the population in the Hellenistic cities, but they were numerous: In the city of Rhodes, for instance, resident aliens and slaves far outnumbered the citizen body. A writer of the Roman period, Athenaeus of Naucratis in Egypt, states that a census held in Athens in 312–308 revealed that there were 21,000 Athenian citizens, 10,000 resident aliens, and 400,000 slaves. Athenaeus lived five centuries after the census that he reports, and the number 400,000 cannot be exact. Yet even if we reduce it tenfold, the number of slaves remains remarkably high. The island of Delos, which in the second century became a place where slave dealers traded their human cargoes, could process 10,000 slaves in a single day, though that probably marked the upper limit. Macedonian slaves, both male and female, fetched the highest prices, and house-born slaves, bred and trained for slavery from the cradle, sold for more than slaves who had been captured in war and reduced to slavery. And the treatment of slaves varied enormously. Mining in the Hellenistic world was done by slaves, both men and women, and the conditions were brutal. House slaves, on the other hand, might be well treated. The pedagogues who escorted their young charges to school and back home again may have found their lives boring, but probably not unpleasant.

If a slave was not the child of a slave woman who had become pregnant—the father did not matter—how did he or she fall into the clutches of a slave dealer? Some were prisoners of war. If a city was captured by an enemy, and destroyed, it was quite regular for the victors to sell the women and children into slavery, and perhaps the male survivors as well. It has been claimed that warfare was more humane in the Hellenistic period than in the past, but when the conquering armies of the Romans arrived, the treatment of captives reverted to unqualified brutality. In 167, the Roman general Aemilius Paullus sent a punitive expedition to Epirus in northwest Greece, the homeland of Olympias, Alexander the Great's mother, and it destroyed 70 cities and sold 150,000 persons into slavery. In 146, the Romans sacked Corinth, killed the men, and sold the women and children into slavery. A lucky few may have been ransomed by their families or friends and freed. But most of them must have been auctioned off to slave dealers who took them to the slave markets and sold them.

There were other sources besides war. Piracy was an important contributor to the slave trade. In the theater, the plots of the dramas frequently centered on a person of good family who was captured by pirates, sold as a slave, and later reunited with his or her parents. The percentage of the slave trade supplied by pirates is hard to estimate. Some of the captives were ransomed, and there was a network of agreements among some cities, which offered a chance of rescue. Yet it is clear that the chief slave markets in Aegean Greece, Rhodes, Delos, and Crete were fed by pirates. Greeks had no qualms about enslaving fellow Greeks, though, all things being equal, they preferred non-Greeks.

Another source was the practice of infanticide. Infanticide was a brutal method of birth control but it seems to have been practiced everywhere in the Hellenistic world except among the Jews and the Egyptians. Unwanted children were exposed by the roadside, often tucked into earthenware vessels—ancient Greek even has a word, *chytrizein,* which means to put a baby in a pot and expose him or her. The child would perish unless it was rescued. The rescuer might be a slave dealer; if he found a healthy baby, he might raise him as a slave, and in due course, sell or lease him. Infants exposed because of some physical defect generally did not survive. Girls were more frequently exposed than boys, and the sex trade in ancient Greece was supplied by foundling baby girls who were raised to be prostitutes. This is the seamy side of Hellenistic life;

there is no doubt that infanticide was practiced, and that girls were victims of it more than boys. Among the papyrus documents found in Egypt is a letter from an absent husband to his wife, who is pregnant. He instructs her to keep the baby if it is a boy, but should it be a girl, to expose her and leave her to die. The letter dates to just after the Roman conquest of Egypt, but the husband's instructions to his pregnant wife reflect earlier practice.

Non-Greek slaves often came from countries on the fringes of the Hellenistic world that were willing to sell surplus population, frequently children, in order to buy trade goods from the Greeks. The Greek historian Herodotus,[7] writing in the fifth century, noted that the Thracians, living in what is now northern Greece and Bulgaria, sold their children for export abroad. With the profit, they bought imports from Greece. They had not changed their ways in the Hellenistic period, and they were not alone. The kingdom of Bithynia, across the Dardanelles from Byzantium, modern Istanbul, was an exporter of slaves; there are accounts of hunts organized there to kidnap human merchandise for the slave markets. Finally there was slavery for debt. Athens had a law, which went back to the early lawgiver Solon at the beginning of the sixth century, that prohibited selling an Athenian citizen into slavery for debt, but not all states followed the Athenian lead. In fact, the great majority did not.

From a purely economic point of view, slavery had two drawbacks. First, the slave had no incentive to work hard. The slave's master might discipline him with a host of brutal punishments, but the results were never entirely satisfactory. A better remedy for slacking on the job was to allow the slave to acquire money of his own. A slave, particularly one who was skilled at a craft, might work on the *apophora* system: that is, he paid an agreed sum to his owner, and then worked on his own. There must have been cases where the owner advanced his slave credit. The *apophora* system was an example of free enterprise applied to slave labor. The slave had an incentive to work hard, for whatever was left over after he paid off his master would go into his own pocket.

The other drawback was that the slave was a wasting asset. The slave represented a capital investment that decreased in value as he grew older. Yet there was a way for a slave owner to protect his investment: it was to allow the slave to purchase his freedom. Slaves, as we have seen, could earn money, and though legally a slave's savings were his master's property along with the slave himself, it was good policy to allow a slave to acquire a nest egg and use it to buy his freedom. Inscriptions show us how manumission operated in Greece, and it was not a simple, straightforward transaction. A visitor to Delphi, the site of Apollo's oracle in central Greece, will be impressed by the number of inscriptions that cover the walls, especially the great retaining wall that contains the platform where the foundation of the temple of Apollo stands, many of them recording manumissions. The master did not free his slave directly; instead he made a fictitious sale of the slave to the god. Apollo purchased the slave from his owner for a price that was agreed upon, and then the slave bought his freedom from the god for the same price. Thus the owner got back at least some of the capital investment that he had made when he bought the slave in the first place, but the manumission itself was a straightforward deal with Apollo as the middleman. But there were also conditional manumissions that were not so straightforward and demonstrate the sort of exploitation that slaves often suffered.

The conditional manumission had a clause attached to the sale contract that subjected the ex-slave to obligations to his former owner that continued after he or she was freed. In one example from Delphi, dating from about 157, Diotima freed her slave girl named Melissa for the price of one mina of silver, no small sum. Yet, after Melissa is freed, she is to continue to remain at Diotima's side for Diotima's lifetime and to do whatever Diotima commands her to do. Melissa is legally free, but remains at her former mistress's beck and call. She is still a quasi-slave. This is not the worst example of a conditional manumission. A slave woman might be required to supply a slave, or even two slaves, to replace her as a condition of her freedom, and it is hard to imagine how she could fulfill such a contract unless she became pregnant herself and her children replaced her as slaves. Roman manumission was much fairer: in Rome, a manumitted slave became a freedman with most of the rights of a Roman citizen and his child would be a full Roman citizen. Greek cities, however, jealously guarded their citizenship. A freed slave in a Greek city would at best become a resident alien, and aliens became citizens only as special favors.

Slave Labor

Slaves provided the muscle for Greek manufacturing. A citizen with some money to invest might set up an industrial establishment that consisted of an overseer with several slaves working under his direction, producing something like shields for the army.

The overseer might himself be a slave, or a freedman. The kingdom of Pergamon was famous for its exports of woolen cloth, which were produced by large companies of slaves who spun and wove it. But most industrial establishments were small. Craftsmen with a few slaves would set up shop in their houses. Workers in the same trade tended to congregate: Shoemakers might take over one street in a city, metal workers another. The smiths in Athens were to be found in the neighborhood of the temple of Hephaestus, the god of the forge, whose well-preserved temple still overlooks the site of the ancient agora. Potters were in the *Kerameikos*, the potters' quarter, near one of the city gates. Yet there were no regions zoned commercial, or residential; houses and shops might be on the same street.

It is not clear why slaves were preferred to free labor, but they were. Perhaps it was because a free laborer could learn his employer's trade and then set up his own shop in competition. It may have been because free Greeks felt that working for a wage infringed upon their liberty and it may also have been because the trades were held in low esteem by the upper classes. Slavery was built into the psychology of ancient Greek society.

To persons of the twenty-first century, there is something very odd about Greek attitudes to slavery. It is as if certain tasks were considered proper only for slaves, not for free citizens, and not all the jobs that free citizens avoided were menial. In classical Athens of the fourth century we are relatively well informed about bankers and banking, in contrast with Hellenistic Athens, when we are ill informed, and it appears that all these fourth-century bankers were slaves, ex-slaves, or resident aliens. One of them, Pasion, had the good luck to be purchased by two Athenian bankers, who put him to work at first as a porter handling heavy bags of coins, and from there he rose to be chief clerk. His masters learned to appreciate his services so much that they freed him, and when they grew too old to take an active role in the business themselves, he took over the bank. He prospered, invested in shipping and manufacturing, and became a generous benefactor of the city until some six years before his death, as his health was starting to fail and he began to go blind, Athens bestowed on him the rare honor of citizenship. When he retired, he turned his banking business over to his general manager, also an ex-slave, named Phormio. Banking made Phormio wealthy too. Why did no Athenian citizens follow his career path? An Athenian might have replied that banking was not something that a free citizen did. It is an answer that sounds odd to modern ears.

Yet the same point is illustrated by a story about Socrates that was reported by Xenophon. He was a disciple of Socrates for a brief period, and produced a work titled *Memorabilia* wherein he collected a miscellany of tales about Socrates. Socrates lived and died in Athens before the Hellenistic period began, but the attitudes that this tale illustrates lived on. Socrates was approached by a citizen who was hard-pressed for money, for he had to maintain a number of penniless female relatives in his household and they were eating him out of house and home. Socrates suggested that he turn his dwelling into a little production unit by putting the ladies to work spinning and weaving, and the sale of the cloth they made would contribute to their support. But, the Athenian replied, his relatives would object, for producing cloth for sale was the sort of work that slaves did, and no self-respecting free woman would stoop to it. Nonetheless, suggested Socrates, the snobbish ladies should yield to necessity. It is not at all likely that they did. Slaves' work was not for them. Respectable poverty was better than losing status.

Prejudice of this sort meant that the trades were dominated by slave labor or ex-slaves, and free labor could not, or at least did not, compete with it. One consequence was that there was a gap between the rich and the poor that, in some cities, grew dangerously wide. We know that one city on Crete, modern Palaeokastro, made all its citizens take an oath not to take part in or support a revolution aimed at redistributing the land and abolishing debts. The oath has survived on an inscription. Here was one city that was nervous about the number of indigent persons on its citizenship rolls, and fearful of social unrest.

NOTES

1. Austin, no. 118.
2. Acts 17:17.
3. The simplest meaning of *deme* (*demos*) was "district," but the word had a special meaning in Athens where all Attica was divided into counties called *demes* that formed the basic units of the Athenian democracy. *Deme* might also refer to the citizen body, as in the word *democracy*.
4. Rhodes, p. 229.
5. Aristotle, *Nicomachean Ethics*, 8.11, *Politics*, 4.4.
6. Epistle to Titus, 2:9–10.
7. Herodotus, *Histories*, 5.60.1.

8

Hellenistic Women

WOMEN IN ATHENS, SPARTA, AND MACEDONIA

The classic description of the role of women in Athens comes from a little work by Xenophon, the *Oeconomicus,* on the proper management of an estate. Xenophon died about 354, and did not live to see Alexander the Great embark on his conquest of the Persian empire, but the definition of male and female roles in the domestic life of Athens cannot have changed much by the end of the fourth century, when the Hellenistic age was a generation old. The passage is worth quoting. Ischomachus, a wealthy Athenian who seems almost too sober and didactic to be an authentic example of a Greek bridegroom, is relating to Socrates the instructions that he gave to his young wife, who was not yet 15 years old when she became his bride. Earlier in the story, Ischomachus has already explained to his wife that it is seemly for a woman to stay indoors whereas a man should attend to work outside. Ischomachus then told his wife,

> It will be up to you...to stay indoors and send out those household servants who have work outside, and superintend those who must work at tasks indoors. You must receive the goods that are brought into the house, and measure out whatever portion of them must be spent. You must take care, too, that the goods which have been stored away to last a year are not spent within a month. When

you are supplied with wool, you must see to it that those in need of them get cloaks. You must see to it that the grain is kept dry so that it is in good condition for making bread. (7.35–36)

Ischomachus goes on at length, and finally he explains to his wife the layout of the house.

It does not have a lot of wall paintings, but the rooms are built with this purpose in mind, that they provide the most convenient space for what is to be placed in them, so that each room calls for what suits it. Thus the bedroom, which is the most secure space, asks for the most valuable bedding and furniture. Dry, roofed rooms are what is required for grain. There are cool rooms for wine and well-lit rooms for products and storage vessels that must have light. I showed her the beautifully-adorned living rooms that are cool in the summer and warm in the winter. I also showed her the women's quarters, separated from the men's quarters by a door locked with a bolt, so that nothing may be taken out of it which should not be, nor may slaves breed without our permission. For worthy slaves generally become more trustworthy when they have families, but scoundrels with partners become all the more ready for misbehaviour. (8.2–5)

Ischomachus's wife was clearly in charge of everyday life and work in the house, and it was no light responsibility. The domestic slaves had to be supervised; they were not to be allowed to breed without the permission of their masters, though Ischomachus concedes that when good, reliable slaves have children, they become more loyal. But let the bad ones breed, and there will be trouble. But one point in particular is to be noted. There are women's quarters in Ischomachus's house, with a door that could be locked. Xenophon is not the only author to mention women's quarters. An Athenian orator in the fourth century named Lysias refers to them in a speech he had written for use in a murder trial. It should be explained that defendants in Athenian law courts could not hire lawyers to represent them; they had to speak for themselves, but they could hire an orator to write a speech for them. In this case, the defendant had murdered his wife's seducer and was brought to trial. He lived in a small house, with only two rooms, one on the ground floor and the second in the upper story. But the upper room was the women's quarters. It appears that even in a little house, a woman in Athens had her own space.

Yet, as we have already seen, there is no good archaeological evidence for separate apartments in Greek houses that can be clearly identified as women's quarters. The remains of many Greek houses have been excavated by now, and no women's apartments with locked doors have been found. This may be because women's quarters were often on the second floor, and second floors are almost never found intact. But we may also misunderstand the meaning of women's quarters, for which the Greek word is *gynaikonitis*. The *gynaikonitis* in a house may simply have been the rooms that the women of the house customarily used for women's work, such as spinning and weaving. It was where the mistress of the house slept along with her female servants, both slave and free. It was usually not a separate apartment. Men and women in Athens seem to have led parallel lives. But we should not think that Athenian customs were universal throughout the Hellenistic world. For instance, husbands might come home for lunch, but did they eat with their wives? In Athens, it seems they did not. Yet in some other cities, the evidence suggests that they did.

Girl Children

When a child was born, it was not the mother who had given birth to it but instead the father who decided whether or not it should be accepted into the family and reared. If the child was rejected, it was exposed and left to die, though sometimes infants were saved by passersby, most of them, no doubt, slave dealers who reared the children to sell, or sometimes, if they were pretty girls, to work in the sex trade. Female babies were more likely to be rejected than males. The city of Miletus, on the Aegean coast of modern Turkey, provides statistical evidence about what went on from inscriptions. Some thousand families from Greece received Milesian citizenship in the 220s, and census details for 79 of them have survived. They had 118 sons and 28 daughters. This disproportion cannot be due to natural causes. The reason for it must be that the families wanted boys, and female infants were exposed to die in far greater numbers than males. Inscriptions found elsewhere bear out the evidence from Miletus. Families often had two sons, but rarely is a family to be found with more than one girl. Infanticide was not the only method of birth control. Greek doctors knew various medicines that were supposed to induce abortions, and sometimes they must have been successful.

One result of this was a decline in the population of old Greece, the Greece that was the cradle of classical civilization. When Alexander conquered Persia, Greece had a surplus of population. A century later, the surplus had disappeared. Emigration accounts for some of the decrease, but birth control and infanticide were important factors.

Dowries and Marriage Contracts

One reason for the reluctance to rear girl children was that when they got married, their fathers had to provide them with dowries. The earliest dated papyrus document that we have from Egypt,[1] written only 12 years after Alexander the Great's death, is a marriage contract between two Greeks who have immigrated to Egypt, and since they had recently arrived, the marriage contract follows the customs of the Greek world of the time, without Egyptian influence. The bride is from the island of Cos, and the bridegroom from the little city of Temnos on the Asia Minor coast. Heracleides, the groom, received Demetria, his bride, from her father and mother. Demetria's dowry was clothing worth 1,000 drachmas. Heracleides promised to supply Demetria with everything a freeborn wife should have, and to consult his father-in-law about where he and Demetria would live. If Demetria brought shame on her husband, she would lose her dowry, but Heracleides would have to prove any accusation that he made against his wife before a three-man panel approved by both of them. Heracleides promised not to insult Demetria by marrying another wife, nor to beget children by another woman, nor to injure Demetria, whatever the pretext. If he did, and the evidence was clear, then he had to return Demetria's dowry and pay a hefty fine as well. Heracleides and Demetria each kept a copy of the contract, and like typical Greek contracts, there were six witnesses.

This particular marriage contract was between Greeks recently arrived in Egypt, and followed Greek customs. What was unusual was that the bride and groom were citizens of two different cities; in the Greek homeland, that would have been unusual in the classical period, though in the Hellenistic age old interstate barriers were breaking down. Yet in Athens, marriage contracts were similar to the one that bound Heracleides and Demetria in wedlock. A father sought to protect his daughter in marriage and the dowry, which a bridegroom would have to return if he injured his bride, was a method of protection. Then, after the contract, there was a marriage ceremony. In one of Menander's plays, there is a brief marriage formula that served the purpose. The father of the bride says to the groom, "I give you my daughter to sow for the purpose of producing legitimate children." The groom replies, "I take her." The father added, "I also give you a dowry of such-and-such." The groom replies, "I take it too, gladly."

Equality and Power

But customs were not the same everywhere. Athens was not typical. Outside Athens, we find women who could inherit and bequeath property, and sell and buy land, whereas in Athens, they could not. In Macedonia, women played a role in public life that would have shocked the Athenian Ischomachus. The Macedonian queens in the Hellenistic monarchies were a series of remarkable women. They were no shrinking violets. One of Philip II's wives, an Illyrian princess named Audata, fought beside her husband on the battlefield. The Ptolemaic dynasty, which was Macedonian, produced a series of remarkable women. Arsinoe II, the sister and wife of Ptolemy II Philadelphus, who reigned 285–246, was one of the most successful, if we count success as the ability to wield power. She was coruler of Egypt from about 275 to her death in 268. The Ptolemaic queen whom we know best is Cleopatra VII, the last of the Ptolemaic monarchs to rule Egypt, and though she is most famous as the romantic heroine of a love story, she was also an able administrator of her country who seems to have inspired the loyalty of both her Greek and Egyptian subjects. But we need not go to Egypt to find women whose lives contrasted sharply with those lived by Athenian women. We need only go to Sparta.

Spartan women, unlike their Athenian counterparts, could own land. Spartan girls were given an education modeled on that of the boys. Like the boys, they exercised and danced naked, and marched naked in religious processions. Infanticide took place, but boys were probably its victims more than girls, for when a male child was born, the father took it to a club house where the elders of his tribe examined the boy and gave permission to rear him if he promised to be a robust youngster. If not, he was exposed to die. We cannot prove that female infanticide was never practiced in Sparta, but at least it seems to have been more infrequent than in Athens. Nor do we hear of women's quarters in Spartan houses. Spartan men, however, were raised as warriors, and ate their meals in their regimental messes; until they reached the age of 60, when they were too old to fight, they had little home life. Spartan women, however, must have found their home life not unpleasant. One of the tasks of the

Athenian housewife was to weave cloth; in Sparta, slaves looked after the weaving. Helots did the hard work on the farms.

For Sparta, even in the twilight of its power in the Hellenistic age, was a stratified society where all authority was in the hands of a class of elite warriors called the Spartiates, whose income came from their estates: parcels of land that serfs called helots cultivated for them, giving them half the produce. Helots lived on their little farms with their families. The women whose lives I have described above were Spartiate women; the helots faced a dreary existence of hard work. They resented the Spartiates, but the Spartiates had brutal but effective methods of maintaining control. Yet, by the Hellenistic period, the famous Spartan constitution, which was supposedly drawn up by an early lawgiver named Lycurgus, was showing its age. By the mid-fourth century, two-fifths of the estates that were supposed to support Spartiate warriors were owned by women, and the revenue from them supported their lifestyles instead. Reform was necessary, but what happened was revolution.

About 244, Agis IV came to the throne of Sparta, or rather to one of its thrones, for Sparta had two royal families and two kings. Agis attempted reform but his enemies among the Spartiates closed ranks to resist him. He was outmaneuvered and killed. But his widow, Agiatis, married the king of the other royal house, Cleomenes III, who ruled from 235 to 222, and converted him to her late husband's cause. Agis had cancelled debts, but Cleomenes took the next step that Agis had not lived long enough to accomplish: he redistributed the land. He also freed some 6,000 helots in Spartan territory in return for a manumission fee payable in cash. Revolution was in the air. The landless poor in the Greek *poleis* began to hope for a better life. Property owners in the states neighboring Sparta became frightened, so frightened that they appealed to the king of Macedon, Antigonos III Doson, who marched south and defeated Cleomenes at the Battle of Sellasia in 222. Cleomenes's reforms were annulled.

The two reformer kings, Agis and Cleomenes, were linked by a woman, Agiatis, who had married Agis first, and then converted her second husband, Cleomenes, to Agis's cause. Agis was also supported by his mother and grandmother, who were immensely wealthy. They were reputedly the richest of all the Spartans, including men as well as women. Cleomenes's mother also threw her support behind her son. This was a failed revolution, but nonetheless

it illustrates the influence that women could exert in Hellenistic
Sparta.

THE EMERGENCE OF EDUCATED WOMEN

From Akharnai, outside Athens, a gravestone has survived that
depicts a seated woman with her name, Phanostrate, inscribed over
her head. She stretches her right hand toward a standing woman
who wears a veil. Shown around them are children, both boys and
girls. Epigraphers, who study inscriptions, are skilled at assign-
ing them a general date, and the date given this one is the second
half of the fourth century, as the Hellenistic age was beginning. But
what attracts our attention to this inscription is that Phanostrate is
described as a midwife and a doctor.

There had always been midwives in Greece, but a woman who
was a doctor, evidently specializing in gynecology, was a new development. Phanostrate was not alone. Some women wrote treatises
on gynecology, and two of those documents have survived. Unfortunately, we cannot assign secure dates to these treatises. We know
nothing about the authors, and we cannot be certain that they
belonged to the Hellenistic period. However, this was a time when
we find not only women doctors, but also women who were philosophers, poets, and scholars.

In the classical age, the voices of women seem to have been mute.
When the Athenian statesman Pericles gave his great funeral speech
at the end of the first year of the Peloponnesian War, which took up
the last three decades of the fifth century, he dealt briefly with the
role of women at the end of his speech: The great glory of women,
he said, was not to fall short of what Heaven made them, and their
greatest glory was to be least talked about by men. Pericles was
referring specifically to the proper role of Athenian women in the
classical period; there were women poets in earlier periods and in
other places. Sappho from the island of Lesbos is the most famous
of them, and she was not alone. But in the classical period women
seem to have fallen silent. This may simply be an impression given
us by the evidence that survives, which consists of battered stones
with inscriptions carved on them and references in ancient texts.
But by the fourth century, a change had taken place.

We begin to hear of women philosophers, though none of their
writings have survived. Many of them were attracted to neo-
Pythagoreanism, which was a late-Hellenistic revival of Pythagorean

thought. Pythagoras himself had lived in southern Italy in the sixth century, and though we nowadays associate him with the Pythagorean theorem—that the square of the hypotenuse of a right-angled triangle is equal to the squares of the other two sides—he was during his life the founder of a cult that had accepted women as well as men. Neo-Pythagoreans glorified Pythagoras as a semi-religious figure who had founded a perfect way of life and they inherited Pythagoras's fascination with the symbolism of numbers. However, neo-Pythagorean thought came into its own under the Roman empire, though its roots were in the Hellenistic age. Other women were attracted to the Academics, the followers of Plato. As for the Peripatetics, who were disciples of Aristotle, women intellectuals found nothing attractive about them, which is understandable, for Aristotle believed that the minds of women lacked the rational element. Nor did women find much that was appealing in Stoicism, for the Stoics considered motherhood the proper role for women. On the other hand, Epicurus, the founder of the Epicurean school, admitted women into his company on equal terms with men. We have a number of anecdotes about female philosophers, but the evidence, though tantalizing, is meager. Yet it is enough to show that, in the Hellenistic period, women were beginning to take part in the intellectual life that was once the preserve of men.

There were women poets and musicians. Some went on tour and gave public performances. An inscription, dating to 218 or 217,[2] survives from the little city of Lamia in Aetolia, and records a decree of the people honoring the poetess Aristodama from Smyrna in Anatolia. She came to Lamia and gave a reading of her poems—her specialty was epic poetry—that flattered the heroic past of the Aetolians and the ancestors of the Lamians. The grateful Lamians made her a *proxenos,* or honorary consul of their city, and gave her various other rights, including citizenship, all of which were granted to herself and her children, and to her brother and his children as well, for it seems that her brother accompanied her on her tours. One hopes that the Lamians paid Aristodama a fee as well as the honors, but the decree fails to mention it. Women also took part in music and poetry competitions. One woman poet, Aristomache, from the city of Erythrae, entered the competition for epic poetry at the Isthmian Festival and won two prizes. And from Delphi comes an inscription honoring Polygnota, a harpist who came to Delphi to take part in the Pythian Games of the year 86, and when they were cancelled because of a war with Rome, she stayed and gave a free concert which so pleased the city fathers that they invited her to play for three more days for a fee.[3]

We may wonder what sort of education an ordinary woman, neither rich nor poor, could receive, and how many could read and write. In two places, Pergamon and the city of Teos, there is specific evidence that girls went to school. There is no specific evidence that girls went to school elsewhere, but we can assume that they did. The survival of evidence is a happenstance affair, and when evidence does survive, it must be interpreted. When an inscription mentions children going to school, does the word *children* mean just boys, or boys and girls? It is clear in many contexts that both boys and girls are meant, and I believe we can assume that in most of the cities of the Hellenistic world, elementary education was open to girls, and that there were some girls whose education went beyond the elementary level.

What proportion of the women in the Hellenistic world were literate? That is a question that is impossible to answer, not merely for women but for men as well. Pictures of women reading are common enough, particularly on vases, but we can only guess what percentage of women could read. From Egypt many papyri have survived with letters or petitions written by women, but this is treacherous evidence, for there were professional scribes to whom a person who was illiterate or whose penmanship was poor might dictate a letter. Not everyone who wrote a letter penned it himself, or herself. It is also clear from the papyri that there were a great number of persons whom we can classify as semi-literate: they read and wrote only with difficulty. Yet it seems likely that the great majority of women belonging to the propertied class could read and write.

That said, however, if we had only the fragments of the situation comedies that were produced in Greek theaters as evidence for the status of women, we would infer that there were only two roles open to them. They could get married, become respectable housewives, and give birth to legitimate children, like the young wife of Ischomachus in Xenophon's *Oeconomicus*. Or they might be courtesans or prostitutes. Thus far, we have been considering only respectable women, and we should remember that there were courtesans who were often accomplished women, able to sing, play musical instruments, and hold conversations on equal terms with men. *Hetairai*, they were called. They seem to have lived on the fringes of respectability. Nor should we forget the prostitutes at the bottom of the social scale. They also existed in every city of the

Hellenistic world, except for a lucky few, they lived lives of quiet desperation.

NOTES

1. Bagnall and Derow, no. 122.
2. Burstein, no. 64.
3. Burstein, no. 82.

The Philppieion at Olympia, Greece, site of the Olympic Games. A monument begun by Philip II of Macedon after his victory at Chaeronea (338 B.C.E.) and finished by Alexander the Great. Within it were five gold-and-ivory statues: Philip, his father, his mother, and Philip's son, Alexander the Great. Courtesy of Eleanor Evans.

Athens, Greece. The Stoa of Attalus, erected on the east side of the Athenian agora as a gift of Attalus II, King of Pergamon (159–138 B.C.E.). Reconstructed by the American School of Classical Studies, Athens, in the early 1950s for use as a museum and dedicated by King Paul of Greece in 1956.

Athens, Greece, the Theater of Dionysus. Rebuilt in stone by the Athenian statesman Lycurgus (346–326 B.C.E.) to replace an earlier structure. It was extensively
modified in the Hellenistic and Roman periods.

Priene in modern Turkey. The remains of the *Bouleuterion* (council house) with seats
for the councilors and an altar in the center. Originally it had a wooden roof.

Priene. The theater, showing the raised stage where the actors performed.

Didyma, in modern Turkey. Temple and oracle of Apollo. The temple was destroyed by the Persians in the early fifth century, but when Alexander the Great arrived, a sacred spring that had long been dry flowed with water again, and the oracle predicted Alexander's victory at Gaugamela. Alexander ordered the temple rebuilt and the construction continued for 500 years before it was abandoned, still incomplete.

Didyma. The interior of the temple, which was open to the sky.

Pergamon, in modern Turkey. The Hellenistic theater had a wooden stage building, unlike most contemporary theaters, which had permanent stage buildings constructed of stone.

Bergama, Turkey, the modern town beneath the acropolis of ancient Pergamon. The *Kizil Avlu* (Red Hall) was originally built as a temple to Sarapis, where he was worshipped along with Isis and Harpocrates. This attribution is not universally accepted; one archaeologist, Sir Mortimer Wheeler, thought it housed the great Pergamene Library.

Belevi, Turkey. A mausoleum that is thought to be the tomb of the Seleucid king Antiochus II Theos (261–246 B.C.E.). The sarcophagus, which shows the deceased resting on his elbow, has been removed to the Selçuk Museum.

Athens, Greece. The Temple of Olympian Zeus was begun in the sixth century B.C.E. and brought close to completion by the Seleucid king Antiochus IV Epiphanes, 175–163 B.C.E. It was pillaged by the Romans in 85, and finally completed by the emperor Hadrian (117–135 C.E.).

Athens, Greece. Andronicus of Cyrrhus built the Tower of the Winds around 2 B.C.E. as a sun dial and a water clock. Though built a generation after the end of the Hellenistic period, it exemplifies the Hellenistic technological tradition.

Claros, Turkey. Site of an oracle of Apollo that was active at the beginning of the Hellenistic period, but neglected towards the end of it. However, its popularity revived under the Roman Empire. The site is prone to flooding.

Dodona, northwest Greece, site of the oracle of Zeus. The theater shown here was built by Alexander the Great's cousin, Pyrrhus of Epirus (297–272 B.C.E.). It was destroyed in 219 B.C.E., and rebuilt by Philip V of Macedon.

Ephesus, Turkey. Hellenistic Theater, enlarged in Roman times.

The *Nekyomanteion* at Ephyra. This was an oracle of the dead dedicated to Hades, the king of the Underworld, and his wife Persephone. It is a labyrinth of corridors and underground and above-ground rooms. The masonry is Hellenistic. The sanctuary was ruined by fire in 168 B.C.E. Worshipers came to this sanctuary to consult the souls of the dead. Courtesy of Eleanor Evans.

The Temple and Oracle of Apollo at Delphi. The temple was destroyed by an earthquake in 373 B.C.E. and rebuilt between 366 and about 329 B.C.E. with international cooperation and funding. The oracle continued to be patronized in the Hellenistic period. Courtesy of Eleanor Evans.

Columns of the fourth-century temple at Delphi which have been re-erected. Courtesy of Eleanor Evans.

The stadium at Delphi, at the highest point in the sanctuary of Apollo. On the north side of the track, the seats are hewn out of the rock. On the south side, the seats were artificially supported. Courtesy of Eleanor Evans.

An early Hellenistic Tanagra Figurine. These little figures made of terracotta showing women wearing the latest fashions were the Royal Doulton figurines of the Hellenistic world. This lady wears an outer cloak called a *himation*. With permission of the Royal Ontario Museum © ROM.

Probably an image of the last queen of Egypt, Cleopatra VII, sculpted in black granite. With permission of the Royal Ontario Museum © ROM.

An example of a Hellenistic house on Delos used by a wealthy businessman during the second century B.C.E. Courtesy of Hector Williams.

Statue of Queen Arsinoe II, from the Ptolemaic Period, after 270 B.C.E. The queen's striding pose is traditionally Egyptian, while her representation incorporates Hellenistic elements such as the hairstyle and the cornucopia, which is a Greek symbol for divinity. The Metropolitan Museum of Art, Rogers Fund, 1920 (20.2.21) Photograph © 1982 The Metropolitan Museum of Art.

9

Making a Living

TRADE AND COMMERCE

The eastern Mediterranean is a vast region, and we must avoid sweeping generalizations about trade and commerce. Egypt and the southern Ukraine both exported wheat, though the Ukraine's exports fell behind in the Hellenistic period. The olive tree could not be grown in the Black Sea regions, however, and so merchants peddling wine and olive oil were a familiar sight in the Black Sea ports. Some places had export specialties. The island of Thasos in the north Aegean Sea was famous for its honey, and indeed, still is. The Phoenician city of Sidon in Syria was famous for its linen, and Tyre was known for its purple dye. Purple cloth was a profitable commodity that peddlers sold with a generous markup: Saint Paul, on his travels, encountered a Jewish woman at Philippi who was a seller of purple goods.[1] Egypt exported papyrus, the writing paper of the ancient world, though Pergamon managed to compete with parchment made from sheepskins. From Pergamon too came exports of timber and pitch for shipbuilding, and its sheep also supplied wool for fine woolen cloth. Macedonia, like Pergamon, exported timber and pitch. Arabia exported dates and incense and transshipped spices. From the Black Sea there were exports of cattle, slaves, honey, wax, and dried fish.

The Hellenistic world sent three important exports to Rome: wine, cooks, and tutors, and one might also count slaves, though many of these came to Rome as the spoils of war. Italy produced good wine, but the vintages from northern Syria and the coastal region of Ionia in modern Turkey were especially prized there. The cooks, who brought Greek cuisine to Italy, and the tutors, who introduced Rome to literature and art, may have come as slaves, but the Romans granted freedom to slaves far more generously than the Greeks ever did, and the achievements of these Greek tutors was impressive—one of them, Livius Andronicus, founded Latin literature with his translation of Homer's *Odyssey* into Latin. This merely scratches the surface of a complex picture of trade and commerce.

The standard container of the Hellenistic world was the amphora, an earthenware jar with a pointed end that could be slung over a donkey's back, or carried, one amphora on each side, or stacked like cordwood in the hold of a ship. A great number of these jars have survived, and they tell us something about Hellenistic trade and commerce, partly because individual trading cities often had amphoras with distinctive shapes, but even more because of the practice of stamping amphora handles with marks of their cities of origin. Not every city stamped its amphora handles, but enough did to allow us to make some estimates of the volume of trade. The statistics can be deceptive, however, for every amphora need not have been shipped full of oil, wine, or the like; Rhodes seems to have shipped empty amphoras to Egypt, which lacked good clay to make high-quality pottery of its own. But the number of amphoras found indicates that a large labor pool was employed in trade: Stevedores loaded and unloaded the ships, sailors manned them, and traders delivered the imports to customers. Let us look at two trading cities in particular, Alexandria in Egypt and Rhodes. Alexandria was where Alexander the Great lay in his great mausoleum and the Ptolemaic kings had their great, sprawling palace. It was a showplace capital as well as a great trading city that gave access to the Nile Valley. The *polis* of Rhodes resulted from the union of three city-states on the island of Rhodes in 408, and unlike Alexandria, it was a democracy. Let us take Alexandria first.

Greek Imports in Alexandria

The royal government of Egypt retained strict control of the economy of Egypt so far as it could—and that was remarkably far. Foreign coins could not circulate in Egypt; foreigners entering the country had to exchange their money for Egyptian currency. Alexandrian citizenship was a favor granted by the king only to a restricted group; most immigrants remained resident aliens, citizens of their cities of origin. Yet Alexandria was a magnet for immigrants from all over the Mediterranean world, including Italy in the later Hellenistic period. But the cultural tone was distinctively Greek: Native Egyptians were not supposed to become citizens, though it was impossible to keep them out of the city. They were, in fact, there from the beginning, for before Alexander founded Alexandria an Egyptian village named Rhakotis occupied the site, and the name Rhakotis continued to be used for the Egyptian quarter in the southwest of the city. But Greeks set the tone, and the Ptolemaic kings promoted Greek culture as a way of asserting their prestige in the Hellenistic world. Even the large immigrant Jewish community in Alexandria forgot Aramaic, the language of its homeland, and spoke Greek, even in the great Alexandrian synagogue in the Jewish quarter.

The Greek immigrants to Alexandria remained loyal to Greek cooking, and Egypt could not supply all the foodstuffs they needed. Olive oil was a staple. It provided fuel for lamps; in cooking, it took the place of butter and lard; and in the gymnasium, athletes rubbed themselves down with it before exercising, and then scraped it off their bodies with strigils before taking a shower. In Egypt, however, the staple vegetable oils were sesame-seed oil and castor oil, and even though the royal government encouraged olive oil production, it seems to have been inferior to the Greek variety. So Egypt was a good export market for olive oil. Similarly with wine: Egypt had produced wine long before Alexander the Great arrived, but the favorite drink of the Egyptian natives was beer. The Ptolemaic government encouraged the Egyptian wine industry, but even so, Alexandria was a ready market for Greek vintages.

Wood had to be imported, too. The Nile Valley produced no good timber for ship building and could never become self-sufficient even though the government planted trees along the dykes of the irrigation canals. One commodity that was perennially in short supply in the whole Hellenistic world, and particularly in Egypt, was fuel—not only for cooking, but for heating bathwater, for wherever the Greeks settled, even in Egyptian villages, they wanted public bathhouses. Straw, dried grass, reeds, twigs, and even dry dung from camels and donkeys was used, but probably Egypt had to import some wood for fuel. Then there was the eastern trade, some of which flowed through Alexandria, and as time went on it grew in importance. Alexander's expedition to India had opened trade routes to the north of the subcontinent, but about 100, a mariner from Egypt discovered how to use the monsoons to sail to southern India and thus opened up trade with the Tamils in the south. Soon Indian spices were no longer expensive rarities in Alexandria, and from there they were transshipped to the Mediterranean world. International trade made many a Greek entrepreneur rich.

A document dating to the mid-second century has survived that sheds light on how foreign trade was conducted in Egypt. It is a maritime loan contract for the import of perfumes from the land of Punt, modern Somalia, which was known for its incense production. It appears that an association of traders contracted with a banker for what in maritime law is called a "bottomry loan" to import a cargo of perfumes from Somalia. The nationalities of these Egyptian residents who made the contract are a cross-section of multicultural Alexandria. They include immigrants from Massilia—that is, modern Marseilles in the south of France—from Carthage, Thessalonica, Sparta, and Italy, too, for the banker has a Latin name. Two of these entrepreneurs had apparently come to Egypt initially to serve as mercenaries in the Egyptian armed forces. Their business became the import-export trade in goods with a high mark-up. With luck, it could be very lucrative for the merchants and the banker, for though bottomry loans were risky—if the trading vessel was wrecked, it was the banker who absorbed the loss—they could also be very profitable.

The Prosperity of Rhodes

Rhodes is a remarkable example of a city that owed its wealth to trade, particularly the transit trade in grain and slaves. Its great period of prosperity began in 323: When it heard of the death of Alexander the Great in Babylon in that year, it expelled its garrison of Macedonian troops, and managed to preserve its independence while Alexander's successors struggled for power. It survived one famous attempt to conquer it: in 305, Antigonos the One-Eyed, who until his defeat in 301 seemed the most likely of the successors to take over the bulk of Alexander's empire, instructed his son, Demetrius Poliorcetes ("the Besieger"), to capture Rhodes, which was allied to his rival, Ptolemy I of Egypt, and Demetrius brought the latest developments in siege warfare to bear against it. Yet the siege failed. To commemorate their deliverance, the Rhodians erected a colossal bronze statue of the sun god, Helios, at the entrance to their harbor, where it stood until a great earthquake toppled it in 228 and destroyed much of the old city into the bargain. The great statue of Helios became known as the Colossus of Rhodes, and it was one of the seven wonders of the ancient world during its brief life span. But after its fall, the Rhodians did not attempt to erect it again; instead it lay where it fell until the Arabs plundered the city in 654 C.E. and the remains of the great statue were sold for scrap.

Huge numbers of amphora handles stamped with the hallmark of Rhodes and made of the easily recognizable fine, light-colored Rhodian clay have been found all over the Hellenistic world. A vast number have turned up in Egypt, so many that we suspect that some may have been shipped empty to Egypt to be used for Egyptian exports. Second only to Egypt is the number of them found in the Black Sea region. A large share of the grain exported from what is now the Ukraine was carried in Rhodian bottoms to customers in the Hellenistic world, and it was Rhodian money that financed them and Rhodian shipyards that built them. As a mercantile power, Rhodes had a vital interest in seeing to it that the sea-lanes were safe, and so it was the Rhodian fleet that kept pirates in check over the eastern Mediterranean during the third and early second centuries. The Rhodian navy was never large, for keeping a fleet shipshape was expensive; the cost of maintaining a trireme, which was a type of warship used in the Rhodian fleet, was 120,000 drachmas per year at the end of the third century. That was no small amount even for a wealthy city like Rhodes where harbor dues alone during the same period brought in about one million drachmas annually. But her fleet was superbly trained and highly effective.

Rhodes's great period of prosperity came to an abrupt end when the Romans began to suspect her of anti-Roman sentiments. During the so-called Third Macedonian War, when Rome defeated the last king of Macedon and eliminated one of the great Hellenistic monarchies, Rhodian sympathies were with the unfortunate Macedonian king, Perseus, and Rhodes tried to mediate a peace between him and Rome. The Roman senate was not amused even though Rhodes gave Perseus no military assistance. It punished Rhodes for its presumption by making the island of Delos a free port and giving it to Athens, with the result that Delos became a transit center for slaves and grain in competition with Rhodes. Merchants flocked to Delos, and the houses they built there have survived well enough to allow us to see what the dwellings of well-to-do Hellenistic businessmen were like. But Delos grew prosperous at Rhodian expense, and Rhodes suffered a sharp drop in revenues, so much so that she could no longer afford to maintain a fleet effective enough to keep the pirates in check, and in the years that followed, piracy became rampant.

Piracy eventually became such a scourge in the Mediterranean that Rome could no longer ignore it. After some false starts, she entrusted the task of ridding the sea of pirates to an ambitious young politician and army commander, Pompey, who at this point was looking for any chance to make a reputation as a great general. Pompey was swift and efficient. Piracy was suppressed so effectively that the prices of imported goods plunged in Rome, to the delight of the Roman consumer. Pompey's career of conquest continued until all the east except Egypt was absorbed into the Roman empire by the time he returned to Rome in 63. The last Seleucid king, whose empire had shrunk to barely more than the city of Antioch itself, was deposed in 64. Egypt alone survived as an independent kingdom. The Ptolemaic dynasty was winding down and Ptolemy XII, the "New Dionysos," clung to his throne only at the sufferance of Rome, but under his daughter, Cleopatra VII, the Ptolemies would make their exit from history in a blaze of glory.

SOLDIERING AS A CAREER

The self-important mercenary soldier was a figure of fun in the Hellenistic theater. There is one famous example in a comedy by the Latin playwright Plautus, the *Miles Gloriosus* (*The Boastful Soldier*). Plautus wrote for the Roman stage, but his plays were translations and adaptations of Hellenistic comedies, with more music and dance added to suit Roman tastes. Plautus's boastful soldier is a nice example of exaggeration for comic effect; he swaggers on to the stage and tells tall tales of his exploits in exotic locales. In real life, soldiering was an occupation that attracted many young men who were physically fit and had no better prospects. The pay was anything but princely, but there were other rewards: adventure, booty, and perhaps a land grant in a new city founded by a king. In ancient warfare, the victors took the spoils, and Aristotle reflected the opinion of his day in his *Politics*,[2] when he cited war as one method of acquiring wealth, and evidently a respectable one.

Soldiers for hire were not new. Greek mercenaries fought for the last independent pharaohs of Egypt—those of the twenty-sixth dynasty—before the Persians marched into the Nile Valley in 525 and ended Egyptian independence. The Persian kings had employed their services in great numbers in the fourth century. Philip II of

Macedon, Alexander's father, also used them, paying their wages with gold taken from mines near Philippi that he controlled. When Alexander met king Darius of Persia at the battle of Issus, the toughest soldiers in the Persian army were the Greek mercenaries, and a few of them remained faithful to Darius even after his flight from the battlefield and fought for him again in his last battle, at Gaugamela. In the Hellenistic world after Alexander, mercenaries were plentiful and in great demand.

There were good reasons why. Neither the Ptolemaic nor the Seleucid kings were anxious to recruit their native subjects into their armies. Pharaonic Egypt did have a native warrior class that the Ptolemies could have used, but they preferred imported soldiers, such as Greeks, Macedonians, Jews, who came from Judea to Egypt in large numbers, and even Gauls, the formidable Celtic warriors who swept into Greece in 279 and got as far south as Delphi before they were turned back. Since standing armies were expensive to maintain, the Ptolemaic kings resorted to the tried and true method of granting soldiers allotments of land to exploit. Thus the burden of supporting them did not fall on the royal treasury. A shortfall of troops could be made up by recruiting more soldiers at one of the mercenary employment centers, the most popular of which were at Cape Taenarum and Cape Malea, the southern tips of the Greek peninsula, where mercenaries who wanted employment gathered and recruiting agents came to hire them.

The system did not always work as well as was intended. In 215, Egypt under the young king Ptolemy IV was threatened by Antiochus III, the greatest of the Seleucid kings after Seleucus I himself, the founder of the dynasty. Egypt was the underdog; its armed forces had suffered from neglect under the previous king, and there were not enough mercenaries available for an army large enough to match the Seleucid one. So Egypt had no choice but to recruit native Egyptians and when the two armies met at Raphia in southern Palestine in 217, it was the Egyptian troops that won the battle for Ptolemy. Raphia was a turning point when the interface between Greek and native Egyptian underwent an important adjustment. Thereafter the Ptolemies found it increasingly necessary to appease the nationalism of the Egyptians and their growing resentment directed at their Macedonian overlords.

Why did the life of a mercenary soldier attract so many young men? A skilled workman made better wages, but there were many men in Greece with little to offer but hard muscles and experience in warfare. Many mercenaries must have been wounded in battle and probably did not survive their wounds, for unlike modern warfare—where military action leaves many survivors who are maimed and traumatized, but continue to live long lives—it was usually the fate of a wounded soldier in the ancient world to bleed to death or die of infection. Yet some mercenaries had long careers, and some found generous employers. The Ptolemaic kings had good reputations. Pergamon was also a liberal employer: In fact, a contract[3] offered by Eumenes I, king of Pergamon, survives, dating to about 260, and it gives the student of the ancient world the sort of terms a mercenary could expect. Eumenes offered a 10-month campaign year, with the remaining two months unpaid, a fixed price for wheat and wine at the royal commissary—mercenaries usually bought their own food—special tax breaks, welfare provisions for soldiers who failed to find employment when their contracts were completed, and provision for the orphans of men killed in service. In addition, there might be a share of booty, and the prospect of retirement with some old wounds and a host of stories.

Yet, for all that, we must balance the attractions of the professional soldier's life against the dangers. Let us, for instance, imagine the fate of most of the troops who followed one of the most brilliant military leaders of the early Hellenistic period—Alexander the Great's cousin, Pyrrhus, king of Epirus. In 280, after some reverses in Greece, he came to Italy with 25,000 troops and 20 war elephants, on the invitation of Taras, modern Taranto, a Greek *polis* in southern Italy that was at war with Rome. In that year he defeated a Roman army, but his losses were such that the maxim "Pyrrhic victory" came into our vocabulary. The next year he won another expensive victory. Then he moved to Sicily to serve a new employer in a war against Carthage. In 275 he was back in Italy and fought a drawn-out battle with the Romans at Beneventum, modern Benevento, and his retreat after the battle was a brilliant feat of military tactics. But he got home with only one-third of his expeditionary force. Pyrrhus did not have the wherewithal to reward his soldiers, much less make provision for the orphans of his fallen troops. His veterans may have had stories to tell, but not much else. We need not wonder that, as the Hellenistic age wore on, the supply of soldiers for hire diminished.

BANKING

The evidence for banking in the Hellenistic world is not as abundant as we would like. In Athens of the fourth century, before the

Hellenistic period began, we know the names of about 20 bankers, including Pasion, who was probably the wealthiest man in Athens when he died in 370 or 369. In Hellenistic Athens banking no doubt continued, but the names of the bankers are unknown. We do have abundant evidence for banking elsewhere in the Hellenistic world, where banks became common fixtures of everyday life. The best known are those in Cos, Ephesus, and Sardis. Some cities, such as Miletus, set up state banks. Temples, which had always taken deposits for safekeeping, became deeply involved in lending money at interest. Some of our best evidence comes from Apollo's birthplace, the island of Delos, where a large number of inscriptions have been found that throw light on the temple of Apollo's banking business. The holy island of Delos was under the domination of Athens in the fifth and fourth centuries, until 314. Then Delos enjoyed a period of independence until 166. Delos had been neutral during the so-called Third Macedonian War, when Rome terminated the Macedonian monarchy, but the sympathies of the Delians were with the last Macedonian king. Rome was unforgiving. She forced the Delians to leave their island, taking their belongings with them, and the real estate that they owned was confiscated. It was an atrocity that benefited the temple of Apollo. At least, after the Delians were forced to leave, Apollo's property seems to have increased substantially. Athenian settlers took the place of the Delians forced to leave, for Rome gave the island back to Athens, which had followed a pro-Roman policy, and Delos became a free port.

Apollo lent money at 10 percent interest, the usual rate in the Hellenistic world except in Egypt where it was more than twice that. His clients were other cities on the Cyclades Islands that borrowed to meet shortfalls in revenue. When Athens lost control of Delos in 314, the Cyclades Islands remained major clients, but soon the city of Delos itself was borrowing money from Apollo, who, it seems, demanded a guarantor for the loans. Banking was not without risks. After 280, we find Delos ceasing to make loans to foreign states—evidently they were too difficult to collect—and about the same time, Apollo began to get into the business of making small loans to small-time borrowers.

How difficult were these loans to collect? We know that in the last two decades of the third century, the number of defaults increased sharply. Was the cause an economic downturn? Or was it negligent supervision of Apollo's business? When Athens took over Delos again in 166, it looks as if the fresh management of Apollo's temple was a broom that swept the place clean. Apollo called in his mortgages and mortgaged property was added to the god's considerable property portfolio. And Apollo's loans were henceforth limited to five years.

Temple banks became widespread in the Hellenistic world, both as lending institutions and places to deposit money. For 600 years, from the fourth century to the second century C.E., the great temple of Artemis at Ephesus maintained its reputation as a safe place to deposit money and valuables. It was by no means the only temple in the business. The temple of Asclepius on the island of Cos had a secure crypt intended to keep valuables safe and secure. In the Seleucid empire temples were deeply involved in banking, and when some of the later Seleucid kings who were desperate for money laid their hands on temple wealth, they faced an outraged citizenry, for much of the wealth in the temple hoards was made up of private deposits that belonged to citizens. An incident in Hellenistic Jerusalem illustrates the angry protest that any attempt to confiscate the wealth of temple banks aroused. The wealth of the temple of Yahweh was well-known, but when king Antiochus IV sent a royal deputy, Heliodorus, to seize it, the high priest protested that the treasure of the temple consisted largely of deposits, some of them belonging to widows and orphans, and when Heliodorus persisted in his attempt, popular resistance forced him to retreat.[4]

It is in Egypt that we find the most sophisticated banking system in the Hellenistic world. The kings of Egypt ran the country as if it were a large corporation that had larger and ever larger profits as its chief objective. The banks were part of the corporation. Egypt minted coins on a standard about 20 percent lighter than the Athenian standard that had been adopted by Alexander and remained the standard in general use in the Hellenistic world. Newcomers to Egypt, whether traders or tourists, had to exchange their foreign money for Egyptian currency, and exchanging money was a profitable business for the banks. Like the rest of the Egyptian economy, banking was centralized and carefully controlled. We find a network of royal banks with the central head office in Alexandria. In the provinces, or nomes as they were called in Egypt, every nome capital had a bank, and in smaller villages there were branch banks, as well as private banks that were strictly regulated by the state. When a man wanted to borrow money, he could approach one of these banks, or one of the temples that also were in the business of making loans, or he might go to a private lender such as the owner of a large estate.

The banking business in Egypt employed thousands of accountants and clerks who kept voluminous records, for the manufacture of paper from papyrus was a royal monopoly, and it was relatively cheap inside Egypt. The parched desert soil of Egypt preserves papyrus very well, and banking records are among the many documents from Hellenistic and Roman Egypt that have survived. So have many other records, such as business letters, petitions from injured parties seeking justice, instructions from bureaucrats to other bureaucrats further down the bureaucratic ladder, land surveys, and receipts for taxes written on pieces of broken pottery called *ostraka,* for one did not waste a sheet of papyrus on a tax receipt.

Banking was generally accepted in the Hellenistic world as part of business life. The attitude towards both trade and banking is illustrated by a parable Jesus told with slight variations in two books of the New Testament.[5] A man who was setting out on a long journey entrusted some of his capital to three of his servants—probably slaves or freedmen. To one he entrusted five talents, two to another, and only one to the third. The first two went into trade and doubled their master's capital. The third buried his talent in a hole in the earth. When the master returned, he praised the first two servants, but he reproached the third angrily. Why, he asked, had he not at least deposited his talent in a bank where it might earn interest? We should note two points. First, banks paying interest were considered secure depositories. But it was the servants who went into trade and doubled their master's capital who won their master's greatest praise. Second, the master did not sully his own hands at trade. To be sure, he was an absent investor, but in his use of servants for his business dealings he was following common practice. For the respectable citizen, there was something a little sordid about trade and commerce, much as he might like to see his capital grow.

MAKING A LIVING IN HELLENISTIC EGYPT

Thanks to the discovery of great numbers of papyri from Egypt, we are relatively well-informed about the well-ordered life of the Egyptians, both native Egyptians and immigrants who flocked there after the Macedonian conquest. Most of the papyri come from the region south of the Delta of the Nile, where the river runs between two narrow strips of fertile land, and on either side of it, desert. The Nile was the lifeblood of Egypt. It was the annual Nile flood that made the river valley fertile, and the Egyptians had learned to maximize the arable area by irrigation. The Ptolemaic kings made it their business to bring as much wasteland as they could under cultivation. They even made the experiment of planting two crops a year, probably with no great success. Life in Egypt revolved around the annual flood. The land that the floodwaters did not reach was desert, and since arable land was too precious to waste on houses, we find most of Egypt's villages sited on the edge of the desert.

One document preserved on papyrus[6] illustrates what the economy of Egypt was like in the late third century, when the document was written. It is a long memorandum written by the *dioiketes*, who was the chief minister in charge of the state economy, and it was addressed to a subordinate who was the overseer of a nome of Egypt. It was probably a standard memorandum sent to all such overseers, or *oikonomoi*, as they were called in Greek, and anglicized as *oeconome*. The beginning of the papyrus is broken off, and the legible portion begins with an instruction to check the irrigation canals, in particular the water intakes. Farmers were to plant their crops according to a sowing schedule, and the *oeconome* was to see to it that the schedule was followed. The amount of grain that the nome was to bring to the market in Alexandria was prescribed, and the *oeconome* should see to it that the quota was met. The looms in all the royal weaving factories should be producing their quotas of linen, and if looms were idle, they should be stored in the chief village of the nome and sealed, so that no one might use them for illicit weaving. Tax accounts should be audited, village by village if possible. Taxes in money should be paid only to the royal bank, but if they were taxes paid in grain or oil, the proper receiver was the officer in charge of the royal storehouses. Oil was a royal monopoly and the *oeconome* was instructed to supervise the oil presses in the factories with particular care. As for the cattle in the nome: there were both royal and private herds, and both should be registered. The best time to do this was at the height of the Nile flood, for then the cattle breeders had to drive their cattle to high ground, and there was no hiding them from the inspector's eagle eye. Some goods had ceiling prices, and the *oeconome* should see to it that no merchant exceeded them; even when the goods had no ceiling price, the *oeconome* should see to it that the markup was fair. There was to be no gouging of the poor countrymen. The dykes along the canals should be planted with trees—willows, acacias, mulberries, and tamarisks. Native Egyptian soldiers or sailors who had deserted should be arrested if they were discovered and sent to Alexandria; the memorandum does not indicate what would happen to them there, but we may infer that whatever it was, it would be unpleasant. The *oeconome* was in charge of all these duties. No doubt he had a large staff to help him.

As the *oeconome* or his staff went from place to place, they were instructed to cheer everybody up. The minister in charge of the economy admitted that not everything had been perfect in the past. There had been dishonest officials. But that was all in the past. Everyone—so the minister directed his *oeconomes*—must believe that wrongdoing had stopped. The minister concluded with an exhortation to his *oeconomes* to behave properly and avoid bad company, and if they did, they could expect promotion.

We get a vivid picture from this document of a controlled economy where all production was supervised. There was some room for private enterprise, but it was carefully controlled. The chief interest of the civil service, which was headed by the king's minister in charge of the economy, was to maximize profits. The minister expressed concern for the native Egyptians who worked the fields or wove linen in the weaving factories, for in Egypt, unlike Greece, men sometimes did the weaving. Without the native Egyptians' labor, Egypt could not have been the money-spinning business that it was. The minister wanted everyone to be happy, yet what was really important was to keep the wheels of commerce turning smoothly and profitably.

PRIVATE ENTERPRISE

Yet there were private entrepreneurs who found profitable niches for themselves, and by chance an archive of an entrepreneur's private papers has survived to throw light on his business dealings. His name was Zenon, and he was a Carian by origin; that is, he came from the little enclave of Caria in southwest Asia Minor. Long before the Hellenistic age began, the Carians had been assimilated to Greek culture, and in Egypt, Zenon counted as a Greek. By 261, the date of the earliest document in the Zenon archive, he was the general factotum of Apollonius, the minister of finance and much else in the government of Ptolemy II Philadelphus (282–246), and we find him traveling through Syria on business for Apollonius. But by 258, Apollonius had been granted a large estate in the Fayum near a recently founded village called Philadelphia, after king Ptolemy II Philadelphus and his sister-wife, Arsinoe II, and we find Zenon in charge of this estate by the spring of 256. He remained as manager for nine years, until he left Apollonius's service to devote himself to his own business in association with his brother. A new king, Ptolemy III, "the Benefactor," came to the throne in 246, and Apollonius dropped out of the picture. His estate at Philadelphia was confiscated. Zenon lived on, but his brother died in 243 and Zenon no longer seemed as interested in his business as he had once been. Another brother was in charge of his dossier of papers by 240, and our last dated document of Zenon's belongs to early 229. At some point the dossier was discarded, and as chance would have it, a large part of it survived to give us an intimate record of a businessman in Hellenistic Egypt.

As Apollonius's agent, we find him involved in trade in Syria and Palestine. One letter to Apollonius that went through Zenon's hands was from the Jewish sheikh Toubias, the head of the Toubiad clan in Jordan. He was sending Apollonius slaves: one eunuch and four boys, two of them uncircumcised. Another document from Toubias records his gifts of horses, dogs, mules, and donkeys to Apollonius and horses, dogs, mules, and two white Arab donkeys to king Ptolemy. There are a great many documents concerning Apollonius's estate at Philadelphia. Irrigation had to be supervised. The sluices were to be opened at a precise date in August to let the floodwater on to the fields. Only the land that the water reached could be cultivated, and so the water supply has to be measured precisely. Then, too, Zenon was an important man and important men received requests and petitions. Zenon's countrymen back in Caria wrote to him to ask his help in business deals. Zenon's everyday life was taken up with all sorts of business.

But for some reason, Apollonius fell from favor. His estate at Philadelphia was a *dôrea*, that is, land gifted to him by the king. It was never private property. A new king came to the throne and took back the gift.

EVIDENCE OF OTHER OCCUPATIONS

Other dossiers of documents belonging to individuals have also survived. They give a vivid picture of everyday life. Village clerks at work in their offices wrote countless memoranda and receipts, and when they were out-of-date they were discarded, or recycled as wadding for mummies. Irrigation engineers digging new canals sent messages back and forth. Egyptians filed petitions complaining about being cheated, or suffering assault and battery on the streets. In most villages, particularly in the Fayum, Greeks, Macedonians, and Egyptians lived side-by-side, and the royal government recognized the right of the Egyptians to use their own laws. General dishonesty in the bureaucracy was common. Yet crops were sown and harvested, taxes were paid, and the royal officials went about their appointed tasks.

In fact, we get the impression that the bureaucracy that ran the day-to-day life in Egypt acquired a life of its own. Since more and more papyri written in the Egyptian language—demotic—are being published, it is becoming clear that more native Egyptians found employment in the government civil service than scholars once imagined. The government in Alexandria grew weaker in the last hundred or so years of Ptolemaic rule, but in the *chôra*, the Nile valley beyond the limits of Alexandria, we see little evidence of it. The civil service conducted business as usual.

NOTES

1. Acts 16:14.
2. Aristotle, *Politics*, 1.8.
3. Austin, no. 196.
4. 2 Maccabees 3:9–30.
5. Matthew 25:14–30; Luke 19:12–27.
6. Bagnall and Derow, no. 85.

10

Eating and Drinking

SHARED FEASTS

Eating was a serious business. Men eating meals together could be engaging in both a civic and religious ritual in the city-state. The town hall (*prytaneion*) of a city had a space for dining, and those members of the city council who had to be on call all the time would gather there to eat meals together. The meals were prepared by professional cooks called *mageiroi*, who knew the right religious rituals for butchering animals and preparing the meat for eating. A victor at the Olympic games might be honored in his home city with free meals in the town hall for the rest of his life, and so, too, might a citizen who had done great service to the state. Very important people from other city-states could be entertained there. Aristotle in his *Politics*[1] stated that it was generally agreed that in a well-governed state there should be communal meals for all citizens, though he acknowledged that a poor citizen might have a problem paying for his contribution to this meal and at the same time meeting his own household expenses.

In Sparta there were communal meals (*syssitia*) for the full citizens, the Spartiates, who were a warrior elite trained to be soldiers from the age of seven, and the Spartiate participants were expected to maintain their eating clubs with per capita contributions. If a Spartiate failed to pay, he was dropped from his club and ceased to be a full citizen. In the Hellenistic period, so many Spartiates lacked the wherewithal to pay that the communal meals were abandoned, but not forgotten. As we have seen, in the late third century, king Cleomenes III (235–222) tried to revive the old Spartan way of life. On Crete, too, we also find cities with the custom of communal meals for male citizens, but there it was the state that paid for the cost, and evidently the meals were generous enough that a man could take home leftover food for his wife and children. Eating together gave a sense of community, for men who ate together stuck together.

Shared feasts were a way for a wealthy man to advertise his status for all to see. One of the parables Jesus tells is the tale of how a rich man whose expensive clothes proclaimed his wealth feasted daily on fine food, while just outside his door there crouched a poor man named Lazarus who ate "from whatever fell from the rich man's table."[2] Lazarus was one of the wretched street people of the Hellenistic city, and the parable states that he and the rich man received rewards in the afterlife that were the inverse of their lives on earth. The tale was a warning to the affluent classes that however great an impression they might make with their wealth on earth, death would level the playing field. But the parable also reminds us that food left over from a grand banquet was not thrown into the garbage. A guest might take it home, or it would be given to the slaves who attended the wealthy banqueters, and the leavings might reach street people like Lazarus. This was an example not only of conspicuous spending but also of the redistribution of food. The rich man feasted to display his wealth and status, and he gave food to his guests to show that he could afford to do so. Thus needy folk like Lazarus got food enough to live.

It should not surprise us to find in Hellenistic cities a class of hangers-on known as "parasites"—the literal meaning of the word is "a person who sits at your side." Parasites are stock characters in the situation comedies that were common in the theaters. A parasite was a man in search of a free meal, that attached himself to a well-to-do citizen who supplied his meals, and in return he furnished his patron with various services, one of which was to keep him abreast of local gossip. Hellenistic kings, whose feasts were famous, also attracted parasites. "Flatterers," they were called, for they stroked the royal ego, and they supplied the king with information, but they were reluctant to give unwelcome news even when it was important that the king should know it. Yet sharing food was a way in which wealth trickled down to the poor in ancient society, and it created a bond between those who wielded power and the vulnerable classes. Lazarus in the parable was too far down the social scale to concern a rich man, but the parable makes a point that few men could ignore: the same end awaits both rich and poor.

Bread or polenta, wine mixed with water, olive oil, and seasonal vegetables and fruits were the staples of the Greek diet. But the city market offered a great variety of vegetables for sale. The market gardens outside the city walls produced onions, garlic, turnips, broad beans, kidney beans, lentils, chickpeas, artichokes, and fruits including figs, dates, pomegranates, apples, grapes, and pears. Alexander's conquests introduced the Greeks to peaches and cherries. Absent were modern staples such as tomatoes, potatoes, some varieties of beans, and maize or "Indian corn," all of which became known to Mediterranean cooks only after the discovery of the Americas. In early spring, women gathered the greens of plants such as mustard and nettles, which sprang up on uncultivated land, and used them fresh for salads or boiled and eaten cold with olive oil. Spring through early summer was a time when the stocks of stored food ran low, and salad greens, the *horta* of modern Greek cuisine, were a valuable addition to the diet. For those above the poverty line, there might be salted fish, cheese, and eggs. The markets of cities close to the sea offered fresh fish, though the Mediterranean has never been a rich fishing ground.

The well-to-do had a greater variety of food on their tables, including meat and a variety of fish. A market of the first century or even earlier might have a round, colonnaded building called a *makellon* (Latin: *macellum*), which was a place where meat, fish, and poultry were sold. The usual meats were pork, mutton, and goat, for beef was not for everyday, though when cattle were slaughtered for sacrifice in religious festivals, some meat from the beasts that were sacrificed might find its way on to the market. To add flavor, Greek cooks had an assortment of herbs such as thyme, sage, fennel, parsley, oregano, rue, dill, and coriander, and once merchants began to ply the trade routes to India, new spices such as cinnamon and pepper appeared. The Greeks used pepper as a medicinal herb when they first encountered it; at least, it first appears in the medical writings of Hippocrates and his school, but Greek cooks soon discovered that it added zest to food, and after Alexander's conquests opened the trade routes to northern India, pepper was no longer difficult to obtain. A fish sauce called *garos* (in Latin, *garum*) tickled the Hellenistic palates. There is a fish sauce in modern Vietnamese cuisine that is similar. One ingredient that flavored Greek cooking is not to be found nowadays. It was a variety of wild fennel called *silphion* that grew in Cyrene in North Africa, now part of Libya, and it paid a high price for its popularity, for it is now extinct.

COOKING TOOLS AND MEAL CUSTOMS

What sort of kitchen did Greek houses have? There were no chimneys, and the modern chef who slaves over a hot stove has it relatively easy compared to a Greek cook preparing a meal over a hearth in a poorly vented kitchen. Excavated Greek houses provide rather puzzling evidence. One would expect to find a room in them that was clearly set aside for cooking, and at a site such as Olynthus, which is in northern Greece, some houses—though not the majority—do have cooking rooms. But Olynthus is the exception rather than the rule. In the remains of the private houses that are found on many sites, no kitchen can be identified. Some cooking was probably done in the courtyard of the house, where the cook could use a little earthenware stove that burned twigs or charcoal. There, at least, the cook did not have to worry about ventilation. But we must suspect that often, if a Greek cook wanted to serve an oven-baked meal at home, he would take it to the oven of a nearby bakery, where it would be cooked and delivered back to the house.

Greek cooking pots yield some clues. Greek cooks had two standbys—a large, bulbous pot, sometimes with a lid, that was used for stews, soups, and boiled vegetables, and a wider, shallow casserole with a lid that was used for cooking fish in sauce, oil, or water. There was also a covered earthenware vessel, wider at the bottom than the top, in which bread was baked by half burying it in the embers of a fire. Alexander the Great's conquests brought Middle Eastern cuisine to the Hellenistic world, as well as new fruits such as peaches and cherries. Cooks began to roast meat in ovens and to bake stuffed-meat dishes, and new varieties of bread from Syria and Cappadocia delighted the Greeks. Honey cakes—like modern baklava—cheese, fruits, and nuts served as dessert. A well-to-do Greek's dinner could be an elaborate affair. But for the Greek working man, meals remained simple. Fresh meat, for instance, was prepared and roasted by a professional cook, a *mageiros*, who butchered the animal that was to be eaten, and a middle-income citizen could not afford to hire his services every day.

Probably most Greeks, for most of the time, sat on chairs or stools to eat, and though no Greek chairs have survived we do see them depicted in relief sculptures and vase paintings; so they can be reconstructed. Some of the chair designs, with their curved legs and seats of leather thongs covered with cushions, would be the last word in elegance nowadays. But at some point in the sixth century, in what we call the archaic period, the Greeks adopted the practice of reclining on couches when they dined. It was a custom that the Greeks probably borrowed from the Persians who in turn borrowed it from the Assyrians, who dominated Mesopotamia and even conquered Egypt before their empire crashed in the late seventh century. Formal dining on couches became the style in classical and Hellenistic Greece. Greek art shows more than one variety of couch. One was a simple chaise lounge: a chair with an extended seat so that a man could sit on it and stretch out his legs horizontally in front of him. Another was a sofa with a large pillow or bolster at one end where a diner could recline on his elbow. Some sofas were large enough for two diners.

But the Greeks never abandoned the custom of sitting as they dined. In the agora of Athens there was a circular building called the *tholos* where 50 councilors from the executive council known as the Council of 500, plus a few magistrates, met to eat, and along with them perhaps some victors in one of the important athletic festivals. The *tholos* has been excavated, and clearly it could not have accommodated couches for between 55 and 60 guests, even if we calculate two diners to a couch. Probably the guests ate their free meals as they sat on stools or on benches around the periphery of the building. We are familiar with one famous meal where the guests sat on chairs. The Last Supper of Jesus and his disciples took place in an "upper room," not in the *andron* of a private house, and in the earliest depictions of it in Christian art the disciples are shown sitting in a semi-circle around Jesus. The dining arrangement that we see in Leonardo da Vinci's famous painting *The Last Supper* may be more or less accurate.

The day began at sunrise, and about noon the Greek took a light meal. The heavy meal of the day took place in the evening. If the master of the house was entertaining guests in the *andron*, a small wooden three-legged table, scrubbed clean, would be placed before each couch where a guest reclined, and first, loaves of bread in baskets would be brought in, and then a course of appetizers. The guests put their food on the tables or on chunks of bread that they tore off a loaf. They ate with their fingers, for forks were unknown. Then came the second course, which might be poultry, fish, or a shish kabob of fresh meat, roasted by a professional cook. If there was a dessert course, there might be sweetmeats—honey cakes like baklava, perhaps, for honey was the common sweetener for food. Sugar was unknown.

Then the dirty tables were removed, the floor was swept clean, and the wine was brought in and mixed with water. The Macedonians, whose heavy drinking was famous, liked their wine earlier in the meal and preferred it straight, or at least with less water than the Greeks, who thought that drinking unmixed wine was a barbaric custom, and probably unhealthy. The Spartans had a story about one of their kings named Cleomenes, who lived at the end of the sixth century and drank his wine straight. His mind became deranged, and in a fit of madness he killed himself. The Greek custom was to mix wine with water. Half wine and half water was a fairly stiff drink; two-thirds water and one-third wine was a more prudent mix if the guests were to leave the symposium sober. The mixing was done by the host in a great two-handled urn called a *krater*. It would be a fine example of the potter's art, the equivalent of Spode or Royal Doulton china. Once the *krater*, the drinking cups, and the containers for the wine and the water appeared, the symposium could begin.

THE SYMPOSIUM, OR DRINKING PARTY

The word *symposion* means a "drinking party," where guests gathered together and drank wine. By extension, it could refer to the guests at the party, or even to the room where the party was held, which was known as the *andron*, the men's room. To judge by the size of these men's rooms in the private houses that archaeologists have found, the guests at most symposiums must have been a select group—the banquets offered in the palaces and mansions of the Hellenistic world are a separate topic, and so is the banqueting that was an important part of festivals honoring the gods. We have two accounts of symposiums that Socrates attended. Both date to before the Hellenistic period, for Socrates was put to death in 399, but they convey a vivid impression of what the symposium was like. Both were written by pupils, or at least associates, of Socrates, one by the philosopher Plato and the other by the ex-soldier and man of letters, Xenophon. Plato's is better written, but Xenophon's is perhaps more true to life, for in his symposium not only did the host give his guests the opportunity to discuss matters of the day—none of them very intellectual—but he brought in a little troupe of acrobats and musicians to entertain them. Professional entertainers were a regular feature at Hellenistic symposiums, if the host was a generous man who liked others as well as himself to enjoy his wealth.

The *krater* was brought in at the end of the main course. Before the wine was mixed, the host poured a few drops of unmixed wine on to the floor as a libation to the gods, and made a prayer. Then the host decided—or perhaps his guests made the decision by a vote—what the proportion of wine to water would be, and the mixed wine was ladled out into cups. The *krater* was usually a splendid example of the potter's art, and from Athens, which has been extensively excavated over the years, we can glean some idea of the prevailing styles. At the start of the third century, the *krater* was turned on the potter's wheel and embellished with wreaths and necklaces or geometric designs in buff and white on a black gloss background. A century later, *kraters* were beginning to be made in molds, with decorations in relief on their sides and garlands painted on the rim or inside the bowl. By about 25 years later, *kraters* had become smaller, and then potters in Athens seem to have stopped making them. At least, they stopped producing *kraters* with first-rate embellishments, though they continued to make cheaper urns in coarse earthenware while fine *kraters* might still be imported from abroad. But in Athens, which was a fashion leader, clearly a change in drinking customs had taken place.

Nor was it only the *krater* that had changed. Drinking cups grew larger and the pitchers that were used to dip wine from the *krater* grew smaller. Their necks became so narrow that clearly that they cannot have been used as dippers. A new type of vessel appeared— the so-called *lagynos,* a decanter with a single handle and a narrow neck, and it was not suited for communal drinking in a symposium. Did the symposium give way to bring-your-own-bottle parties, where guests mixed their own wine? We cannot say, but clearly fashions had changed. The symposium was adapting to new trends in society as the Hellenistic age wore on.

Moreover, the houses found on the island of Delos, which attracted traders from across the Mediterranean after it became a free port in 167, seem to show that the *andron* was going out of style. In its place was a rectangular room with a door on its long side giving on to the courtyard. It was the principle room of the house, as we can see from its size and the paintings that decorate the walls. It appears that these houses on Delos could accommodate parties where guests brought their own wine, or if the host provided it, at least they mixed it to their own satisfaction. The exclusive dinner in the *andron,* followed by an elegant drinking party and civilized conversation, seems to have gone out of style as the Hellenistic age wound down.

Taverns

At Delos, too, archaeology has unearthed evidence of a new place for drinking: a tavern. Pompeii, near Naples in southern Italy, which was buried by a volcanic eruption of Mount Vesuvius in 79 C.E., had many taverns that were very similar, but the Delian example is the first in Greece that can be clearly identified and it is as much as two centuries earlier than the examples found at Pompeii. It is just north of the agora of the Italians, and it may have catered to the Italian traders who flocked to Delos. There is no doubt about its identification. Amphoras for wine were stacked in the room, along with many drinking cups and various pitchers. Dice and gaming pieces, and jewelry possibly belonging to a prostitute on the second floor, indicate what sort of recreation took place in this tavern. This was an establishment where a man might come for a drink, or perhaps more than one, play at dice and eat a few snacks, and it is the first example of many such taverns unearthed at Delos. But the archaeological evidence from Delos does not tell us when the forerunners of the tavern first appeared in Greece. For that we must turn to the clues that we find in Greek literature.

The comic poet Aristophanes wrote his best work in the last quarter of the fifth century, and in one of his comedies, produced in 411, the chorus pours out its heart in a prayer to the Olympic gods to lay a curse on all persons who harmed the community of women, and among those who are cursed are bartenders who shorted their customers when they poured drinks for them.[3] The reference is casual, but it is clear that in classical Athens there were already shops where a man or a woman could buy a drink. They must have served the same purpose as the Hellenistic taverns, where the publican decanted wine, strained and mixed it with water, and poured it into a drinking cup, adding myrrh, perhaps, if that was to the customer's taste, and sometimes presenting the cup to his customer less than completely full. Plato, in one of his dialogues, the *Gorgias,* mentions a publican named Sarambus who was as skillful at preparing drinks as a fine cook. Was Sarambus the ancient counterpart of a modern bartender who knows how to mix a good martini? To be honest, Plato's Greek is not entirely clear, and there is room for doubt. The word Plato used to describe Sarambus's occupation was *kapelos,* which means simply a shopkeeper, and Sarambus's shop might simply have sold wine by the amphora. But why, then, should he be compared to a fine cook? Add to that some suspicious evidence found in the excavation of the agora of Athens: In an abandoned well in the southeast corner of the marketplace there were found many broken and discarded amphoras, drinking cups, mixing bowls, and cookware. Did they come from a nearby tavern that went out of business about 430?

There is a reason for pursuing this line of reasoning. Taverns—shops selling wine to customers, along with food—were a feature of the Hellenistic city, and one would like to know when they first appeared in Greece. The evidence seems to suggest that it was sometime in the fifth century, in the heyday of the Athenian empire, which encouraged democratic constitutions in its member states. Taverns and democracy seem to go together. Drinking with friends at a symposium was elitist and upper class. It was like having cocktails followed by dinner with a fine French wine, whereas eating and drinking in a tavern was like meeting friends for beer and a hamburger at Joe's Grill. The tavern was more inclusive than the symposium ever was. It was more of a meeting place for the common man, and it is no coincidence that when Aristophanes referred casually to publicans selling drinks in Athens, he was living in a democracy. Nor is it odd that, as society became more open and multicultural in the Hellenistic period, a fully developed tavern should appear on Delos, dating to a time when Delos was a center where businessmen gathered from all over the Mediterranean.

The term *symposium* has been taken over from Greek into English and given a different meaning. The modern symposium is no longer a drinking party. Instead it is a sort of roundtable debate where a group of speakers present prepared statements or papers, and discussion follows. It is a sober affair, and the ancient symposium was not like it at all. The guests drank, and their host might provide dancing girls for entertainment—or the guests might dance themselves. One ancient author remarked that the Athenians had only to take a sip of wine for them to start dancing. Yet it seems that Athenian symposiums were relatively decorous compared with those in Thessaly, south of Macedonia. There drinks and food were served together, and the guests made merry.

COOKS

We have already noted that most Greek houses seem to lack a kitchen. A room used for cooking should have some evidence, such as broken cooking pots, hearths, earthenware stoves, or even tell-tale charred remains of fires, that would give archaeologist a clue that meals were prepared there, but in most houses, there is none. Yet meals were prepared in these houses. It was women's work, and it was mistress of the house who was in charge, though domestic slaves might do much of the work. Domestic slaves were as much a necessity in a self-respecting household as refrigerators are in modern kitchens. To make bread, wheat had first to be milled in a quern, and then the flour kneaded to make dough, which was then baked into bread. There were commercial bakeries in the larger cities, and since they had larger ovens than the small earthenware ovens that were used in the ordinary home, they made better loaves with a more consistent texture. These bakeries had mills where a patient donkey might turn the millstones and grind the grain into flour, but there must have been many places in the Hellenistic world where women had to rise early in the morning to hand-mill the grain, and bake the bread.

For anything more elaborate than the daily meal, there were professional cooks, some free men, and some slaves—when we meet them in the Roman world, they are generally slaves. The *mageiros*, as the professional cook was known, was a man who was hired to produce a spread for a number of guests. He bought the food and provided his own cooking utensils. The cook is a familiar figure in the situation comedies that were popular in the Hellenistic theater. A Hellenistic comic poet, Alexis of Thurii, who wrote an enormous number of plays that now survive only in fragments, has a character set out to hire two cooks who can serve a banquet Thessalian-style, with the tables groaning with food, not as in Athens, where each dish was set separately before the hungry guest. Menander's comedy, titled *The Grouchy Man* (in Greek, *Dyskolos*)—the one play of this writer of comedies to survive almost entire—first staged in Athens in 317, presents us with a *mageiros* who had been hired to cook for a family picnic at the sacred cave of Nymphs at Phyle in the Athenian countryside, where the family had gathered to sacrifice, eat, and make merry, in that order. He arrives leading the sheep that is to be sacrificed and then eaten, but he has forgotten his casserole, and must borrow one from a neighbor. He tells the audience that he is a man with a great many customers who want his services in Athens itself. He provided the sheep to be sacrificed, looked after the sacrificial ritual, butchered the victim, and then cooked the meal using utensils that he brought with him—except that in the play, the cook has forgotten to bring a casserole.

And how did the women fare? In Menander's *The Grouchy Man*, once the misanthropic old farmer has agreed to betroth his daughter to Sostratus, the young man who is desperately in love with her, Sostratus invites everyone to a drinking party, and the women must have their party, too. His father sniffs that it is the women who will do all the drinking. But women ate and drank separately. Yet it was a young girl—slightly tipsy—who led the dance. Did they have the same food as the men, or just the leftovers? That is not clear.

BANQUETS

We have dealt with symposiums in private houses, where the number of guests was limited by the size of the *andron*. There was space, generally, for seven couches, two along each of three walls, and only one along the fourth, and even so, the doorway had to be off center to make space for the couch. In fact, when we find the door of a room in a Greek building off center, it is a clue that the room was designed for dining. A larger dining room might accommodate 11 couches, but the 7-couch room was the norm in private houses. Dining also took place in public spaces: in stoas, for instance. Square and rectangular rooms have been found that were used for dining. At Vergina, the old Macedonian capital of Aegae, where Alexander the Great's father was assassinated, a great palace has been uncovered with remarkable mosaics on the floors, and it has several square dining rooms. They are also to be found in the Macedonian capital of Pella. Banquets among the Macedonians were less decorous than in the rest of Greece: The Macedonians liked lots of food, particularly meat, at their banquets, and they preferred their wine neat. Before a man could recline on a couch to eat at a Macedonian banquet, he had to have first proved his manhood by killing a wild boar without trapping it first in nets. Cassander, one of the ruthless generals who fought for supremacy in Greece after Alexander the Great's death, had to wait until he was 35 years old before he won the right to recline, which probably did not improve his temper—he was the man who murdered Alexander's son, the boy king Alexander IV. Even the pressures of war did not disrupt Macedonian banqueting customs. The baggage train that Alexander took with him on his campaign against the Persian empire included a great banqueting tent that could hold about 100 couches. It was probably in this tent that Alexander held his great banquet of reconciliation at Opis in the year before he died, though if 9,000 guests were invited, they must have spilled out of the tent into a courtyard in front of it.

Some reports of these Macedonian banquets have survived. When the Seleucid king Antiochus III, gave a banquet for his friends, all of them, including the king himself, would put on their armor and dance after their bellies were full of fine food and wine. The old Macedonian general Polyperchon, who championed the cause of the boy king Alexander IV—and died deserted by everyone, including his own son, before the fourth century came to an end—used to dance at banquets, tipsy with too much wine. He would dance nonstop, wearing a saffron-colored tunic and embroidered slippers. Banquets were always an opportunity to display the host's generosity, which may strike us as extravagance, particularly if the banquet marked a great occasion such as a wedding. One wedding banquet given by a rich Macedonian named Caranus was so extravagant that it was recalled almost five centuries afterward by Athenaeus, from Naucratis in Egypt, the learned compiler of odd bits of information.

Twenty men were invited. Caranus was—to use an informal expression—rolling in dough, and he wanted to show it off. As the guests entered the banquet room, they were given gold tiaras to wear on their heads; probably these were peaked caps made of cloth shot with gold thread. Once they took their places on their couches, each was given a silver cup for wine, which they could take home with them after the party was over. The banquet was not only a splurge of food but an extravaganza of gift giving as well; when the guests returned to their homes, they took with them not only leftover food but a small fortune of gold and silver to invest in real estate and slaves. During the dinner, one course followed another: First each guest was served a bronze platter with servings of chicken, goose, duck, and doves piled high on a great loaf of flat bread. The guests took as much as they wanted and then handed the rest to the slaves that stood behind them. Then came a second great platter with goose, hare, pigeon, partridge, and other poultry piled over a huge loaf of bread. The guests again ate their fill and handed the rest to their slaves. Then they washed their hands and put wreaths of flowers on their heads. One of the guests proposed toasts to everybody he could think of until the guests were quite drunk.

It was time for some entertainment before the meal continued. In came singers and girls playing the *aulos,* a woodwind instrument with a reed, or the *sambuca.* The stories about Caranus's banquet were unclear if the girls were stark naked, or were simply wearing skimpy tunics. After the musicians, there arrived girls with perfume jars of gold and silver. Then the dining recommenced: A silver platter holding a roast pig was presented, and baked inside its belly were wild birds, eggs, oysters, and scallops. More drinking, and then a roast kid was served. By now the guests could eat no more, and Caranus provided each of them with baskets made of ivory strips so that they could take leftover food home with them. Then more wreaths, more perfume, and more entertainers: dancers, clowns, naked women who performed sword dances, more drinking out of gold cups provided by the host, and finally many varieties of baked fish. A male chorus of a hundred voices sang a wedding hymn. When night fell, the white linen curtains that lined the banquet room were drawn back to reveal sculptures of assorted gods holding lighted torches in their hands. The banquet ended, Macedonian fashion, with a trumpet fanfare.

Caranus's wedding feast was an extravagant display of wealth and generosity, intended to impress, and it was memorable enough that a written description of it has survived. Feasts like his were not everyday events. Yet eating in the company of selected guests at banquets was part of everyday life in the Hellenistic cities, and an economist would recognize these banquets as a method of redistributing wealth. Most of the benefits went to the well-to-do classes, but the leftovers trickled down to the poor. It was a meager trickle, but when we assess the economic condition of the Hellenistic world, the effect of conspicuous spending cannot be ignored.

NOTES

1. Aristotle, *Politics,* 8.10; 1329b36.
2. Luke 16: 19–31.
3. Aristophanes, *The Women at the Thesmophoria,* line 347.

11

Sport and Spectacle

ATHLETIC AND MUSIC FESTIVALS

The four great sacred athletic festivals, the Olympian, Pythian, Isthmian, and Nemean games, retained their prestige and popularity in the Hellenistic period. They were "sacred" games, for they honored a god, but what lent them an aura of prestige was that they were *stephanitic* games, after the Greek *stephanos* meaning "wreath," for the prizes were only wreaths—a wild olive wreath for the Olympic Games, a wreath of laurel for the Pythian Games, wild celery for Nemea, and a pine wreath for the Isthmian Games, though later the Isthmian Games switched to dried celery, following the example of Nemea. The youngest of the four was the Nemean Games, founded about 573, and it had a checkered history, but Philip II, Alexander the Great's father, seems to have brought it new life. Between 415 and 410, while the Peloponnesian War was grinding on with neither side accepting defeat, Nemea's neighbor, Argos, appropriated the Nemean Games, but Philip brought them back to Nemea about 330. A new temple of Zeus and a new stadium were built. However, by 271 Argos had annexed the games again, and the site of the Nemean Games, which has been excavated and can be visited by tourists, hosted the games for only about a quarter of its history.

The other three *stephanitic* games were more fortunate. The Olympic Games, begun in 776, became the model for athletic contests. The Pythian Games at Delphi included musical contests, which was fitting, for Apollo, whose oracle was at Delphi, was a patron of music. The Olympic and Pythian games were held every four years, and the Isthmian and Nemean games every two. These were all sacred games under the protection of a god, whose temple dominated the site. For the Olympic and Nemean games, the god was Zeus, for the Isthmian Games, Poseidon, and for the Pythian Games, Apollo. Wars were supposed to pause for the sacred games and a truce was observed while they were held, though there were occasions when it was broken.

It was not the wreaths that made victory profitable at these *stephanitic* games. Victors won immense acclaim. Their home cities greeted them as heroes when they returned and awarded them free meals in the town hall, and in the Hellenistic period, the prestige and profitability of an athletic victory did not diminish. Four sacred games were not enough; there was a luxuriant growth of new festivals founded by cities ambitious for fame. In addition, Hellenistic kings founded festivals that emulated the great *stephanitic* games. For instance, one Seleucid king, Antiochus IV, founded Olympic Games at the park of Daphne, a short distance from Antioch in Syria, and not only the program of the games, but even their administrative details, reproduced the Olympic Games in the Greek homeland. In the second century, as Rome began to make its power and influence felt in the Hellenistic east, there was a rash of eager cities that founded festivals called Romaia in honor of Rome. Their aim was to flatter Rome and win her esteem, and Rome received this homage with a mixture of pleasure and contempt. The first in line was Delphi, eager to ingratiate herself with the rising superpower in the west with a Romaia festival.

The founders of most of these new festivals allowed themselves freedom to be creative, but they all coveted titles such as iso-Pythian or iso-Nemean; that is, on a par with the Pythian or Nemean games. They claimed to be the equals of the great *stephanitic* festivals. Thus when king Ptolemy II of Egypt founded a magnificent festival in Alexandria in 279, which he named the Ptolemaieia, he declared it iso-Olympic and invited delegates from across the Greek world. To give another example, the Nikephoria Games in Pergamon, which, like the Pythian Games, included both athletic and musical contests, was acknowledged as equal to the Pythian Games in music and equal to the Olympic Games in its athletic and equestrian events. The Delphic council granted its seal of approval to this status in 182.[1] The king of Pergamon, Eumenes II, must have been pleased, for he provided the wherewithal to finish the theater at Delphi, where construction had been started in the late third century, but had been interrupted when Delphi ran out of money.

Cities that already had festivals might nurture ambitions to have them recognized not just as *equal to* one of the *stephanitic* games, but as *stephanitic* festivals themselves. They sent out envoys, called *theôroi*, who canvassed the cities of the Hellenistic world seeking recognition. They did not always get what they requested, but we know of five annual festivals that achieved this status and became great quadrennial celebrations, for inscriptions have survived recording decrees passed by various cities that were willing to recognize the heightened status of these games. For instance, we have the decrees of 70 cities that consented to recognize the *stephanitic* status of a festival in honor of Artemis Leukophryene ("white-browed" Artemis) at Magnesia on the Maeander River in modern Turkey. It seems that it was in 221 or thereabouts that the Magnesians made their first attempt to upgrade their festival. They got nowhere. But they tried again in 208, and succeeded. The kings of Egypt, Pergamon, and of the Seleucid empire all replied positively to the Magnesian request that they recognize Artemis's festival as sacred games with the same rank as the Pythian Games at Delphi. Inscriptions that reproduce the royal letters of consent have survived.[2]

The Deliverance Festival (in Greek, *Sôteria*) at Delphi secured the same status. In the winter of 280–279, a horde of Gauls invaded the Balkan peninsula, swept aside a Macedonian army, and might have destroyed the oracle of Apollo at Delphi, except that the Aetolians who inhabited the nearby mountainous region harried the invaders, forcing them to make a disastrous retreat as a snowstorm swirled about them. Delphi founded an annual Deliverance Festival of music and drama contests to commemorate its salvation, and about the middle of the century, at the urging of the powerful Aetolian Confederation, these games were refounded as a quadrennial pan-Hellenic festival. Athletic contests and chariot races were added to the program, and the cities of Greece were invited to recognize it as a *stephanitic* festival. The response was generally favorable.

The famous Great Panathenaia at Athens had ambitions to become pan Hellenic, but it never became *stephanitic*. The Panathenaia was an annual festival, and as its name suggests the contests were open to Athenians only. But every four years there was a great celebration known as the Greater Panathenaia, and non-Athenians were invited to compete. Not every event was open to competitors who were not Athenian citizens; yet envoys were dispatched with invitations to the various cities of Greece, and valuable prizes were offered. There were amphoras of olive oil for the athletic contests and cash awards for the music contests. First prize in the youth's wrestling contest was 40 amphoras of olive oil, which was no small amount. For the second prize, there were offered eight amphoras, and the first prize for the chariot race with a two-horse team was 30 amphoras. There was a contest in the famous pyrrhic dance, a ritualized war dance where youths, naked except for helmets and shields, maneuvered in formation. There was also a boat race: the winners received 300 drachmas, three bullocks, and 200 meals in the town hall. The bullocks no doubt provided the winning boatmen with meat for a victory feast, though some might be sold.

Professional Athletes

The commercialization of sport had already been creeping into athletic festivals before the Hellenistic period began, but as the number of festivals increased, it became possible for an athlete with a string of victories to turn professional—or at least, that is what we would call it. Star athletes toured from festival to festival. Pausanias,[3] who toured Greece sometime after the mid-second century C.E. and wrote a guidebook based on his observations, tells a story of a boxer from Alexandria who was fined for arriving late for his fight at Olympia because he was collecting prizes at games elsewhere in the Hellenistic world. Athletes trained under the direction of professional trainers, who prescribed a training program that included eating large amounts of red meat, which was not usually a large part of the Greek diet. Bodybuilding had been foreign to the Greek athletic tradition in the past, but soon all that changed. Wrestlers and boxers bulked up with muscle and developed massive shoulders. The philosopher Plato remarked that these muscle-bound athletes were no use at all as soldiers, but the crowds that watched them perform cheered them on. At the same time that professionalism in sport increased, the general level of physical fitness seems to have declined, though in a society where the easiest way to travel from one place to another was to walk, there were few couch potatoes.

Charioteers

Anyone who has seen the 1959 film *Ben Hur,* starring Charlton Heston, will remember one of the classic scenes of cinematic history, depicting a chariot race which supposedly took place in Jerusalem— in Lew Wallace's novel, the venue was not Jerusalem but Antioch— in the first century c.e., less than three-quarters of a century after Cleopatra of Egypt committed suicide and the Hellenistic period came to an end. Chariot racing never reached the height of popularity that it did in ancient Rome, where there were four companies called factions, distinguished by the colors that their teams sported—red, white, blue, or green—that entered their chariots in races that took place before thousands of cheering spectators. The great hippodrome at Rome known as the Circus Maximus held 150,000 spectators and later reconstructions more than doubled its capacity. In the Hellenistic world, there were no factions, and hippodromes were more or less improvised. Well-to-do owners of teams entered them into races as they had done in the great *stephanitic* games in the past, and sometimes they drove the teams themselves, though more frequently they hired professional charioteers. However there was no social stigma attached to being a charioteer, as there was in Rome, where the charioteers were generally slaves who, even though they became enormously popular, remained at the bottom of the social scale. The chariots themselves were light, weighing no more than the light two-wheeled carriages in which the drivers sit in modern harness racing. But the driver had to stand, not sit, on these flimsy chariots, and guide a team of two or four horses. An unskilled charioteer courted disaster, to say nothing of the scorn of the spectators. But the chariot races maintained their prestige. In the classical period, men of standing had used them to display their affluence and power, for only the wealthy could afford the luxury of maintaining a stable of racehorses. In the Hellenistic period, kings and queens joined the ranks of those who entered teams in the races. Even the favorite mistress of Ptolemy II, Bilistiche, won a prize in the two-horse chariot race in the Olympic Games of 268.

SPECTACLE

Grand processions that projected impressions of wealth and power were a way to impress the masses. When a Roman general arrived back in Rome after conquering one of Rome's enemies, he would hold a triumph to celebrate his victory, even when the victory was of no great consequence. Captives and booty were paraded through the streets of Rome and up to the temple of Jupiter the Best and Greatest on the Capitoline Hill, which overlooks the Roman Forum, and the victorious general himself brought up the end of the parade. Hellenistic kings also staged grand processions, though not necessarily to celebrate victory. As it happens, we have an account of one of the grandest parades of all, which was staged by Ptolemy II to celebrate the inauguration of the iso-Olympic Ptolemaieia, in honor of Ptolemy I. We have a description of it in the voluminous work of Athenaeus of Naucratis titled *Philosophers at Dinner*.[4] The narrative begins with a description of the great pavilion where Ptolemy's guests feasted. It had space for 130 couches, and the luxury surpassed the imagination even of Hollywood. But it was the great procession that was truly impressive. It was held in the stadium of Alexandria, or to be more accurate, it terminated in the stadium, for a procession of its size would with only difficulty be accommodated within a stadium.

At the head of the procession marched regiments of the army, beginning with the regiment of the Morning Star and terminating with the Evening Star regiment. A Dionysiac procession came next, with silens to keep back the gawking crowds, and after them came satyrs carrying torches; 20 took up position at each end of the stadium. Then came women costumed as winged Victories, and 120 boys dressed in purple tunics carrying frankincense and myrrh. Then there were more satyrs and silens, along with figures representing the year and its seasons. The Dionysiac actors from the Alexandrian guild were all there, as well as all the paraphernalia of a Dionysiac procession. There was a float with a 15-foot-tall statue of Dionysos, clothed in purple and gold, and shown pouring a libation from a golden cup. Another float carried a figure representing Nysa, Dionysos's birthplace, as a woman. Nysa was not only richly dressed; she was a robot that could stand up, pour a libation of milk, and then sit down again. Another float carried a great wine press, with satyrs treading the grapes and singing as they worked, and the new wine streamed out on to the road. Then came a wagon with a great wineskin that poured out wine, and following it, satyrs and silens, some with golden pitchers and others with cups, and after them there was a wagon bearing an enormous silver *krater*, a bowl for mixing wine with water. These floats were so heavy that each took 600 men to pull it. Then came silver racks to hold cups, more basins and mixing bowls, cauldrons, silver wine presses, even pan-Athenaic amphoras. It was all a garish display of wealth.

The procession continued. There were more gold and silver utensils. Next in the procession marched 1,600 boys wearing white tunics and wreaths of ivy or pine, carrying pitchers of silver or gold, and after them came boys with vessels for carrying candies. Then there were dioramas: one showed the bridal chamber of Dionysos's mother Semele, another showed Dionysos returning from India, riding an elephant. There was a display of exotic beasts: elephants pulling chariots, antelopes, wild asses, leopards, one rhinoceros, and six teams of camels trailed by carts drawn by mules. Camels loaded with frankincense, myrrh, saffron, cinnamon, and other spices followed along and in their train were black Africans, bearing elephant tusks, ebony logs, and mixing bowls brimming with gold and silver coins and gold dust. There were statues of Alexander the Great and Ptolemy the Savior, both crowned with gold ivy crowns. Infantry numbering 57,600 troops and 23,200 cavalry marched in the parade. The total cost of this display was 2,239 talents and 50 minas. It is impossible to translate that sum into modern currencies, but perhaps if we estimated it at 72 million U.S. dollars, we would not be too far wrong.

It must have been an incredible display of pomp and circumstance. Nor was it the only effort to use a public spectacle to express power, The Seleucid king Antiochus IV (175–164) put on a remarkable display of pageantry at games he held at Daphne outside his capital at Antioch. The Seleucid empire was in decline and Antiochus's wealth was nowhere near a match for the full treasury of Ptolemy II Philadelphus. Yet he paraded an impressive number of troops, 100 chariots drawn by six horses and 40 drawn by four, one chariot drawn by four elephants and another by a team of them, and then 36 war elephants in single file.[5] Rome had sadly depleted the elephant corps of the Seleucid army, and yet Antiochus showed that he could still muster a respectable contingent. He was aware of the comparison between his parade and a Roman triumph, for the Roman general Aemilius Paullus, who had overthrown the last king of Macedon, Perseus, had just staged an impressive victory display. Antiochus was anxious that his spectacle should not pale by comparison with that of Paullus.

Parades and spectacles were commonplace in Hellenistic cities, though they were generally modest compared with the two that have been described, and most of them were connected with religious festivals. Ptolemy II's lavish procession was unusual in that its purpose was more political than religious, but it signaled an impression of power and wealth.

NOTES

1. Burstein, no. 87.
2. Welles, nos. 31–34.
3. Pausanias, *Description of Greece*, 5.12–14.
4. Athenaeus, *Deipnosophistae*, 5.196–203b.
5. Athenaeus, *Deipnosophistae*, 5.194c–f.

12

The Theater

A modern visitor to the site of a Hellenistic city will almost invariably find one structure that has survived time's ruination better than the rest and that is the theater. Or at least the *cavea*, or the seating area, of the theater survives, for they were usually built against a hillside that provided support for the seats; the stage building was generally less fortunate. The size of these theaters is impressive. To judge from their seating capacity, they offered entertainment for the masses. Some could accommodate a significant percentage of a city's population: Priene, which perhaps had a population of 5,000, had a theater that could seat most of them. It is one of the best-preserved ancient theaters; we can still see its raised stage resting upon pillars and can imagine the scenery they once supported when a play was being staged. About 330, thanks to an Athenian statesman named Lycurgus, who also saw to it that official copies of the dramas produced in the dramatic festivals of Athens were stored in the city archives, the Theater of Dionysos was rebuilt in stone, and it could accommodate about 14,000 spectators.

Priene's neighbor, Miletus, built a more modest theater that could seat about 5,000 in the fourth century, though in the Roman period its capacity was tripled, and Magnesia, where the *stephanitic* festival of Artemis Leukophryene was held, had a theater seating about 3,000. Many of the Hellenistic theaters were remodeled in the Roman period and some were adapted for productions more to Roman taste, such as gladiatorial games. One, however, that escaped Roman remodeling is the well-preserved, 14,000-seat theater at Epidaurus, the sanctuary of Asclepius, the god of healing, which is still in use today for summer festivals of plays. It was built in the fourth century, as the Hellenistic age was beginning, and it served to accommodate the visitors to a festival in honor of Asclepius held every four years. How much it was used when there was no festival is hard to say. Epidaurus was an out-of-the-way place, and though its sanctuary attracted great numbers of persons suffering from one illness or another, it stretches the imagination to believe that they could have filled the theater to see the shows, week in and week out. Of course, shows were not all that was presented in these theaters; there were also civic events and visiting speakers—the Greeks liked a good orator.

STAGE PRODUCTIONS

Yet the staple fare of these great Hellenistic theaters was drama, music, and dance produced by touring companies of Dionysiac *technitai,* that is, performing artists such as actors, musicians, and dancers whose patron was Dionysos, god of tragedy and comedy as well as the god of wine. The most famous of these productions was the Great Dionysia of Athens and it provided the model—with variations—for the mushroom growth of drama festivals in various Hellenistic cities. We find them springing up everywhere. They seem almost to have been an emblem of Greek culture.

Most of the evidence for these new Dionysia, where there were both dramatic and musical competitions, comes from inscriptions that have survived and are still more or less readable. The information they provide is tantalizing, but we are never told as much as we would like to know. Prizes were offered for the best presentations; successful actors and playwrights could expect generous rewards. Moreover, not all the new drama festivals took Dionysos's name; at Argos, on the Greek mainland, where the patron deity of the city was Hera, a Heraia was held. We know of another Heraia at Samos, where there was a great temple to Hera that was never finished. At Dodona in northwest Greece, where there was an oracle of Zeus, there was a festival called the Naia that Pyrrhus, king of Epirus, supplied with a new stone theater. Delphi had a Soteria, little Tanagra in central Greece had a Sarapieia in honor of the Egyptian god, Sarapis, even the little sanctuary of the hero Amphiareus in the northeast tip of Athenian territory, with a theater seating only about 300, had a festival. Where we find the remains of a theater, we may infer a drama festival, though how frequently it may have been held is an unanswered question.

The stars of the theater moved freely from festival to festival. One, who came from Tegea in the Peloponnesus, set up a series of dedications in his native city to commemorate his prizes: in the Great Dionysia at Athens he carried off first prize in a revival of Euripides' *Orestes*, in the Delphic Soteria he won another prize for a revival of a Euripides tragedy, at Argos and at Dodona revivals of Euripides brought him more prizes, not to mention 88 other victories at sundry Dionysiac festivals.[1] He also fought a boxing match at the Ptolemaieia in Alexandria and won. This actor had more than one string to his bow!

Students of Greek culture are often left with the impression that theater reached its high point in Athens in the fifth century, when the great tragic poets Aeschylus, Sophocles, and Euripides produced their plays, and Aristophanes produced some of the most ribald comedies ever written. After Euripides and Aristophanes, darkness descends. This impression is wrong, but it is nourished by an accident of survival. Most of the plays produced on the Athenian stage in the fifth century have perished with the passage of time, but at least some masterpieces have survived—Euripides fared best, for his tragedies continued to have a following in the Hellenistic period. But the accident of survival has been cruel to the dramas of the Hellenistic age. Yet if we look at the seating capacity of Hellenistic theaters, which were filled with spectators who came to see the performances, we realize that drama continued to attract a mass audience. Football games in the modern world can attract similar flocks of spectators, but a theater with 1,500 seats in the twenty-first century is considered large. Athens continued to be the Broadway of the Hellenistic world, or London's West End— the place that set the style—but the Dionysiac artists moved across the Hellenistic world, adored by their public and courted by kings.

We might like to think that what motivated the founding of all these new drama festivals was art for the sake of art. Not entirely. Festivals, whether they were athletic competitions, dance, music, drama, or a combination of them all, were part of the economic life of the Hellenistic world. Traders flocked to them, set up their tents, and displayed their wares. Business deals were made. Love affairs blossomed, as we may infer from the plots of the New Comedy. At the Dionysia in Athens, the names of the benefactors who had helped to foot the bills for public projects were proclaimed for all to hear. Festivals in the new cities that had been founded in Asia affirmed their Greek character. All in all, a festival was a good thing for a city to promote.

Yet the plays these festivals presented have almost dropped out of sight. We know that new tragedies, comedies, and even satyr plays continued to be written for the stage, and old masterpieces were revived as well. At the Dionysia in Athens, by the last quarter of the fourth century, revivals of tragedies and comedies from the classical period became an annual event, and in the next century, the order of the presentations at the Dionysia was first new comedies—plays by playwrights with names such as Diphilus, Philemon, and Menander, the acknowledged master of the so-called New Comedy—then came revivals of old comedies by masters such as Aristophanes; then satyr dramas, some old and some new; and then, closing the festival, tragedies, some of them revivals and others new productions. Time has been unkind to tragedies written in the Hellenistic period. None of them have survived. We know the names of some writers—over 60 of them, in fact—and the titles of their plays show that they were not afraid to deal with historical or mythological subjects, such as the romance of Aphrodite and Adonis, which never appeared on the classical stage. There was even a tragedy written by a Jewish writer named Ezekiel that told the story of Moses and ended with the crossing of the Red Sea, where the waters divided to let the Israelites through on dry land. We would like to know how the Red Sea crossing was staged in an ancient theater. Ezekiel meant his tragedy to be performed, and probably it was, though we do not know where. A theater in Alexandria was a likely place for it, for one of the city's quarters had been taken over by Jewish immigrants who would have provided an audience for the tragedy of Moses. Portraying the crossing of the Red Sea would have been a difficult challenge for a set designer, but tragedies in Hellenistic theaters were sometimes produced as public recitation by famous actors who were accompanied by music and song. Ezekiel's tragedy may have been a recitation piece where an actor with a well-trained voice created the spectacle in the imagination of the audience. There are great gaps in our knowledge. But the enduring tradition of Greek tragedy is born out by the words for "singing" and "song" in modern Greek. "Song" is *tragoudi* and "I sing" is *tragoudô*.

Playwrights of the New Comedy

At one time, our information about Greek New Comedy, which was the staple of the Hellenistic theater, was not much better than for Hellenistic tragedy, except that a number of the new comedy plays were translated and adapted for the Roman stage by Plautus and Terence. Plautus was a popular playwright in Rome in the last part of the third century and the start of the second, and his life overlapped with that of the African immigrant to Rome, Terence, who produced his first play in 166. Both men borrowed heavily from the Hellenistic stage. They took their plays from contemporary theater in Greece, not even bothering to change the settings from Greece to Rome. They were not slavish translators; they might make a play out of a combination of two Greek plays. Plautus in particular never missed a chance to insert a joke and raise a laugh, for he knew that his Roman audience liked a belly laugh, along with a lot of song and dance, and he gave it what it wanted. But the modern world got a taste of the Hellenistic theater from Plautus and Terence. Thanks to their Latin adaptations, Hellenistic comedies never dropped out of sight, as Hellenistic tragedy has done.

But the situation has improved. In the last century, finds of papyri from Egypt have given us substantial fragments of Menander, the most famous writer of the New Comedy, including one complete play, *The Grouchy Man*. Menander's aim was to give his audience a slice of contemporary life. War, and the breakdown of law and order that seems to characterize the age, did not affect the world of the New Comedy. Some other playwrights of the New Comedy chose parodies of classical myths and their plots, but Menander's subjects were the everyday dramas of domestic life. In his *Grouchy Man*, a citified young fellow of good family falls desperately in love with the daughter of Cnemon, a poor farmer with a vile temper who hates visitors, and after various adventures—for example, Cnemon tumbles into a well and is saved by his daughter's suitor—the play ends with two weddings and much merriment. We have most of another of Menander's plays, *Girl from Samos*, which was one of his masterpieces, and a mosaic found in a house excavated at Mytilene on the island of Lesbos depicts a scene from it, labeled by the mosaicist so that we cannot mistake it. Three characters are on stage: a cook who has been hired to cater a wedding feast, the master of the house who is confused and choleric in equal measure, and his mistress, whom he suspects of hanky-panky.

Masks and Presentation

All the actors wore masks made of linen and cork. In Menander's *Girl from Samos*, the cook's mask, as it is portrayed in the mosaic from Mytilene, depicts him as an African with dreadlocks. In classical Athens, comic actors sometime wore masks that were portraits of citizens in the audience who were being burlesqued on stage. When *Clouds* by Aristophanes, which satirized Socrates, was produced, the actor playing Socrates wore a mask that reproduced Socrates's ugly features so well that Socrates himself stood up in the theater so that the audience could see how true to life the mask was. But in the Hellenistic theater, masks became standardized. The evidence indicates that the Hellenistic theater had 43 or 44 standard masks for comedy, which is a feasible number for an acting company to take on tour.

The theater buildings themselves were adapted to new styles of presentations. The orchestra or dancing floor, the semi-circular space in front of the scene building, was little changed, but the scene building developed into a structure with two levels. The upper level served as a raised stage, which was supported by a row of pillars with painted panels of scenery in the intervals between them. Thus the painted scenery formed a backdrop for the dances in the orchestra. The dramatic action took place on the raised stage. Perhaps because they wanted to heighten the dignity of tragedy, tragic actors wore a boot with a thick sole called a cothurnus, which made them appear taller on the raised stage. Earlier, in the classical period, tragic actors had also worn the cothurnus, but it had been a soft shoe without the thick sole. Comic actors always did without the thick-soled cothurnus. They wore low-heeled slippers.

Music and Dance

Besides drama, there was dancing. Dancing and music were among the attractions that filled the seats of the theaters. The favorite musical instrument was the *aulos,* a woodwind that must have sounded rather like the modern oboe. A skilled *aulete,* as we can call a musician who played the *aulos,* could play two of the pipes at the same time, using a mouthpiece and a harness that he slipped over his head to give him control, and thus he could play the treble and bass or tenor line at the same time. There was also the kithara or lyre, which had a sound rather like a zither, though its appearance was quire different: The kithara was held upright as it was played, whereas the zither is held horizontally. Thanks to discoveries of musical scores preserved on fragments of papyrus from the sands of Egypt, we do have some examples of ancient music, and we can guess how popular musical performances must have been from the fact that some Hellenistic cities built *odeions:* theaters with roofs, intended for musical entertainments. The interiors of these buildings must have been lit to some extent by artificial lighting, but the audience still sat in semi-darkness as they listened to singers and musicians, and sometimes to little dramas that might be pantomimed by dancers on stages that had curtains—not curtains that rose as they do in modern theaters to reveal the stage set, but rather rolled down into a channel at the front of the stage.

Interpretative dance developed into a style of pantomime that was introduced to Rome by two dancers from the Hellenistic east, Bathyllus and Pylades, both in the reign of the emperor Augustus, the Roman who terminated the Hellenistic age in the year 30. Bathyllus came from Alexandria and the pantomimes that he danced in Rome must have been similar to the performances that were popular in his home city. While an actor recited or sang a story, the pantomime dancer interpreted it in solo ballet dancing, accompanied by a small orchestra of musicians. The story lines often came from the great repertory of Greek mythology, and might be tragic or comic. They might also be quite irreverent, for though the Greeks feared the gods and did not willingly offend them, they cheerfully told ribald tales about them. They did not have our modern concept of blasphemy.

Satyr Plays and Tragedies

In classical Athens, the tragic poets who were competing in the two festivals, the Great Dionysia and the Lenaea, where new tragedies were presented, were each expected to present three tragedies and a satyr play, all in a single day. A satyr was a mythical creature who loved making mischief; he looked human except that he had the tail and ears of a horse. About the beginning of the fifth century, as the classical period began, a tragic poet named Pratinas had introduced burlesques with satyrs as the characters, and they became a feature of the great dramatic festivals. They continued to be staged in the Hellenistic period, and they appear to have been popular.

The great tragedies of Aeschylus, Sophocles, Euripides and the tragic poets who were their contemporaries also continued to have an audience. Euripides was particularly popular, for he was more in tune with the feelings of the Hellenistic age. We may wonder what the reaction was of a Hellenistic audience to the classical tragedies, and it is a question that can never be answered, for only a few fragments of the musical scores for these productions have survived.

Sitting in a theater today and watching Sophocles's *Oedipus the King* unfold on stage is like seeing a production of Puccini's opera, *Tosca,* without the music. The Hellenistic audience could have heard the music as well as the powerful poetry of Sophocles, but we may wonder if they felt the same shiver of horror that a classical audience felt as Oedipus learned that he had killed his own father and married his mother. What would an audience have felt in Egypt, where the Ptolemaic kings and queens practiced brother-sister marriage? When Ptolemy II married his sister Arsinoe II—he was the first of his house to marry his sister—a poet scribbled a few lines denouncing the incestuous nuptials, and the admiral of the Ptolemaic fleet took him out to sea and drowned him. We hear of no more protests.

Yet many women—and some men too—watching Euripides's *Medea* must have felt greater sympathy for Euripides's terrible heroine than an audience earlier in the classical period. Medea was an outsider, a barbarian, as the Greeks would have called her, from Colchis at the eastern end of the Black Sea. It was still on the fringes of the civilized world in the Hellenistic period. Her husband, Jason, was a genuine native Greek—a citizen, not a foreigner who had learned to speak Greek and had only a smattering of Greek culture—and when the opportunity for some social climbing was offered him if he discarded his barbarian wife and married a princess, he seized it. Why should the discarded wife resent it? Medea could take this chauvinism no longer, and her revenge was terrible. In the Hellenistic period, there must have been many women who understood Medea's feelings. One of Alexander the Great's last acts was to wed 80 of his army officers to Asian wives, and after his death, most of these bridegrooms who married at Alexander's command discarded their wives, just as Jason did with his wife Medea. How did the discarded wives feel? The Hellenistic age was a time when it was discovered that women had feelings, and yet Euripides had made that discovery even before the age began.

Yet, all in all, the Hellenistic audiences preferred the comedies of manners that Menander wrote, presenting a slice of middle-class life or else light-hearted treatments of Greek myths. Or they preferred mimes with music and dance.

ACTORS' GUILDS

There were professional actors before the middle of the classical period, but in the last half of the fourth century, performers and entertainers got something similar to trade unions. "Trade union" is an inadequate translation of the word *synodoi*, which is the label they themselves used, but the English word *synod*, which derives from the Greek *synodos*, refers to a meeting of Christian clergy. Let us call them "professional associations." They probably got their start in the fourth century, though the evidence for them, which for the most part comes from inscriptions, becomes abundant only in the third century. However, the fourth century, when Philip of Macedon and Alexander the Great were alive, was a time when permanent theaters built of stone were beginning to spring up everywhere, and along with them, new festivals where culture was harnessed to the service of commerce. It is probable that these professional associations had their beginnings then.

There were six of these artists' associations; the four main ones were the Athenian, the Isthmian-Nemean, the Ionian-Hellespontine, and the Egyptian, and there were two others about which we have scanty information, the Dionysiac Artists of Rhodes, and the Artists of Sicily and Magna Graecia, that is, the region of Italy south of Naples that had been colonized by Greek settlements, some dating as early as the mid-eighth century. The membership included actors, musicians, rhapsodes, trainers of choruses called *didaskoloi*, who might themselves be actors or musicians, and costume masters, who looked after the troupe's wardrobe of costumes and masks, but *mimoi*—that is, performers of mimes—seem not to have been included. Mimes were skits that presented a slice of life; the players included women and no masks were used, though probably there was heavy makeup. The Hellenistic poet Theocritus wrote a mime that presented two women in Alexandria visiting a festival of Adonis in the royal palace and chitchatting with each other. It is the dialogue rather than the sketchy plot that captures our interest.

These associations were immensely powerful corporations. They operated with constitutions that were completely democratic, and their headquarters served as lodges, banquet halls, travel bureaus, and shrines for the worship of Dionysos, for the associations were *thiasoi*—clubs with religious links (as mentioned in chapter 6). Shows were their business, whether they were festivals of drama, music, dance, or all three. The actors were an unruly lot, but they were experts in the entertainment business. They could take charge of the organization of a festival, or they might organize it in cooperation with local authorities, or in a place where the festivals had a history and the pattern of the festival was well established, their role would be simply to perform. It must have been a rare festival,

however, where the Dionysiac artists had no hand at all in the organization. A city that had a festival to produce would send officials
with a sum of money to spend, and they would negotiate for the
best deal they could get. Once both sides were satisfied, a contract
would be drawn up.

THE POPULARITY AND PREVALENCE
OF THEATRICAL PERFORMANCES

Even small places had drama festivals. In Athens, for instance,
not all the theater was in the city. There were also rural Dionysia:
festivals held in the townships of Attica known as *demes*, where stone
theaters were sometimes built, most of which have disappeared.
However, one has survived at the mining town of Thorikos, where
the form of the *cavea* is unique, for it is an irregular ellipse rather
than the usual two-thirds of a circle with a round dancing floor
called the orchestra in the center. Acting troupes visited theaters
like these, and though festivals seem to have been the lifeblood of
Hellenistic show business, a civic theater would not remain empty
when there was no festival. There were lectures by visiting speakers, amateur performances of drama, sometimes with professionals
taking the leading roles, and there were mimes, acrobatic performances, and stand-up comedy shows. What was necessary was a
good audience.

Theater as a Political Tool

The Dionysiac artists were purveyors of mass media in the
Hellenistic world. The kings found them useful links with their
subjects. The Ptolemaic royal house in Egypt was perhaps the first
to realize their potential as instruments of propaganda, for the
Ptolemies claimed descent from Dionysos, but the Attalid house
of Pergamon and the Seleucid house of Asia were not far behind.
The Dionysiac artists were happy to cooperate and grease the propaganda machinery of generous royal patrons. Actors had to make
a living. Yet, decrees survive, carved in stone, that praise the piety
of the Dionysiac artists, for they were votaries of Dionysos, and
they sometimes lent their talents to religious celebrations with no
immediate cash reward. We have already noticed that the Alexandrian synod of Dionysiac artists was out in full force to take part in
the lavish procession that king Ptolemy II of Egypt staged in Alexandria to celebrate the inauguration of the Ptolemaieia. We are not

told what rewards they got for their participation, but the procession had a generous budget.

The Dionysiac associations did have one privilege, and it is proof of their pan-Hellenic status. They were *asyloi:* that is, they had the right of asylum, the right to travel the roads or sail the sea unmolested, and the right was recognized by the Hellenistic world. Pirates and bandits were common, and travel was unsafe for most people. But even bandits recognized that shows had to go on, and they spared the troupes of actors as they traveled with their props and costumes from one drama festival to another.

NOTE

1. Austin, no. 122.

13

Hellenistic Kingdoms

KINGS AND ROYAL FAMILIES

With the Hellenistic period, a new institution appeared in the Greek world: hereditary kingship, along with palaces, courts, courtiers, propaganda, and all the pomp and circumstance of charismatic monarchy. Greece had known kings before; in the epic poems of Homer, there were *basileis,* which we translate as "kings." Agamemnon, the leader of the Greek expedition against Troy, was king of Mycenae, and he bore the title of *anax,* which in classical Greek was reserved for the gods, for he was the overlord of the other Greek chieftains, called *basileis,* who seem to have been vassal princes in his army. But Agamemnon and the other Greek chieftains who fought at Troy belonged to the distant past. In classical Greece, the only state with kings was Sparta and it was peculiar: it had two kings ruling concurrently. We cannot call the Spartan government a monarchy, for a monarchy implies a single king, whereas Sparta had two royal families. Spartan kingship survived into the Hellenistic period, but it found no imitators.

In Macedon, on the fringes of the classical Greek world, there were kings belonging to the royal house of the Argeadai that claimed descent from the hero Heracles. But Macedonian kings were never absolute monarchs surrounded by pomp and circumstance. Rather they were first among equals, and when Alexander

the Great attempted to introduce some of the ceremony of the
Persian court, his Macedonians resented it bitterly. Macedonian
kings might belong to a royal family, but they were elected by the
Macedonian army; they owed their position not simply to heredity
but to the approval of the troops. The Hellenistic kings, by contrast,
were descended from mere Macedonian army officers who managed to grab a slice of Alexander's empire, and they ruled their
kingdoms by right of conquest. In other words, their realms were
whatever they managed to hold, and they held them ultimately
by force. But they sought to give themselves legitimacy by what
we would recognize as personality cults, using all the propaganda
vehicles that they possessed to present themselves as larger than
life to their subjects.

One technique that they used was coinage. Before the Hellenistic
age we do not find coins with portraits in the Greek world. The
Persian empire of the Achaemenids had minted gold coins called
darics showing king Darius, but they were intended as pay for Greek
mercenary soldiers whom the king hired. Coins were not used for
commerce within the Persian empire itself. Yet in the Hellenistic
age all the kings, beginning with Alexander himself, minted coins
showing royal portraits of kings, living or dead. In Ptolemaic
Egypt, coins bearing the image of Ptolemy I continued to be minted
until the end of the Ptolemaic royal dynasty; the message seems to
have been that this royal family radiated stability. In the far-off Bactrian kingdom, the kings were shown on their coins fully armed,
for they wanted to be seen as kings who defended their kingdoms
and their subjects with military might. In an age that knew no
illustrated magazines or television, coin portraits served as a powerful instrument of communication, for coins were symbols of a
ruler's power.

Art was also harnessed. It, too, was put in the service of creating
a personality cult. Alexander himself took extraordinary care of his
public image. He had a favorite portrait painter, Apelles, and a favorite sculptor, Lysippus, and both used their art to project Alexander's
persona as a heroic young man with superhuman qualities. Apelles,
for instance, painted a portrait that showed Alexander as Zeus,
complete with the thunderbolt that was the exclusive weapon of
the king of the gods. It was put on public display in the temple of
Artemis at Ephesus, where it illustrated for all to see the godlike
quality of the Macedonian king. The sculptor Lysippus, who was
famous for his statues of nude male athletes, developed an image
of Alexander that had the king's approval: It showed the king as a

well-developed youth with long, tousled hair—before Alexander, Greek young men usually wore their hair short. Alexander's gaze fixed upwards toward the heavens, hinting at a special relationship with the divine, and on his head were the horns of Zeus Ammon. Following Alexander's example, the Hellenistic kings tried to create images of themselves that conveyed the message that they were extraordinary men, but at the same time did not grate too much upon the sensibilities of their subjects.

In Egypt, the royal house begun by Ptolemy I found itself in a kingdom with ancient traditions of its own—far more ancient that anything Greece possessed. The monuments of the pharaohs were to be seen everywhere. Egypt's days of greatest glory were almost over by the time that Greek history began. The Great Pyramid, built by a pharaoh whom the Greeks called Cheops (his Egyptian name was Khufwey), dated from almost 2,500 years before the conquering Macedonian troops of Alexander arrived. The reception that these Macedonian intruders received was at first not unfriendly, for they liberated Egypt from the hated Persians, but Ptolemy knew that if he wanted the Egyptians to accept him, he had to come to terms with their traditions. So he and his successors presented themselves to their Egyptian subjects as pharaohs, and like all pharaohs before them, they were the sons of Re, the sun god, and thus also gods in the mindset of their Egyptian subjects. The Ptolemies treated the Egyptian gods with conspicuous respect and devotion. We have to go back to the early twentieth dynasty of pharaohs, who ruled Egypt in the twelfth century before Christ, before we find kings as generous to the Egyptian temples and priesthood as the Ptolemies were. The result was that the temples never encouraged any widespread insurgency directed against the Ptolemaic kings, much as the native Egyptians might resent their foreign conquerors.

Yet Ptolemaic power was based on alien settlers: Macedonians, Greeks, Jews, and immigrants from the Hellenized populations of Asia Minor who had come to Egypt. The Ptolemies did not recruit Egyptians into their armed forces until they were forced to do so in 217, when the Seleucid king, Antiochus III, attacked Ptolemy IV, and Ptolemy, desperate for soldiers, recruited native Egyptians and trained them to fight like Macedonians. When the two armies met, Ptolemy IV owed his victory to his Egyptian recruits, and the Ptolemaic regime had to adjust to a new balance of power. There was unrest at the end of Ptolemy IV's reign and during the reign of his successor. Between the years 206 and 186, two native rulers, father and son, broke away from Ptolemaic rule and took control of Thebes in Upper Egypt, and after the death in 180 of king Ptolemy V, Egypt was torn by strife for 60 years, some of which was due to quarrels over the succession within the royal family. But it was also fed by the need to placate the native Egyptians' aspirations. The famous Rosetta stone,[1] an inscription recording a resolution approved by a synod of priests meeting at Memphis on the occasion of Ptolemy V's coronation, which provided the clue for deciphering hieroglyphic script, belongs to this period of insurgency and reflects an almost pathetic desire to present Ptolemy in a favorable light.

The Ptolemaic capital was Alexandria, and there the immigrants attempted to insulate themselves from the native Egyptians, who had their own quarter—the old village of Rhakotis, which was there before Alexandria was founded. The Ptolemies tried to make Alexandria a great Greek city and a center of Greek culture, with a great library and research center that attracted scholars and scientists from all over the Greek world. But the native Egyptians could not be kept out, and they soon made up a large percentage of Alexandria's population.

The Seleucid empire faced a different situation. At its height under Seleucus I (311–281) and his son Antiochus I (281–261) it ruled a vast region. It is occupied now by 13 modern states: Turkey, Syria, Lebanon, Israel, Jordan, Iraq, Kuwait, Afghanistan, Iran, and much of Armenia, Uzbekistan, Tadjikistan, and Turkmenistan. Just before his assassination Seleucus had added Macedon to his empire, but his son could not hold on to it. Seleucus's assassin seized the Macedonian throne, but he did not enjoy it for long, for he was defeated and killed by a horde of Celts that swept down into the Greek peninsula. The empire that Antiochus inherited was a patchwork of ancient customs and traditions, though the one that was dominant, and with which the Seleucids had to come to terms, was the Babylonian.

Babylon, where Alexander the Great died in Nebuchadnezzar's palace, was already an ancient city when Nebuchadnezzar reigned (604–562). The chief god and patron of Babylon, Bel-Marduk, whose great temple, the Esagila, dominated the city, conferred the rule of Babylonia on the man who grasped his right hand in the New Year's Festival. When the founder of the Persian empire, Cyrus, captured Babylon in 539, he treated Bel-Marduk with respect, as well he should, for Bel-Marduk's priests had helped betray the city to him. But Babylon revolted under Xerxes, whom we remember for his failed expedition against Greece in 480, and though we no longer believe that Xerxes destroyed Bel-Marduk's temple as punishment for the revolt, there was a story, which is probably true, that he robbed it of a huge golden statue and slew the priest who tried to stop him.[2] When Alexander took Babylon, he was careful to treat Bel-Marduk with respect, and Seleucus followed his lead: At the New Year's Festival of 312, he grasped the right hand of Bel-Marduk's cult image. He thus became Bel-Marduk's choice as king of Asia, though there was hard fighting ahead before he made good his claim. Seleucus's son, Antiochus, was brought up in Babylon and was familiar with it before he became king.

In Egypt, there were only three cities: Alexandria, the greatest of the Hellenistic cites; Ptolemais Hormou, which Ptolemy I founded in Upper Egypt: and Naucratis, which had been founded as a Greek trading post long before Alexander entered Egypt. The Seleucid kingdom was dotted with cities that were islands of Greek culture. In Anatolia, more than a third of which was controlled by the Seleucid kings at the height of their power, some of the cities that owed them allegiance were ancient Greek foundations. Asia Minor, too, had temple estates, where temples owned large holdings of land that were cultivated for them by dedicated temple slaves. Then there was Macedon, the homeland of the Macedonians. The ancient royal dynasty to which Alexander the Great belonged was now extinct, terminated with the murder of Alexander the Great's son in 310, but a new dynasty had begun: the Antigonids, which went back to one of Alexander's generals, Antigonos the One-Eyed, and his son, Demetrius the Besieger. Antigonos and Demetrius were both brilliant generals who lost their last battles, but Demetrius's son, Antigonos Gonatas, vindicated his right to be king of Macedon by defeating a terrifying horde of Celtic invaders who had swept into Greece and killed the latest claimant of the Macedonian throne. Antigonos's descendants ruled until the Romans dethroned the last of the line, and under the Antigonid kings the traditions of Macedonian kingship continued. Divine kingship was not one of those traditions. Seleucid and Ptolemaic kings were worshiped as gods. Macedonian kings were not.

THE NATURE OF HELLENISTIC KINGSHIP

The Greek political scene had never encountered anything like Hellenistic kingship. The city-states had known tyrants: dictators who seized power by force and kept it for relatively brief periods by manipulating their friends and murdering or exiling their enemies. But the Hellenistic kings were not tyrants, though they were all absolute rulers, and none of them were constitutional monarchs. They adopted the title of *basileus* after the old royal dynasty of Macedon became extinct, and philosophers and political thinkers wrote treatises on what the characteristics of an ideal king should be. A good king was supposed to reverence what is right, show concern for the welfare of his subjects, win victories, and give due honors to the immortal gods. The kings liked to suggest that they owed their kingship to their outstanding virtue, but they were practical men, and they knew that outstanding virtue was not enough to keep them in power.

Hellenistic kings could not claim to belong to ancient dynasties that went back to semi-mythical heroes. The past kings of Macedon had belonged to a dynasty that claimed descent from Heracles. History and tradition vindicated their right to rule. These new kings could make no such claim, though in the first generation after Alexander's death, a connection to the old Argead royal house of Macedon was still considered an asset. Ptolemy I, for instance, promoted a tale that he was actually the son of Philip II of Macedon, Alexander the Great's father. Yet for all of them, their right to rule rested ultimately upon conquest; they were the survivors who emerged from the turmoil after Alexander's death with their kingdoms intact. But kings who have won their kingdoms by conquest must win the allegiance of their subjects. How could a ruler persuade his subjects to accept him as a rightful king?

Military success was important. A king had to appear strong and able to protect his subjects. Antigonos Gonatas established himself as king of Macedon in 276 only after he inflicted a sharp defeat on the Gauls the previous year. These Celtic invaders had invaded Macedonia in 279, killed the current king of Macedon, and pushed south as far as Delphi before they were stopped. Greece was terrified of them. They moved into Asia Minor in 278 where they were equally dreaded as foes, as restless and unruly as they were terrible. But Attalus I of Pergamon defeated them soundly in 237, after which he took the title of king. Attalus made sure that his victory was well advertised. He commissioned statues of vanquished Gauls to commemorate it, and set them up in Pergamon with copies in Athens, and though the originals have not survived, we have fine Roman copies. One shows a well-muscled Gallic warrior sinking to the ground as death overtakes him, though his expression is still fierce. Another shows a Gaul who has killed his wife rather than let her fall into the hands of the victors. With one hand he holds the limp body of his wife and with the other he stabs himself beneath the throat. Anyone who saw statues such as these would remember Attalus's great victory that saved Anatolia from the Gauls.

Yet military success was not enough. Kings had to be seen as good shepherds of their people. They had to be acceptable to the gods, particularly in places such as Egypt and Babylon that had ancient kingship traditions of their own. They had to show that they were friends of the non-Greek gods that commanded the devotion of their non-Greek subjects, and they had to show an interest in their traditions, however alien they might seem to a Greek. In Egypt, Ptolemy I encouraged a bilingual Egyptian priest named Manetho to write a history of his country in Greek using Egyptian records, for Egyptian temples had libraries and priests called "sacred scribes" to look after the archives. In Babylon, a priest named Berossus wrote a history of Babylon for king Antiochus I. But at the same time, the kings could not forget that their power was based on the loyalty of their immigrant subjects, the Greeks and Macedonians who had settled in their kingdoms and provided the backbone of their armies, and for them, they had to be seen as defenders and promoters Greek culture. They built libraries and supported philosophers and poets who in turn promoted a climate of opinion that was favorable to kingship. They had to use whatever pomp and circumstance they could command to show that they were no ordinary people. If necessary, they had to be able to defend their right to rule by force of arms. They could become gods themselves. In the Hellenistic kingdoms, it was important to inculcate loyalty to the king's person, and religion was a useful instrument. Paganism recognized a multitude of gods, and there was no theological reason why a divine king could not be added to their number. Only the Jews adhered to a religion that was strictly monotheist, but the Greeks preferred not to notice that the Jews refused to recognize their gods.

KINGS AS GODS

If mythology told of mortal men long ago who became heroes after death, what of men of the present day? Alexander the Great's best friend, Hephaestion, died in 324, a year before Alexander himself, and Alexander heaped honors upon him. He asked Zeus Ammon that Hephaestion be worshipped as a hero. What of Alexander himself? The evidence is ambiguous, but as he approached the end of his short career it is clear that he found divine kingship an attractive idea, either because he came to believe that he was divine, or because he realized that a great imperial ruler would find it useful as a device for winning the allegiance of the diverse ethnic groups that he had conquered. While Alexander was in Egypt, he visited the temple of Zeus Ammon at the oasis of Siwah, and the high priest had greeted him as "Son of God." So, at least, some said. The pharaohs of ancient Egypt had always been gods, in life as well as in death, and Alexander was slipping into their shoes. But he was also slipping into the shoes of the Persian kings, who had never been divine, though they were surrounded by the pomp and circumstance that, in Greek eyes, befitted a divine king. As for Greece, it recognized no divine kings, but Greek philosophers had speculated about the nature of ideal monarchy before the Hellenistic age began. Aristotle himself[3] speculated that a man of preeminent virtue had a natural right to rule as a king.

In 305, Rhodes beat off an attack by Demetrius the Besieger, son of Antigonos the One-Eyed, who brought all the latest technology of siege warfare to bear against the city, and to commemorate its survival it erected the famous Colossus of Rhodes. Not so well known is that fact that in 304 the Rhodians established a cult of Ptolemy I, who was their savior. Ptolemy had helped the Rhodians, and after Demetrius withdrew, they consulted the oracle of Zeus Ammon at Siwah in Egypt and asked if it would be right to worship Ptolemy as divine. The oracle approved, and Ptolemy Soter ("the Savior") received sacrifice in Rhodes. It was the Rhodians, not Ptolemy, who initiated the deification. Then, in 290, Demetrius, who advertised himself as Athena's brother, reoccupied Athens. During an earlier occupation, he had made the back room of the Parthenon his living quarters and treated Athena as his elder sister, which gave him the right to raid her treasury. Greece had suffered greatly from the turmoil that took place after the death of Alexander the Great, and when Demetrius reoccupied Athens, the Athenians were ready to acclaim Demetrius as a divine being who could save them from the enemies that threatened them. A hymn to Demetrius[4] survives that hails him as the "greatest and dearest of the gods come to the city!" The hymn continues, "It is in majesty that [Demetrius] appears, with his friends all in a circle around him and he in their midst, as if they were the stars and he the Sun. . . . For the other gods are far away or else they have no ears, or they do not exist, nor pay any heed at all to us, but *you are present,* and we see you, not in wood or stone but in reality" (italics mine). The hymn then prays first for peace, and secondly, that Demetrius would free them from the fear of their enemies, the Aetolians, lawless hill tribes from west central Greece. The hymn nicely captures the Greek attitude to divine kings. Mortal men prayed to gods because they thought them able to offer help. Why not, then, pray to a king such as Demetrius, who really could help?

Each royal family had its patron god. The Seleucid dynasty claimed descent from Apollo, who was supposed to have visited the mother of Seleucus I, the founder of the dynasty, and left a ring in her bed with the sign of an anchor on it. Seleucus was born with an anchor-shaped birthmark on his thigh, which proved that Apollo was his father, and all legitimate members of the Seleucid royal family bore the same anchor-shaped mark on their thighs. At least, so the royal propaganda claimed. The Antigonid royal house of Macedon assumed the trappings of the old Argead house to which Alexander the Great belonged. The Argeads had claimed descent from Heracles and the Antigonids took over their claim. The Attalid royal family of Pergamon claimed a special relationship with Athena, and in Egypt, the Ptolemies made Dionysos their patron. The father of Cleopatra VII, the last Ptolemaic monarch to rule Egypt, called himself the "New Dionysos." Kings who claimed descent from gods were commonplace in Greek mythology. Divine kingship was not a revolutionary concept.

Divine kings may seem odd to us. Judaism, Christianity, and Islam are all monotheistic religions and they have no place for monarchs as gods. But hereditary rulers in monotheist religions have sought to make themselves appear more legitimate by wrapping themselves in religion—in the "divinity that doth hedge a king," as Shakespeare put it in *Hamlet*. In eighteenth-century France, the king called himself "his most Christian Majesty" and the king of Spain called himself "his most Catholic Majesty." Kings claiming a divine right to rule were direct heirs, at least in principle, of divine kings. In the everyday life of the Hellenistic world, the common man probably held the divine kings in no more or less esteem than a subject held a king who ruled by divine right in seventeenth-century Europe. However, though prayers might be offered in churches on behalf of Christian divine-right monarchs, they were never worshiped, whereas the Ptolemies and the Seleucids did receive sacrifices and worship.

Ptolemy I died in 283, and three years after his death, his son, Ptolemy II, declared him a god and established his worship as Ptolemy the Savior. When his queen, Berenice, died the next year, she was included in the cult of the "Savior Gods." The Seleucid king, Antiochus I, did likewise for his father, Seleucus I, when he died two years after Ptolemy I, and built him a temple in northern Syria at the city of Seleucia-in-Pieria. Then, sometime before 274—the exact date is uncertain—Ptolemy II married his older sister, Arsinoe II, and when she died in 270, he deified her. According to the court poet Callimachus, Castor and Pollux wafted her off to heaven. She was identified with Aphrodite, and she and her brother became the "Brother-Sister Loving Gods." Hitherto, the vintners of Egypt had paid a portion of their wine production— usually one-sixth of the crop—to the temples, but once Arsinoe became a goddess, this tax, which was known as the *apomoira,* was diverted to her worship. (In fact, the *apomoira* seems to have gone into general revenue.) Regulations were published for sacrifice to the divine Arsinoe: The victims must not be male or female goats, but any other animal or bird would do, and the altars for the sacrifices were to be made of sand.

By the end of the third century, the worship of the Ptolemaic kings of Egypt had developed into a full-fledged cult of the royal dynasty, which included Alexander who lay in his coffin in his magnificent tomb in Alexandria. Alexander had his own priest, and so did each pair of deceased Ptolemaic monarchs, and the reigning king and queen as well. The new gods became *synnaoi theoi,* that is, "gods who share the sanctuary." The meaning of the title must be that images of the king and queen were placed in all the temples of Egypt, where they were worshiped.

For the native Egyptians, this was no great innovation. Their pharaohs had always been gods, and the Ptolemaic kings had stepped into the shoes of the pharaohs: Ptolemy II had taken an Egyptian title—*Meryamun Setepenre,* "Beloved of the god Amon and chosen of the god Re." The ruler cult of the Ptolemaic kings was meant primarily for their Greek subjects. Divine kingship had never been part of Greek tradition—nor Persian tradition, either, for that matter. The ruler cult changed all that: it demanded that the Greeks recognize the Ptolemaic kings as divine, just as the native Egyptians had always recognized their pharaohs.

The Seleucid kings were not far behind. When Antiochus III, surnamed "the Great," came to the throne in 223, he undertook to restore the Seleucid empire to what it had been under its founder, Seleucus I, and he succeeded so well that he would have come down in history as the second founder of the empire had he not run afoul of Rome. As he reconquered the eastern provinces that had slipped away from Seleucid rule, he organized a royal cult with a royal priesthood in each of them. The living king, as well as his ancestors, was worshiped. The kings of Pergamon were less enthusiastic, or more cautious: They did not institute an official royal cult until 188, and the kings became gods only after they were dead. Living kings were not worshiped. In Macedonia, there was no royal cult at all.

How seriously did the Greeks take king worship? No doubt it brought the presence of the kings into everyday life. Shrines to the royal cult were to be found in gymnasiums where students went for their education. Did they offer a pinch of incense to the royal images? If they did, was their offering merely a sort of patriotic gesture, like saluting the flag? We cannot say. But we should not dismiss the royal cults as so much sham and political propaganda. The royal cult was aimed at two levels: one was the army, where it cemented fidelity to the royal dynasty, and the other was the masses, whom it taught to accept the kings as legitimate rulers, the equals of the gods. On the practical level, the royal cult gave the kings great powers of patronage and supervision. The priests in the temples dedicated to the divine kings were royally appointed and served as contacts with the people in their province. Yet we know of only one Seleucid king who took his divinity seriously. He was Antiochus IV Epiphanes, and, for reasons that we do not quite understand, he wanted everyone in his empire to make a formal sacrifice to him as a god. The sacrifice was, in his eyes, a kind of loyalty oath that would enhance the security and dignity of his reign. The general reaction to this sacrifice was that it was harmless, if slightly odd. Antiochus's subjects gave him a new, unofficial surname: not Epiphanes, which means "God Manifest," but Epimanes, meaning "raving mad"—in the Greek alphabet, only one letter had to be changed. Yet in Judea, where we are relatively well informed about the reaction, some of the Jews in Jerusalem made the sacrifice willingly, but in the country villages, which were relatively untouched by Hellenistic culture, there were many who saw it as sacrilege. The result was a full-scale revolt, which we shall deal with later.

KINGS AS CHAMPIONS OF GREEK CULTURE

A student visiting the ruins of ancient Greece with a guidebook in his hands will be impressed by the generosity that the kings showed to the old city-states that were no longer of any great importance in the international politics of the Hellenistic world but still had a high profile. In Athens, two stoas were built by the kings of

Pergamon. Between the theater of Dionysos and the Roman *odeion* of Herodes Atticus was a stoa funded by Eumenes, king from 197 to 159. On the edge of the agora is the Stoa of Attalus, which had been restored as a museum; it was built by the second-to-last king, Attalus II, who ruled Pergamon from 159 to 138. Ptolemy III built a temple of Sarapis in Athens and Ptolemy VI built a gymnasium. The temple of Olympian Zeus was begun in the sixth century, but the main structure was the work of the Seleucid king Antiochus IV (175–164). It fell to the Roman emperor Hadrian (117–135 C.E.) to complete the building, and what the visitor to Athens sees nowadays is the spectacular remains of a great Hellenistic temple erected over the course of nearly seven centuries.

Delphi, the oracular sanctuary of Apollo, also benefited from the generosity of the kings of Pergamon. The theater there remained unfinished until Eumenes II sent stonemasons and money to complete the construction. Attalus I donated a small stoa, and Attalus II (159–138) and Eumenes II (197–159) both erected statues of themselves. But Athens was the main beneficiary, and it is easy to understand why. Athens may have lost its power in the international arena, but it became, in a sense, the homeland of Greek culture. It had been the artistic center of classical Greece, and in the Hellenistic period it became the intellectual center. There were other cities with lively cultural traditions, such as the islands of Rhodes and Cos, and toward the end of the Hellenistic period, Tarsus, but Athens remained the teacher of Greece. Philosophers from all over the Hellenistic world migrated there. Besides the Academy, founded by Plato, and the Lyceum, founded by Aristotle, there were the schools founded by newcomers. Epicurus (341–270), the founder of Epicureanism, came from Samos where his father, an Athenian expatriate, had been a schoolmaster, and when Epicurus came to Athens he set up a community of disciples that included women and slaves. The Stoic school was founded by an immigrant from Cyprus named Zeno who came to Athens and lectured in the so-called Painted Stoa on the edge of the marketplace because he could not afford to rent a lecture hall. It is remarkable how many of the great Stoic teachers were not Athenians by birth but rather immigrants. The Cynics represented a strand of thought that went back to Socrates; the founder of the school, Antisthenes, was a disciple of Socrates. But the most famous Cynic was Diogenes, who came from Sinope on the south coast of the Black Sea. He went out of his way to shock conventional public opinion. There are many stories told about him; one of the most famous relates that while he was living in a great storage jar, Alexander the Great visited him, and asked if there was anything he could do for him. Diogenes asked the king to step aside so as not to block the rays of the sun. Diogenes compared himself to Heracles, who triumphed over monsters, for did not he, Diogenes, triumph over the conventions that constrained mankind?

Most of these philosophic schools had ideas about what an ideal king should be. The treatises on kingship that they inspired have for the most part been lost, but we have echoes of them. The ideal king should be able, first and foremost, to rule himself. He should rule justly and promote peace; he must show qualities such as forbearance, gentleness, and humanity, or as the Greeks called it, philanthropy—the basic meaning of *philanthropist* is "lover of mankind." The Cynics developed the idea that a king should emulate Heracles and use his power to make life better for the human community. Most of these treatises titled *On Kingship* were addressed to kings, and some of the kings may have read them. The king of Macedonia, Antigonos Gonatas, had a resident court philosopher, and he went out of his way to make Macedonia hospitable to philosophers.

The Ptolemies in Egypt went even further. They made Alexandria an intellectual center. They established a research center, the Mouseion—that is, a haunt of the Muses—which was built on the palace grounds, and connected with it was a great library. In fact, there were two libraries in Alexandria, the Great Library connected with the Mouseion, and its daughter library at the Sarapeion, the temple of Sarapis in Alexandria. There had been earlier libraries; both Plato's Academy and Aristotle's Lyceum in Athens had modest collections, and the Egyptian temples had always housed libraries. The temple libraries and the Lyceum probably both provided models for the Alexandrian library, for Ptolemy I's consultants on cultural affairs were Demetrius of Phalerum, a disciple of Aristotle, and Manetho, a bilingual Egyptian priest from Sebennytus near modern Cairo. Demetrius was the first librarian, but he was no favorite of Ptolemy I's son, Ptolemy II Philadelphus, who had him arrested when he came to the throne. His successor was Zenodotus of Ephesus, who edited Homer's epics and is the scholar whom we must thank for the texts of the *Iliad* and the *Odyssey* that we have today. Next was the poet Apollonius of Rhodes, who tried to prove that epic poetry had not gone out of style; he wrote an epic in four books that told the myth of Jason and Medea and the voyage of the *Argo* to fetch the Golden Fleece. His epic, titled the *Argonautica*, was moderately successful, and it had one careful disciple who would be more famous than Apollonius: the Roman poet Vergil, who wrote the national epic of the Roman empire, the *Aeneid*. Next was Eratosthenes, who calculated the circumference of the earth and was not far off the dimension of modern scientists. The last important scholar to hold the post was Aristarchus, who was dismissed by Ptolemy VIII in 145, and fled from Egypt.

However, it must be admitted that, though much has been written about the Alexandrian Library, the amount of trustworthy evidence is rather small. We do not know how many books it had—by "books" we mean scrolls of papyrus, which was an exclusive product of Egypt. Estimates have been as high as half a million, which we cannot believe. Another story is hard to believe as well: that all trading vessels coming to Egypt had to surrender any books on board for the benefit of the Alexandrian Library. One story could be true. The great statesman of Athens, Lycurgus, who put the finances of Athens in order during the battle of Chaeronea in 338 that made Alexander the Great's father master of Greece, had official copies made of all the Greek tragedies and placed in the state archives. Ptolemy II, it is said, borrowed these texts to make copies for the Great Library, and as a pledge for their safe return, deposited in Athens the princely sum of 15 silver talents. But he kept the originals and returned the copies, thus forfeiting his deposit. It was said that the aim of the Great Library was to collect the literature of every nation, with the aim of having foreign works translated into Greek.

The research institute known as the Mouseion provided quarters where its members might live and carry on their investigations. They were a community of scholars and scientists with a priest appointed by the king in charge. Thanks to the generosity of the Ptolemies, the Mouseion attracted the best minds of the age. Membership depended on the king's approval, but nonetheless, the scholars had a high degree of freedom to carry out their research as they pleased. The Mouseion was not a teaching institution, but its members did give public lectures, and it was the centerpiece of intellectual life in Alexandria. There were many scholars and scientists in the city who were not attached to the Mouseion; some had private incomes and some earned a living from their professions as engineers, doctors, and architects. Together they made Alexandria the most brilliant center of scholarship and science of the Hellenistic age. Only Pergamon could rival it; king Eumenes II of Pergamon also founded a library that was the second largest in the world, and the archaeological excavations at Pergamon give us some idea of its appearance. There were three large rooms with wooden cases where the papyrus or parchment scrolls were stored in pigeonholes. Each scroll had a label on a dog tag hanging from the end sticking out of the pigeonhole so that the library patron could use it. The Seleucid kings had a library at Antioch and so did the kings of Macedon at their capital of Pella, but neither of these had the resources to rival Alexandria.

The question of what happened to the Great Library in Alexandria is a vexing one. One possibility is that it was destroyed, or at least badly damaged by fire, in the winter of 48–47, when Cleopatra's brother was leading an insurgency against the Romans led by Julius Caesar, who was besieged in the royal palace along with Cleopatra herself. However, if so, Cleopatra no doubt tried to restore it when she became queen, and there is a story that Mark Antony gave her the library of Pergamon, which she could have used to replace the lost books. There are many other times in Alexandria's history when the library could have been damaged or destroyed, and there is a tradition that when the Arabs invaded Egypt, they burned what was left of the collection on the orders of the caliph. But we do not know if the library was still in existence at that time. There are some scholars who speculate that the Arabs did not destroy what was left of the library, but rather appropriated the remaining books, and that Arabic translations of these books were the foundation of the brilliant Arabic culture in Abbasid Baghdad.

The Great Library was not the only library in Alexandria. The great temple of the god Sarapis also had a library, smaller than the Great Library but still impressive. Temples to the Egyptian gods had libraries, including temples built by the Ptolemies, and the temple of Sarapis merely followed Egyptian tradition, except that its books were in Greek. We are better informed about what happened to the library in the Sarapeion. The temple was destroyed by a Christian mob near the end of the fourth century, and if the library was still more or less intact at that time, it cannot have survived. We would like to believe that some of the lost books reappeared in secondhand bookstores in Alexandria, but that is mere speculation. The fate of many papyrus rolls in Egypt was to become stuffing for mummies, where, at least, some survived to be read by modern papyrologists.

Resentment among the Non-Greeks: The Case of Judea

We would like to know what the popular reaction was to the cultural imperialism of Greece in the Hellenistic world, particularly in the two superpowers, Egypt and the Seleucid empire. The everyday life of the man on the street could not have been greatly affected by it, but we should never write off divine kingship as meaningless. A country's flag nowadays can provoke strong emotions among the citizens of the country, and saluting the flag is a ceremony that is taken seriously. Sacrifices to divine kings may have provoked similar emotions. Instead of flags in school classrooms or government offices, a gymnasium or public office in Egypt might have an effigy of the king: a portrait head carved from stone—archaeologists have discovered many examples of them—that may have been free-standing or attached to a body made of perishable material. King worship was more than a personality cult, for it was intimately connected with religious belief and permeated everyday life, and like patriotic exercises nowadays on the Fourth of July or Memorial Day, it encouraged loyalty.

What the non-Greeks—the subject masses—felt about the foreigners who came into their countries as conquerors is hard to know. In Egypt, the Ptolemaic king followed a policy of conciliating the native priesthood, and by and large the Egyptian priests remained loyal, though they exacted a price for their loyalty. In the second century the Ptolemaic kings found it necessary to issue a number of what were called *philanthropa*—decrees proclaiming amnesties for wrongdoing and remissions of taxes.[5] In the Seleucid empire, the kings were careful not to offend the religious sensibilities of their subjects, and for the first century of the empire's existence, their policies were remarkably successful. But during the second century, after the Seleucid kings had been forced by Rome to abandon most of what is now modern Turkey and the Seleucid empire began it long decline, we have our best-documented example of a clash of religions. It occurred in Judea under the reign of Antiochus IV, sur-named Epiphanes. Antiochus decided that all his subjects should offer sacrifice to him as a kind of loyalty oath.

It is not clear what the reason was for his action, nor can we say for certain that this move was directed intentionally against the Jews, though it was the Jews who were most affected. However, Antiochus had just suffered the sort of humiliation that could be damaging to a Hellenistic king for whom a heroic persona was important if he was to keep the willing allegiance of his subjects. In 169, Antiochus launched an invasion of Egypt. He reached Alexandria and was preparing an assault on the city when an envoy from Rome, Popillius Laenas, appeared in Antiochus's camp in a suburb of Alexandria and demanded that Antiochus withdraw. Antiochus asked for time to consider, and Laenas drew a circle in the sand around Antiochus and told him that he wanted an answer from him before he stepped out of the circle. Antiochus had no time to save face, but he knew better than to refuse Rome's command. His actions in the aftermath of this humiliation do at times seem erratic, but some of them, at least, were an effort to show that he was still a great and powerful monarch.

Coele Syria and Judea to the south had been part of the Ptolemaic realm until 200, but the Seleucids had always coveted them, and as the second century began, the Seleucid king Antiochus III conquered them. Judea was still a small state; there were already more Jews living outside Judea than within it, and wherever the Jewish population in one of the cities of the Hellenistic world became numerous enough, there were synagogues. We do not know the date of the first synagogue—the earliest that archaeologists have discovered dates to the first century C.E.—but synagogues were a development of the Hellenistic period and the word *synagogé* is Greek. The Greeks probably recognized the synagogue as the type of club known as a *thiasos*. Jews regularly submitted their disputes to the synagogue officials, headed by a ruler of the synagogue, partly because they wanted their cases settled according to Jewish law and partly because they distrusted Greek courts, which was not unusual—so did many Greeks. In cities where the Jewish population was large, it might form a corporation called a *politeuma*, which allowed Jews greater rights than if they were mere resident aliens. Jews belonging to a *politeuma* managed their own internal affairs, and they had one privilege that was refused to non-Jewish *politeumata* as far as we know: the right not only to be judged by their own courts and be exempted from the jurisdiction of Greek courts. Yet the social pressure to conform to the Hellenistic way of life was strong. In Alexandria, Greek became the language of the synagogue, and the books of the Old Testament were translated into Greek. The social pressure was felt even in Judea itself.

In Judea, the Temple of Yahweh on the Temple Mount in Jerusalem was the religious center of Judaism. The daily sacrifices to Yahweh were financed by a half-shekel levy paid each year by all Jews, whether they lived in Judea or not, and like most temples, the Temple in Jerusalem took money on deposit and loaned it. Two families in Jerusalem vied for dominance: the Oniads, who supplied the hereditary high priests of the Temple, and the Toubiads, who also held high positions in the Temple. Just before the Seleucid king Antiochus IV came to the throne, the high priest Onias III went to

Antioch to report the misdemeanors of the rival clan, and while he was away, his brother Jason seized power and won the support of the new king by promising him higher tribute. Both Onias and his brother favored the Hellenistic way of life, but Jason was more radical; he set up a gymnasium for Jewish youth on the Temple Mount in Jerusalem, and got leave from Antiochus to rename Jerusalem Antioch. Jerusalem became a Greek *polis*, and Hellenized Jews were enrolled on its citizenship list. Jerusalem got an *ephebe* program like a Greek city; young Jewish *ephebes* wore the broad-brimmed hat that Greek *ephebes* wore, and stripped themselves of all their clothing to exercise, like the Greeks. It was all very different from the Jewish schools in Judea where the Torah was taught to young Jewish males—no women were allowed.

Nonetheless Antiochus deposed Jason in 170, and made a Toubiad, Menelaus, the high priest. But the next year, while Antiochus was invading Egypt, Jason and his party returned, slaughtered Menelaus's supporters, and forced Menelaus to flee to the citadel of Jerusalem where the Seleucid garrison protected him. Antiochus heard the news as he was encamped in a suburb of Alexandria. It must have sounded to him like a revolt at his rear as he was campaigning against Egypt, and when the Roman envoy Laenas forced him to make a humiliating retreat, he was not in a good mood. On his way back home, he entered Jerusalem, forced Jason to flee, and restored Menelaus, who in return gave him a share of the Temple treasure. Then Antiochus returned to Antioch where he held the great procession and games at Daphne (see chapter 11).

Antiochus's next move may have been prompted by his humiliation at the hands of Rome. The logic of it may escape us, but Antiochus was never known as a levelheaded king. He did not earn his sobriquet Antiochus the Mad for nothing. He imagined that he could strengthen his position by uniting all his subjects in king worship. In 167, a Seleucid army occupied Jerusalem, and a royal decree prohibited the Jewish religion. Pigs were sacrificed on an altar built in the Temple courtyard and the Temple itself was rededicated to Olympian Zeus. Many Jews conformed; others offered passive resistance. But when a royal officer arrived at the little village of Modein to conduct the sacrifice to the divine Antiochus, and called on the priest, Mattathias of the Hasmonean family, to be the first to take part, old Mattathias protested, proclaiming in a loud voice that he and his sons would remain faithful to Jewish law. But not everyone applauded. One Jew, at least, was ready to conform. He stepped forward to sacrifice as the rest of the villagers watched, and Mattathias wrathfully leaped on him and killed him, and then the royal officer. Then he and his sons fled to the mountains.

Mattathias died little more than a year later, but his son Judas Maccabaeus ("the Hammer") continued the insurgency, and in 164 he defeated a Seleucid army of 6,000 men. Antiochus may or may not have heard news of the defeat before he died on an expedition against the Parthians, leaving a child to succeed him. In Jerusalem, Judas took the Temple, purified it, and restored the worship of Yahweh: an event that is commemorated by the Festival of Hanukkah in the Jewish calendar. In 162, Lysias, the regent for the boy king Antiochus V, invaded Judea and mastered it, but the Seleucid dynasty was in trouble. Lysias returned to Antioch to protect his interests, and before he left, he rescinded Antiochus IV's decree outlawing the religion of Yahweh and put to death the unfortunate high priest Menelaus, whose Hellenizing policy was no longer useful. But a new Seleucid prince, Demetrius II, became king and reconquered Judea. Judas Maccabaeus put up a good fight, but he was defeated and killed. His brother Jonathan made peace and the insurgency was over.

Yet the Seleucid grip was growing feebler; Jonathan became for all intents and purposes an independent ruler of Judea, though there was still a Seleucid garrison in the citadel of Jerusalem until after Jonathan's death. When his brother Simon drove out the garrison and made peace with king Demetrius II, the Jews made Simon their hereditary high priest and governor. The Hasmonean family had now become the ruling dynasty of Judea, and though the religion of Yahweh was safe and no king again attempted to introduce king-worship, Judea began to look more and more like a Hellenistic city-state. The language on the street was Aramaic, which had been the lingua franca of the old Persian empire, but many Jews knew Greek. As for the Seleucid kings, between 140, when Demetrius II died, and 63, when the Roman general Pompey terminated the dynasty, there were 16 of them, and for 14 years during that period the Seleucid throne was occupied by the king of Armenia.

Judea was unique in that Judaism was a monotheist religion and recognized no god but Yahweh. Jews might pray for the welfare of a divine king—and for most of the kings, that was good enough—but they would not sacrifice to him. The Hasmonean revolt illustrates one reaction of the non-Greek subjects of the Hellenistic realms to the pervasive Greek culture, which was too attractive to ignore, but by its very attraction threatened the traditional societies of the subject peoples.

NOTES

1. Burstein, no. 103; Bagnall and Derow, no. 137.
2. Herodotus, *Histories*, 1.183.
3. Aristotle, *Politics*, 3.13.
4. Burstein, no. 7.
5. For an example, dating to 118, see Austin, no. 231.

14

Religion

THE SURVIVAL OF THE OLYMPIAN GODS

Most people who are familiar with Greek mythology know the 12 Olympian gods. They were the immortals whom we find in the great epic poems of Homer, the *Iliad* and the *Odyssey*. Their home was Mount Olympus in northern Greece, and, as Homer presented them, they belonged to one extended family. The head of the family was Zeus, whose fearsome thunderbolt was a weapon that no mortal or immortal would withstand. His wife was Hera, presented by Homer as a shrewish partner, but also a goddess to whom pregnant women prayed for a healthy infant and a safe childbirth. Apollo and Artemis were children of Zeus by Leto, who belonged to the race of Titans that ruled the divine world before the Olympians seized power. Leto gave birth to her children on Delos, the central island of the Cyclades archipelago. Demeter—her name means "Earth Mother"—was Zeus's sister, and her special care was agriculture. Her daughter was Persephone, the queen of the underworld, who obviously did not make her home on Mount Olympus and was not one of the Olympians. Nor was her husband, Hades, the dark lord of the underworld, the brother of Zeus. However, Zeus's other brother, Poseidon, god of the sea and of earthquakes, counted as an Olympian, even though he had a palace in the ocean depths. Aphrodite was the goddess of love and sexual passion, and her husband was the ugliest of the gods—Hephaestus, the blacksmith god. He was lame as a result of an incident of male violence: He had once tried to defend his mother Hera when Zeus attacked her in a rage, and Zeus had hurled him down from Olympus and fractured his legs. Ares was the god of war, a handsome, well-muscled god who was unpopular on Mount Olympus, for the other gods did not admire his passion for senseless conflict. Athena, the patron goddess of Athens, was both a warrior goddess and a patron of household crafts such as weaving. Hestia, goddess of the hearth, was a sister of Zeus and a singularly colorless deity, never the subject of scandalous stories. As we have seen, most Greek houses seem to lack hearths. When Dionysos, the god of wine and of the theater, entered the charmed circle of the Olympians, Hestia faded into the background. Finally, there was Hermes, the errand boy, whose statues show him as a well-developed youth with winged sandals and wings on his cap, which was a *petasos,* the hat with a brim that Greek youths wore at the gymnasium. When Zeus issued an edict, it was Hermes who delivered it. It was also he who escorted the souls of the dead to the underworld, crossing over the boundary between the living and the dead. There was something odd and slippery about Hermes: Among his areas of interest were thievery and trading, and mythographers tell a story of how, as soon as he was born, he slipped out of his cradle and stole a herd of cattle belonging to Apollo.

Homer's epic poems, the *Iliad* and the *Odyssey,* shed an aura of legitimacy over these Olympians, for the two epic poems attributed to Homer were the nearest thing that the Greeks had to a Holy Bible. Worship of the Olympians was the universal religion of the Greeks and it defined them as Greeks. There was a great profusion of gods and goddesses, and one of the services achieved by Homer's epics was to gather them together in an extended family that mirrored the sort of extended family that Greeks knew on earth. Homer's near contemporary, the poet Hesiod, tried his hand at a kind of theology; he wrote an epic on the family tree of the gods, which tried to reduce the many deities of Greece to some sort of logical order by giving them a genealogy that accounted for Creation and the generations that followed. First there was Chaos from which emerged Heaven and Earth, and from them were born the first generation of the gods—the Titans, ruled by Kronos, whose wife was Rhea, and from them were sprung the Olympians. Each generation seized power by overthrowing the generation that preceded it and Zeus himself maintained his throne only after terrible battles. Zeus became king of the gods, but Greek paganism was crowded with gods. To list the Olympians is only to scratch the surface.

Hesiod, for instance, sings the praise of a goddess named Hecate, whose statues frequently show her with three heads or three bodies. She was an ancient goddess who presided over the ghostly world, and for that reason her worship took place at crossroads, or where three roads meet, which were haunted places—not only among the Greeks but other peoples as well. And we may wonder where to place Pan, supposedly the son of Hermes, who had a goat's ears, legs, and horns? He was a god that created panic, the sudden irrational dread of something that might be unseen. Neither Homer nor Hesiod knew Bendis, a Thracian goddess shown carrying two spears who had a festival in Hellenistic Athens; resident aliens from Thrace seem to have brought her with them in the mid- to late-fifth century. There were the Cabiri, originally non-Greek deities, whose center of worship was the island of Samothrace, but it spread rapidly after Alexander the Great partly because the Ptolemies of Egypt backed it. Alexander's mother Olympias was a votary. The Cabiri were frequently confused with Castor and Polydeuces, or Pollux, as the Romans called him. Castor and Polydeuces were the Dioscuri—the name means "Sons of Zeus"—and they saved men at peril on the sea.

In addition, there were the heroes, or demigods, men of great reputation during their lifetime who were worshiped after they died and descended into the underworld. They had shrines, called *heroa*, not temples like the gods, and their cults were confined to the localities where they were buried. They received sacrifice, but the sacrificial rituals were not like those of the gods. There were no high altars for them. Sacrificial victims had their throats cut so that the blood ran down into the earth. Heroes were the saints of pagan religion: Like the saints in medieval Christianity, they were persons of great virtue who could perform miracles after death. Heroes had myths that were told about them, but it seems that a hero might be anonymous; in Hellenistic Athens there was a shrine to Heros Iatros ("Doctor Hero"), a demigod who healed the sick. But who was he? We know him only from a little marble plaque, carved in the third or second century, which archaeologists have turned up. He was a nameless divinity that healed the sick. There was also a "Hero General" in Athens known from a dedication: evidently a nameless but divine military officer. Heroes were *daimones* or spirits—we get our English word *demon* from the Greek *daimon*—and they could be either helpful or mischievous, but it was unsafe to ignore them.

The boundary between a hero and a god was never completely clear. Asclepius was a mortal man who was so skilful at healing that he restored a dead man to life, thus crossing a boundary that only a god could cross. Zeus was incensed, and killed Asclepius with a thunderbolt, and thereafter he became a hero who was worshiped like a god. He was not one of Homer's Olympian gods, but by the Hellenistic period he had crossed the dividing line between hero and god. And what of Heracles? According to Greek mythology, he was a mortal of superhuman strength that he used to rid the earth of monsters and make it a better place. In the Hellenistic period, philosophers made him the model of a great man who used his power to make the world a better place, and as such he was presented as an ideal for the Hellenistic kings to emulate. Heracles was received among the Olympian gods according to myth, and was reconciled with his old enemy, the goddess Hera. However, only at one place in Greece, Thasos, did he have a temple where he was worshiped as a god. Elsewhere he was a hero, though he was a hero with no grave. No place could claim the bones of Heracles.

In the Hellenistic period, the divine world became even more crowded. The Greeks had already encountered alien gods before Alexander the Great changed the cultural shape of their world, but when Greek cities were founded in the regions that Alexander conquered, the Greeks found themselves living side-by-side with the worshipers of gods they barely knew. For instance, at Comana, in the kingdom of Cappadocia, which was on the fringes of the Hellenistic world, most of the inhabitants were sacred slaves of the mother goddess Ma, and the priest of Ma was the most powerful man in the kingdom, second only to the king himself.

The rites of Ma included wild, frenzied dancing, which was not completely foreign to Greek religion, but professional priesthoods and wealthy temple-states controlling extensive territories were outside the Greek experience. Greek religion did not have professional priests. The priests who officiated were ordinary citizens; they might be elected to their priestly office, though in some instances certain families had the duty of holding priesthoods in a cult. Thus in Athens, the priests of the cult of Athena, the Guardian of the City, whose wooden statue was the city's most sacred image, came from the family of the Eteobutadai, and for the secret mysteries in the sanctuary of Demeter in Eleusis, west of Athens, the high priest came from the family of the Eumolpidai. But there was no caste of priests with shaven heads and white linen garments in Greece such as attended the great temples of Egypt nor was there anything similar to the Sadducees in Jerusalem, the descendants of King David's priest Zadok, who attended the worship of Yahweh in the Temple.

Delos

A tour of Delos will give us an idea of how the divine world of Greece changed in the Hellenistic period. Delos was the traditional birthplace of Apollo and his sister Artemis; it was where their mother Leto bore her two children as she leaned against a palm tree, and Zeus watched as he sat upon Mount Kynthos, the highest point on the island. Apollo had a great sanctuary there, and so also did Artemis. A temple to Leto had been built very early. This was a sacred island, dedicated to the cult of Apollo. But he had to share space in the Hellenistic period, for Hellenistic Delos had a long terrace reserved for Egyptian and Syrian gods. First we encounter a Sarapeion, sacred to the Egyptian god Sarapis whose cult was promoted by the Ptolemies of Egypt. Sarapis was well served on Delos, where he had three temples. There was a great sanctuary of the Syrian gods Hadad and Atargatis, a fertility cult that was regulated by an Athenian high priest. Atargatis was identified with Aphrodite, thereby giving her a Greek veneer. A small theater was attached to their temple, and on festival days the images of the two gods were taken to it so they could see the ceremonies and presumably enjoy them. The theater could seat 500 spectators if they squeezed close together, and a high wall surrounding the precinct prevented the public from seeing what it was that the images of the two deities were expected to enjoy. Further along was a sanctuary to the Cabiri from Samothrace. We have already mentioned the clubhouse of the Poseidoniasts of Berytus, merchants and ship owners from Syria who worshipped the Ba'al of Berytus. Delos was no longer the reserve of the Olympian gods.

THE NEWCOMERS: IMMIGRANT GODS FROM THE LANDS THAT ALEXANDER CONQUERED

Who were these immigrant deities that appear in the Greek world in the Hellenistic age, particularly in places like Rhodes or Delos or Alexandria, which were frequented by non-Greek merchants and traders? They were numerous, but for most of them, their worshipers were immigrants from their homelands. An example is the Poseidoniasts of Berytus, the ancient name for Beirut; they were worshipers of the Ba'al of Beirut and they were not looking for converts. From Anatolia, the central plateau of Asia Minor, a number of gods with foreign names followed the emigrants from their homelands into the wider Hellenistic world. We hear of gods named Attis, Agdistis, Anahita, Cybele, and Sabazius. Sabazius had several clubs of worshipers in Athens as early as the fifth century; he was sometimes identified with Dionysos, and in the late Hellenistic period he was identified by some Greeks with the God of the Jewish faith. In Pergamon, there was a center of Sabazius worship founded by a princess from Cappadocia, Stratonice, who married king Eumenes II. Attis was a young lover of Agdistis, who was Cybele under a different name, and Agdistis caused him to castrate himself to prevent him from marrying anyone else. Agdistis/Cybele was followed by eunuch disciples, and Attis was the eunuch prototype. Cybele's principal sanctuary was in the kingdom of Pergamon at Pessinus, where there was a *baetylus* or meteoric stone, which was the most venerated object of her cult, but Cybele's impact remained modest in the Hellenistic age. However, at the end of the third century, the *baetylus* along with a company of priests was taken to Rome, where the religion of Cybele and Attis was strictly controlled until the emperor Claudius (41–54 c.e.) allowed it free rein and it became immensely popular. But that was in the future.

From Syria came Atargatis and Hadad; by the third century, the worship of Atargatis had already been carried to Macedon and to Egypt. The great center of the worship of Atargatis was the city of Mabbog in Syria, north of Aleppo, or as the Greeks called it, Bambyce, though it was better known simply as the "Holy City" (in Greek, Hierapolis). Hadad, the patron god of Damascus, was her consort. He was shown seated on a throne that was flanked by bulls, whereas the attendant animals of the throne of Atargatis were lions. Her temple at Hierapolis was rebuilt by the Greek wife of king Seleucus I—he had two wives, one a Greek, the daughter of Demetrius the Besieger, and the other a Bactrian princess. To the Greeks, Atargatis was known simply the "Syrian Goddess." She remained an exotic deity, with her sacred fish and doves, and she appealed most to Syrian migrants who spread over the Hellenistic world in search of trade. Syria was the homeland of the ancient Phoenicians, and they had not lost their talent for seafaring and commerce.

Isis and Sarapis

Two newcomers deserve more attention: Isis and Sarapis, both from Egypt. Isis was an ancient Egyptian goddess whose cult spread beyond Egypt in the Hellenistic period, and the queens of Egypt attempted to assimilate themselves to her persona. Yet she never lost her Egyptian roots. Sarapis, however, was a god created by Ptolemy I and his advisors, and probably the king hoped that he would unite his Greek and non-Greek subjects in one faith. If so, the plan did not work. The native Egyptians showed little interest in Sarapis. But among the Greeks in Alexandria, where the Ptolemies built a great temple of Sarapis, and outside Egypt in the wider Hellenistic world, the Sarapis cult flourished, often in tandem with the cult of Isis.

The myth of Isis told how her brother and husband Osiris reigned in Egypt until he was murdered by his brother Seth, who dismembered his corpse and threw it into the river. Isis searched long and hard for it, and when she found it at last, she brought him back to life. She bore him a son, Horus, or Harpocrates, as the Greeks called him, whom she hid to escape the persecutions of Seth. When he was fully grown, she brought him before the tribunal of the gods where Seth charged him with illegitimate birth and he defended himself. The gods decided in his favor and gave him his father's kingdom. Since then, Osiris ruled the realm of the dead, and the pharaoh was the incarnation of Horus, Osiris's son.

The cult of Isis spread throughout the Greek east, and as the Greek artists portrayed her, she looked like a typical Greek mother, sometimes wearing a typically Egyptian headdress, sometimes with no headdress at all but with a curl or braid of hair hanging down on either side of her face. Sometimes she was shown with the infant Harpocrates; he can easily be recognized because artistic representations show him with one hand raised to his mouth. But Isis kept her Egyptian roots; holy water taken from the Nile River was used in her rituals and she was served by Egyptian priests with shaven heads and white linen garments.

Sarapis was a new god, created by Ptolemy I's theologians, one of them the Egyptian priest named Manetho whom Ptolemy had commissioned to write a history of Egypt, and the other an Athenian, Timotheus, who belonged to the priestly family in charge of the Eleusinian Mysteries at Eleusis, now a suburb of Athens. There is a tradition that Ptolemy I brought a cult statue of Sarapis to Egypt from Sinope, a Greek *polis* on the south coast of the Black Sea, and that Manetho and Timotheus developed Egyptian rites for him, but most of the elements of Sarapis worship seem to have roots in Egyptian rather than Greek religious traditions. Sarapis worship was a development of the old religion of the Apis bull at Memphis, the ancient capital of the Old Kingdom of Egypt in the age of the great pyramid builders. The Apis bull was the incarnation of the spirit of Osiris, and whenever one bull died of old age, a bull calf would be born somewhere in Egypt with identical markings. The bull became Osarapis in the realm of the Afterlife, and Osarapis became Sarapis, or in the Latin language, Serapis.

Sarapis was probably intended to appeal to both Egyptians and Greeks, for he seems to be Osiris refashioned with characteristics and rituals that would strike the Greeks as familiar. The great temple to him in Alexandria seems to have combined Greek and Egyptian traditions. It had a library that was smaller than the Great Library but still impressive, and the cult statue there, by the sculptor Bryaxis, was one of the seven wonders of the ancient world. It showed the god seated, looking very much like Olympian Zeus, with a modius on his head and a three-headed dog by his side. The dog was Cerberus, the watchdog of Hades, as any Greek would recognize. Like Hades and Osiris, Sarapis was a god of the underworld.

The Cult of Aphrodite and Adonis

There was another cult, too, that can be classed among the newcomers, though it was known in Athens in the classical period. It was the cult of Aphrodite and Adonis, which under its Greek trappings is the cult of Astarte and Tammuz adopted from Phoenicia. There are several versions of the myth of Aphrodite and Adonis, but the simplest one relates that Adonis was a beautiful boy whom Aphrodite loved dearly. He was killed by a wild boar in a boar hunt, and Aphrodite put his body in a box and entrusted it to Persephone, the queen of the underworld. But Persephone refused to give him back, and the quarrel between Aphrodite and the queen of the dead went on until Zeus intervened and ruled that Adonis must stay in the underworld for half the year and the World of the Living for the other half. We can recognize in this cult of Adonis the life/death cycle of a vegetation god who disappears once the crops are harvested and comes back to life when the growing season begins. At Byblos in ancient Phoenicia, modern Lebanon, a center of his worship, it was said that the blood of Adonis stained the river that flowed by the city red. Women mourned Adonis by setting out Gardens of Adonis, which were shallow sherds of pottery filled with damp earth in which lettuce seeds were planted. They sprouted quickly and died almost as quickly, as the earth dried out. They symbolized the life and death of Adonis that recurred each year.

We have a poem by the Hellenistic poet Theocritus that describes how two women in Alexandria visited the palace gardens where the festival of Adonis was celebrated each year, probably in September. It is one of our most graphic descriptions of everyday life in Alexandria in the reign of king Ptolemy II and the meaning of religion to the ordinary middle-class citizenry. The festival was a showpiece staged by Queen Arsinoe II, the wife and sister of Ptolemy II Philadelphus. It lasted three days—Theocritus describes the first day, when the tragic love story of Aphrodite and Adonis was retold. On the second day, the worshipers mourned for Adonis in the underworld, and on the last day he left the world of the dead and returned to life.

TEMPLES AND SHRINES

A temple was a holy space, a place where a god wanted to be worshiped and had made his or her desire known somehow—often there was a myth that explained how the holy space was chosen. These were precincts that were set aside as sacred to a god. The borders of the precinct were marked by boundary stones or sometimes by a continuous wall that divided it from secular space. It was an area that was cut off—in Greek, a *temenos*, a word that derives from the verb *temno*, meaning "to cut," and it was the *temenos* that was the sanctuary, lending holiness to the temple building (the *naos*) that was constructed within it. No one could give birth, make love, or die inside a sanctuary, and worshipers purified themselves with holy water before they entered. For this sacred space was inviolable; runaway slaves might flee there for refuge, and goods put there for safekeeping could not be plundered without committing a sacrilege. Anyone who killed a person who had taken refuge in a sanctuary would arouse the wrath of the gods, who might retaliate. A god such as Apollo might send a plague that would punish a whole city for one murderer's sacrilegious crime. Or Zeus might withhold rain.

Within the sanctuary was the *naos*, the dwelling of the god, where the cult statue of the god was housed. In its simplest form, the *naos* was a one-room building with a porch, and as the form developed, a colonnade was added surrounding this single-room building. Temples make splendid ruins and they are found everywhere in the Mediterranean world that was touched by Greek civilization. Sicily and southern Italy have some of the best examples; in fact, the cathedral at Siracosa, ancient Syracuse in Sicily, is a classical temple of

Athena converted into a church. Temples were showpieces, built of marble or limestone covered with white stucco, with the details of their moldings picked out in paint. Their ruins are serene and lofty, but they were garish structures in the heyday of Greek paganism, often surrounded by other buildings such as treasuries, storage places, or stoas with dining rooms where worshipers could eat a meal after a sacrifice. What we have left in many cases now is a sad ruin and a memory.

However, the *naos* was intended to house a god's statue, not to accommodate a congregation of worshipers. The rituals of pagan religion were generally performed outside the temple building. The cult statue of the god was brought out for public view on festival days, but otherwise it remained locked up. In fact, there were statues that were never brought out for public view. The best-known example was the statue of Athena in the Parthenon on the Athenian acropolis: a magnificent statue made of gold and ivory with a wooden core, fashioned by the great Athenian sculptor Pheidias. It was not for public worship. The image of Athena that the Athenians venerated was an ancient wooden statue that lived in the Erechtheion, the neighbor of the Parthenon to the north.

Thus the temple served as a magnificent backdrop for the rituals that went on in the precinct. The altar was always outside it, and generally outside the east end of the temple, for Greek temples usually faced east. It was there that the sacrificial victim was sacrificed and burned. There were sacrifices called holocausts where the entire sacrificial victim was consumed by the fire on the altar, but in the more common sacrificial rite, only the bones and inedible parts were burned, and the rest was reserved for feasting. Sacrifices on festival days commonly ended with a communal meal.

Sanctuaries must have been crowded with dedications made to the god. Statues and inscribed stones commemorating some event might be set up outside the temple. Within the temple itself might be found the crowns of athletes who were victorious in one or another of the great athletic festivals dedicated there. A person who recovered from illness thanks to the intervention of a god might dedicate a terracotta model of the body part that had been cured. Temples of gods of healing, such as Asclepius or Sarapis, were filled with these little earthenware models. Each of them, no doubt, could tell a story if it could speak. Sometimes there were buildings constructed to house the overflow of dedications, but more commonly, the priests had a periodic housecleaning and buried the unwanted votive offerings in trenches that they dug in the earth. When archaeologists excavated the stadium at Olympia, they found large numbers of old, unwanted votive offerings that had been buried there, still within the sanctuary precinct. These dedications were still holy objects, even though the dedicators might be dead and half-forgotten, and when there was no longer any room for them in the temple of Zeus, they were given a decent burial on hallowed ground.

Demigods

We must not forget the demigods, or heroes, who were worshiped in *heroa* or shrines. Real gods were born in the mythic past, and in the classical period demigods, too, had a mythical pedigree. For instance, about 470, the Athenian statesman and general Cimon found the bones of the hero Theseus on the island of Scyros, where he had died. Theseus was a great hero of Athens who had performed a series of labors like those that Heracles had carried out, but his remains had been lost, and since a hero cult centered on a hero's grave, the Athenians could not give their hero an appropriate ceremony without them. Cimon found bones on Scyros of heroic proportions, identified them from the size as belonging to Theseus, and brought them to Athens, where they were reburied in a *heroon*. This pious act, it was said, brought Cimon more acclaim than any of his victories.

But in the Hellenistic period, it became almost a routine event to make a dead man a hero. All that was needed was for the family of the deceased, or his club, to canonize him. The Greek language even had a verb, *aphorizein,* meaning "to set apart" or "make someone a hero." If the deceased became a hero, he would have a *heroon*— perhaps quite a modest one—where there would be a sacrifice once a year. It was an occasion to mourn his passing, and perhaps professional mourners would be hired for the occasion. Most important of all, a banquet would be held in his honor, which the deceased would attend in effigy, reclining on a dining couch. If a departed club member left a legacy to his club to pay for banquets in his memory, it would add to the likelihood that he would become a demigod.

FESTIVALS, PROCESSIONS, AND SACRIFICES

Paganism had no regular sacred days, such as Sunday for the Christians, the Sabbath for the Jews, and Friday for the Moslems. Instead there were festivals in honor of the gods. The calendar was packed with them, and the situation did not improve in the Hellenistic age when new festivals mushroomed and cities sent embassies to each other's festivals. The spirits of the dead heroes also required annual sacrifices on appropriate days. To keep the religious year in some sort of order, cities possessed sacred calendars that set out the festivals scheduled for each month. The Athenian calendar was drawn up at the end of the fifth century when a certain Nicomachus was commissioned to draw up a month-by-month schedule of state sacrifices, and when his job was done, the calendar was inscribed on the wall of a stoa in the Athenian agora. Fragments of this Great Calendar inscription survive, and by combining the data from it with what we know from other sources, we can reconstruct a complete schedule of the festivals in Athens month by month. The number is impressive. In Athens, there were 120 festival days.

The Great Panathenaia

Not every Athenian attended every festival by any means. But let us take one that a significant portion of the population did attend, the Panathenaic festival. It was held every year, and every fourth year the Panathenaia became the Great Panathenaia, a pan-Hellenic festival where non-Athenians could participate. The first day of the Great Panathenaia—the last day of the first month of the Athenian lunar calendar beginning about mid-July—was taken up with a procession representing the population of the city. Young warriors and old men were in it, as well as resident aliens and their wives and children—they and their sons carried trays loaded with offerings, their wives carried jars of water, and their daughters carried parasols. The parade left from the city gate called the Dipylon Gate, made its way through the Potters' Quarter, and then paraded across the agora following a well-marked path, the Sacred Way. Then it wound up the north slope of the acropolis and finally entered the acropolis itself through the monumental entry called the Propylaea. That brought the procession to the rear of the Parthenon, for the Propylaea is at the west end of the acropolis, and the Parthenon, like most Greek temples, faces east. So the procession made its way along the length of the Parthenon until it reached the great altar of Zeus and Athena at the front of the temple.

This procession brought with it a new robe, a *peplos*, for the cult statue of Athena—not the gold-and-ivory statue in the Parthenon, but an ancient statue of Athena carved from olive wood whose origin was lost in time. Such a statue was called a *xoanon*, and they were thought to have a supernatural origin. Every four years, the *xoanon* of Athena was provided with a new saffron-dyed robe embroidered with scenes of Athena's battles woven by chosen daughters of Athenian citizens. The robe was given to the chief priest of Athens, the King Archon who was chosen each year by lot, and he placed the robe on the *xoanon*, which was housed in the Erechtheion next door to the Parthenon.

Then came the sacrifice. The ritual required the beast to submit willingly to its death, and so it was sprinkled with cold water, thus causing it to quiver, and this quivering was taken as a sign that it accepted its death. Then came the blow with the sacrificial knife, and as the blood flowed down the altar, the women attendants screamed. The ritual scream was an important part of the sacrificial rite. We cannot say what it meant; perhaps it marked the departure of the breath of life from the sacrificial victim. Then Zeus and Athena got their share, and the rest of the beast was butchered and cooked for the feast that followed the sacrifice. Banqueting was part of a religious festival, and within the precincts of a temple we often find dining rooms. When the sacrifice was not a holocaust—that is, a sacrifice where the victim was completely consumed by the fire on the altar—only the inedible parts of the victim such as the bones and the skin were reduced to ashes, and the rest was reserved for the worshipers to eat, and the meat that was not eaten might be put up for sale in the market.

Probably no less than 100 cattle and often many more were butchered for the Panathenaia, and it was not the only festival where there was a massive slaughter of beasts. In fact, there were sacrifices requiring massive slaughter for every month of the Athenian year save one. The cost of these festivals must have been enormous, all the more so since the land around Athens was not cattle country. Probably cattle had to be imported for these great sacrifices. For some festivals, the cost was borne directly by the state, but for others—the Panathenaia among them—it was assigned as a liturgy to a wealthy citizen who paid the bill. Liturgies were free services provided to the state by wealthy men, more or less willingly, except that they could not refuse them. In many cases, the burden must have been a heavy drain on the liturgist's savings.

After the Panathenaic procession and the sacrifice came the competitive events. The competitors—boys up to age 18, young men, and older men—competed in athletic events, musical contests, and in public recitations of epic poetry by rhapsodes. Rhapsodes were professional masters of elocution who in early Greece played the lyre to accompany their recitations, but by the Hellenistic period they simply carried a staff as the symbol of their profession. At the Panathenaia, rhapsodic contests were strictly regulated: only extracts of Homer's poetry could be recited and they had to be in correct sequence. Not every religious festival included contests, though all competitions were religious and had a divine patron. Many festivals did have contests, however, though they did not always include athletic events. Take, for instance, the Great Dionysia, held in late March or April. It began with two days of processions. The image of the god Dionysos of Eleutherae was taken from his sanctuary and carried in a parade to a temple near the Academy where Plato founded his school of philosophy. The next day it was carried back again to its sanctuary, and then taken in another procession which ended in the theater, the ruins of which we can still see on the south slope of the acropolis in Athens. A sacrifice and banquet followed, and then the following days were devoted to dramatic contests.

Processions

Processions were important rituals in pagan festivals. They were half publicity stunts and half devotional acts—the votaries of the god would have claimed that they were all a devout religious observance. Cults that had a professional priesthood, such as we find in Egypt, had votaries of the god who were called "bearers of the *pastos*." The *pastos* was a portable shrine displaying the image of the god that was paraded through the streets on a litter carried on the shoulders of the *pastos*-bearers. We have a description of a procession of Isis-worshippers taking part in the festival known as the Ploiaphesia, where the image of Isis was taken down to the sea to bless the waters at the start of the navigation season each spring. The description comes from a novel titled the *Metamorphosis* (the Transformation)[1] by an author who wrote in Latin, Lucius Apuleius, who lived in the second century C.E., long after the end of the Hellenistic period, and yet the Ploiaphesia festival of Isis that Apuleius described in Corinth was probably much the same as it had been a couple centuries earlier.

In the vanguard of the parade were a number of comedians in fancy dress. They were professional actors, and after the parade was over they would probably entertain the crowd in the theater, for performances of dance and mime often followed the parade. Then came the procession proper. At its head were groups of women.

One group in white dresses scattered flowers, another had mirrors tied to the back of their heads, another with ivory combs pretended that they were dressing Isis's hair, another scattered perfume on the road, and finally there came a group of men and women who hailed Isis as "Daughter of the Stars" and carried torches, lamps, or wax candles. Then came musicians and a boys' choir, and behind them, those who had been initiated into the cult of Isis, men and women dressed in pure white clothing. The men's heads were shaven and they carried rattles called *sistra* (singular—*sistrum*) that made a barrage of tinkling and jangling when they were shaken in unison. Next came the leading priests, dressed in white linen, bearing emblems of the goddess. One man carried a wine jar. Following them were men representing other gods from Egypt: Anubis, the jackal-headed god, with one half of his face painted gold and the other half black; then a dancer bearing on his shoulders the statue of a cow, representing the goddess Hathor; then a priest carrying the secret implements of the Isis cult; and finally a priest bearing a golden vessel covered with Egyptian hieroglyphics. The pageant reached the seashore and there a model ship was launched, its hull covered with hieroglyphics, and on its linen sail was written a prayer to Isis to protect the ships that sailed in the upcoming shipping season. A libation of milk was poured into the sea, and the little vessel set sail while the worshipers watched until she disappeared from view.

The priests returned to Isis's temple where they, along with the initiates, were admitted into the temple. At the gate of the precinct, a priest uttered the word *ploiaphesia*, the formula that permitted ships to sail safely on the sea. The people cheered and dispersed, first kissing the feet of the silver statue of Isis that stood on the temple steps.

Dancing and Pantomimes

Festivals often included theatrical presentations: dancing—the festivals of Isis seem to have included wild dancing—or pantomimes, interpretative dances that mimed some of the myths about the deities who were being worshipped. The stories that were mimed could be ribald and bawdy, but no matter: pagan deities were powers to be feared, not examples of rectitude. Sometimes a festival took over the civic theater of a city, but sanctuaries out in the country built theaters of their own. The sanctuary of Asclepius at Epidaurus, which was not near any large center, had a magnificent theater built primarily for a festival held every four years.

The sanctuary of Atargatis and Hadad on Delos included its own small theater. On festival days, the idols of Hadad and Atargatis were taken from their temple to the theater to witness the performances there. We have a relief sculpture that was found not far from Rome, but nonetheless depicts a dance scene in the sanctuary theater of an Egyptian god or goddess. The dancers clack sticks and castanets as they gesticulate wildly with their arms and shimmy violently with their hips, while standing in the front rows of the theater are onlookers, probably worshipers, for they wave their arms apparently in time to the music. There is no doubt that the god or goddess who is being worshiped is Egyptian, for there are ibises, sacred birds in Egypt, shown in the foreground and in the background, a row of Egyptian images. Does this sculpture show a dance honoring Isis or Sarapis, held in the courtyard of a temple or in a theater that was part of the sanctuary? It is clearly something of the sort.

COMMUNICATING WITH THE GODS

Oracles and *Mantikê*

The best-known vehicle for communication between gods and mankind was the oracle, through whom a god delivered his messages to his worshipers. The oracles were numerous and varied. Those we know best were the oracles of Apollo at Delphi in central Greece; at Delos, the island in the Cyclades where he and his sister Artemis were born, according to myth; and at Claros and Didyma in modern Turkey. Zeus had an oracle in northwest Greece, at Dodona. At the oasis of Siwah, in the desert in Egypt west of the Nile, Amon-Re, whom the Greeks identified with Zeus, had an oracle that was consulted by Alexander the Great. But there were many less famous oracles that were consulted in order to see what the future had in store for the seeker, and in the Hellenistic period, local oracles that had been neglected were revived. Cities kept archives of oracles that oracle mongers consulted in times of stress. True believers thought that the gods spoke through oracles, though they veiled their truths in obscure language.

The ways in which the gods chose to communicate were many and varied. When sacrifices were made at the altar of Zeus at Olympia, which was actually a great heap of ash from earlier sacrifices, the priests of Zeus carefully watched the flames rising from the sacrificial fire to discover if the god gave a sign. This is a type of divination called empyromancy. At Delphi, communication came only one day each month, for nine months of the year (the oracle closed for winter). A priestess, middle aged but dressed like a girl, sat on a tripod, and when questions were called out to her, she fell into a trance and uttered words that the Delphic priests put into verse or prose as the case might be. It was believed that fumes rising from a cleft in the rock below the tripod may have intoxicated the Pythia, as the priestess was called, and in fact a close examination of the geology of Delphi indicates that the cleft—which has been identified—may have emitted mildly toxic fumes in classical and Hellenistic times, but it does not now. At the height of Delphi's popularity, three Pythias were kept busy, but in the Hellenistic period one could handle the business, and the questions asked tended to be more trivial. In fact, when the Pythia was not available, the Delphic oracle would answer questions by lot. For an answer to his query, a questioner would pick either a black or a white bean, and receive either yes or no for an answer.

Other oracles had their own ways of communicating. At Dodona in Epirus, the ancient oracle of Zeus communicated through the medium of a sacred oak: Petitioners submitted questions written on little wafer-thin lead sheets, and Zeus answered by the rustling of oak's leaves, which was interpreted by his priests. In central Greece, at Lebadaea, there was an oracular god named Trophonius where the man who wanted to communicate with the god first purified himself with an elaborate ritual and then lowered himself into a cave where he was snatched away to the underworld and then returned again, terrified at what he had seen. Far away in northwest Greece was Ephyra, where Acheron, the river of the underworld, overflowed to form the Acherousian Lake. An ancient oracle of the dead was found there, where the shades of the dead were called up to communicate with the living. There is a strange little Hellenistic shrine there, with ruined rooms and corridors, some above ground and some below, where mediums once played their tricks of necromancy. Sacrifices, too, yielded omens that carried a message. When victims were sacrificed, their viscera signaled good luck or bad, and interpreting these signs for good or bad omens was a specialized skill called *mantikê*.

Dreams

One of the most common means by which gods communicated with mortals was by dreams. Dreams were particularly important in the healing cults. The worship of Asclepius came into its own in the Hellenistic period. There were great cult centers at Epidaurus in Greece, Pergamon in modern Turkey, and the island of Cos. Men and women who were ill slept in the hostel in Asclepius's precinct, and as they slept, the great harmless snakes that were sacred to the god might crawl over them. They dreamed dreams where the god appeared to them and told them what they should do to regain health. The therapy the god prescribed could be a series of ordeals, such as walking barefoot or taking a cold bath, and modern medical science would not have much use for them. Yet clearly some of the sick were cured, for many votive offerings have been found in the healing sanctuaries, placed there by patients who had found a cure for what ailed them. The offerings were often little earthenware models of the body part that was healed: legs, hips, or as was often the case, the male genitalia or women's breasts. Perhaps these were dedications by couples who wanted a child. Whatever the ailment was, we must presume that the patients thought themselves healed.

Magic

We should not forget astrology and magic. Everyone believed in magic, and the authorities feared it, for magic, it was thought, could both kill and cure. From the sands of Egypt modern scholars have found a great number of documents written on papyrus that deal with the pseudoscience of magic, and for a student of ancient Greek religion they are important evidence of what religious belief meant to the common man. For him, the Olympian gods were still alive and well. The speculations of Hellenistic philosophy about the gods meant nothing to him. But the Olympian gods are not the aristocratic, serene deities that we find in Greek art. They are demonic, dangerous forces who waste no love or concern for mere mortals. They must be approached with magic spells and invocations. There are love spells, spells to drive someone to insanity, either a man or a woman, spells to cure a migraine headache, and others asking for a dream oracle or a vision. The gods of Egypt, especially Isis, Osiris, and the jackal god, Anubis, are all invoked, and so is Io, who must be Yahweh, the Jewish deity whose temple was in Jerusalem. In fact, the corpus of magical papyri reminds us that in the Hellenistic period, Jewish magicians were well regarded. On the level of everyday life in the Hellenistic world, a sick person would turn to a physician who claimed knowledge of magic as naturally as his modern counterpart would turn to a medical doctor. In fact, though medical science made great strides in the Hellenistic period, doctors did not understand disease. The popular view was that persons diseased in body or mind were possessed by demons, and they would turn to physicians whom we might label as faith healers, magicians, or even quacks in order to be cured.

NON-BELIEF

There were no atheists in the Hellenistic world. One of the charges laid against Socrates when he was put on trial in Athens in 399 was that he did not believe in the gods that the rest of the Athenians accepted. Socrates defended himself by claiming that he was a believer. He was no atheist. His greatest disciple, Plato, near the end of his life, wrote a constitution for an ideal state titled *The Laws*, and in this state, atheists were to be put to death. Gods could be terrible in their wrath, and if they took offense because a mere man denied their existence and sent a plague or a flood, it would not be only the guilty man who suffered but his innocent neighbors as well.

Yet there was much speculation about the gods and what role they played. They did not like mortals to become too great, for their jealousy was easily aroused. Sometimes it is the gods (*theoi*) whose jealousy is aroused; sometimes it is "the god" (*theos*), as if a god such as Olympian Zeus embodied the power and divinity of all the gods. The god might be angered by unjust acts such as taking an oath and breaking it, but morality was left to the philosophers. But the divine element could not be ignored.

One school of philosophy came close to atheism. The Epicureans took the atomic theory that had been developed by Leucippus and Democritus and used it to show how life came into being without the help of the gods. Originally there were atoms and void, and the atoms fell perpendicularly through void because of the force of gravity. But by chance, some atoms would collide with others, and stick together, creating a mass of atoms, and it was from these atoms that happened to come together that the forms of life came into being. Thus we are all made of atoms and void, and at death, the atoms of our bodies and souls lose their cohesion and rejoin the world of atoms and void.

There seems to be no place for the gods in the Epicurean universe of atoms and void, but Epicurus did not leave them out. They lived off in a world of their own and paid no attention to humankind. But there was another force at work in the Epicurean world—chance, or *Tyché*, which caused the atoms to collide. *Tyché* was one element of Epicurean thought that spread beyond the Epicureans and influenced the way that the ordinary man thought. *Tyché*—chance— controlled his life. *Tyché* was a goddess; she was Lady Luck. On Mount Silpius, the acropolis of Antioch, stood a statue of the *Tyché* of Antioch. She represented the good fortune of the city.

Yet *Tyché* was never blind chance. Sometimes writers use the word in a way that we would translate as "providence," or even "fate." Old modes of religious thought die hard: The early Greeks believed that even the gods could not change a person's fate. In the Hellenistic world, Fate has become *Tyché:* a capricious Fate that makes some lucky and others unlucky. One Greek historian of the second century, Polybius, speaks of Rome's destiny to become a great empire as *Tyché*. Yet a man who believed in the force of *Tyché* did not discard the ancient gods. Everyone believed, but sometimes beliefs took strange forms.

AN EGYPTIAN TEMPLE IN PTOLEMAIC EGYPT

The native Egyptians had their own gods, and the Ptolemaic rulers were careful to respect them. They were as active builders of temples as any of the pharaohs before them. Egyptian priests continued to compose hieroglyphic and hieratic forms of writing used for sacred texts that went back to early Pharaonic times—the script used by the native Egyptians in the Hellenistic period is called demotic. Egyptian gods gave oracles in the native tongue. This continued to be the case until Rome took over Egypt, when the language of the oracles changed abruptly to Greek. It appears that the Roman overlords of Egypt were aware that oracles could foster nationalist unrest, and they wanted them written in a language that they could understand. The Ptolemaic kings, who did not have a military machine like the Romans did to impose their will, had to be careful not to alienate the priests.

What was an Egyptian temple like? Let us take as an example the temple of Soknebtunis at the village of Tebtunis on the southern edge of the Fayum. Egypt was divided into provinces called nomes, and the nomes were divided into *topoi,* and the *topoi* into the villages, and the Fayum is the modern Arabic name for the Arsinoite nome in Ptolemaic Egypt. The Ptolemies, who needed land for the settlers, reduced the size of the lake and increased the arable land by means of irrigation. Tebtunis had been a small village on the edge of the desert in pre-Hellenistic times, but king Ptolemy I built a new temple there, dedicated to the crocodile god, Sobek.

Each nome had its own animal (or bird) god, and the god of the Arsinoite nome was the crocodile. Its chief temple was in the nome capital, but Tebtunis had its own incarnation, Soknebtunis ("Sobek, lord of Tunis"). The sacred area *(temenos)* of the temple was surrounded by a massive wall of coarse brick, and leading up to the main gate on the north side was a processional road. The door was hung on a great bronze hinge and it could be held in one of three positions—closed, open, or half-open.

The would-be worshiper would cross the threshold and enter the first courtyard. On his right was a small circular enclosure for the holy crocodile, and next to it, an acacia tree, sacred to Sobek. Along the west wall of the *temenos* there were a variety of small buildings that probably housed temple workmen such as bakers, linen workers, and sculptors who carried on the industries connected with the temple. From the first courtyard a double door led into the second, in the midst of which was the holy of holies. Left of it was a grove of trees, and to the right, the great altar, oriented east. Around the outside wall of the second courtyard were the priests' houses, usually two-room buildings, one room in front of the other, with a cellar underneath.

In front of the temple, leading up to the main gate, was a paved processional way, about 650 feet long, which began with a monumental gate, and then continued over cultivated ground until it widened to form a vestibule before the entrance to the *temenos*. Along the processional way, the excavators found two kiosks, one of which dated from the Hellenistic period; they were summer houses that had some ceremonial purpose on festival days. There were also 18 dining rooms, for dining was an important part of an Egyptian festival. It was down this processional way that the priests of Soknebtunis carried the image of Sobek as well as the images of the gods housed in the temple, including, no doubt, the effigies of the Ptolemaic kings. They might be portraits or sculptures, but they represented the kings as gods, sharing the temple with the crocodile god.

Every day the crocodile god was offered worship according to a long-established rite. First, the priest prepared for the ritual in the House of the Dawn, performing a rite that followed the pattern of the king's daily toilet, for the priest who carried out the daily ritual acted in place of the pharaoh. Then the priest entered the temple, where he washed to purify himself, and then entered the holy of holies, where he purified the cult-image and placed a crown on it. He offered the image a sacrificial meal and then, once the ceremonies were complete, he left the sanctuary, walking backwards, and assistants wiped away his footprints. Music, both instrumental and vocal, accompanied the ritual.

We cannot say that the daily ritual at Tebtunis followed this pattern exactly. Was there a cult image of Sobek that the priest crowned, or was the sacred crocodile itself kept in the sanctuary? Was it the image of a crocodile, or of a man with the head of a crocodile? When the priests carried Sobek in procession through the village, was it an effigy of Sobek or was it the divine crocodile itself that they carried in a litter on their shoulders? The temple at Tebtunis did not compare with the great temples at places like Karnak or Luxor, ancient Thebes. It probably attracted only local worshipers. The chief temple of the crocodile god was in the nome capital called Crocodilopolis by the Greeks, and it was famous enough to attract a few foreign tourists. Yet in the desert close by the Tebtunis temple was a crocodile cemetery, where thousands of mummified crocodiles were buried. Pious worshipers must have bought the crocodiles, paid for their mummification, and laid them in their tombs with a prayer for their help in the afterlife. The embalmers used large numbers of discarded papyri to stuff the crocodiles, thus gladdening the hearts of modern scholars.

Among the documents discovered in recent excavations at Tebtunis were 300 oracle cards, which the Egyptians submitted to Sobek with requests of what to do in certain situations. Newspapers nowadays regularly carry advice columns where readers can submit questions about gardening, health issues, or personal problems. In the Hellenistic world, oracles took care of similar requests. Among the cards was one that read, "If Thamista was the man who has stolen my bronze pot, give me this card," and there were five others with exactly the same message, but each with a different name of a possible culprit. These cards must have been submitted to Sobek, and he was expected to choose the right one. Just how the old crocodile did it is a mystery, but Sobek's worshipers seem to have been satisfied.

The Egyptian temples were rich and powerful. A generous portion of the land of Egypt was classified as "sacred land" that supported the temples. The priests with their shaven heads and garments of white linen were a closed caste of professionals; an Egyptian became a priest because his father was a priest. Temples sold their chief priesthoods to the highest bidder within the priestly caste, or at least to the most acceptable one, for a priest would take a percentage of the sacrificial offerings and, if all went well, he would soon recover his investment. As well as the priests, there were other temple attendants, among them hierodules—the name means "sacred slaves," and they were persons who dedicated their lives to sacred service. Within the walls of the temples, too, there were libraries that preserved the ancient traditions and literature of Egypt, and the oracles of the gods were delivered in the language of pharaonic Egypt, at least until the Romans decreed that Greek must be used. Even so, the ancient language lived on as demotic—the language of the ordinary Egyptian—until it re-emerged with the addition of some Greek vocabulary as Coptic, the language of the Christian church in Egypt. About 10 percent of the population of modern Egypt are still Copts.

NOTE

1. The popular title of this novel is *The Golden Ass*. A translation by Robert Graves is available in the Penguin Classics series.

15

Science, Technology, and Medicine

THE PROGRESS OF SCIENCE

The great intellectual achievements of classical Greece had been in the fields of literature and philosophy, and the city-states of Greece, particularly Athens, continued to be the most hospitable homes for these fields. But scientific research migrated to the new world of the Hellenistic monarchies, which can take a large part of the credit for the new developments in both pure and applied science. The kings of Egypt and of Pergamon were in the forefront, and the scientific achievements of the age are impressive even nowadays. Since we are charting everyday life in the Hellenistic age, we must at some point ask how much the new scientific achievements affected the workaday world, and that is a valid question. What did the man on the unpaved streets of Alexandria think about the researchers in the royal Mouseion, if he thought about them at all? Were any laborsaving devices invented that improved transport or irrigation in Egypt? These are questions we must defer for the moment. Let us look at some of the achievements. We shall take astronomy first, for Alexander's conquests had put the Greeks in touch with the long astronomical tradition of Babylonia, where astronomers had been watching the heavens long before the Greeks.

Three ancient cities of Mesopotamia had centers of research into astronomy: Uruk, Sippar, and Babylon itself, along with its neighbor,

Borsippa. At Sippar, as Alexander's generals were fighting over his conquests in about the year 300, Kidenas of Sippar, one of the ablest of the Babylonian astronomers, was measuring the length of the year—he calculated it at 365 days, 3 hours, 41 minutes, and 4/16 seconds, which is only 7 minutes, 16 seconds too short. It was probably he, too, who first discovered the precession of the equinoxes, that is, the westward movement of the points where the sun crosses the equator. Presumably there was some transfer of knowledge from the Babylonians to the Greeks. Hipparchus of Nicaea also discovered the precession of the equinoxes, for instance, but whether it was an independent discovery or not cannot be said for certain. The Greek astronomers did not acknowledge any assistance they may have received from Babylonia.

The Macedonian conquest did not interrupt Babylonian research. The Babylonian astronomical diaries, which collected the phenomena of the night sky year by year and coupled it with the important events of the year, continued to be kept without interruption down into the Seleucid period and even after Seleucid rule faded out in Babylon. In fact, Babylonian mathematical astronomy made its most significant advance in the last three centuries of the Hellenistic period. Babylonian astronomers understood the concepts of longitude, latitude, the regression of the lunar nodes, and lunar and planetary periods.

To what extent Babylonian astronomy influenced Greek thought is hard to say, but there is no doubt about the influence of one offshoot of it: astrology. The Babylonians had always taken an interest in omens that appeared at the time of a person's birth, but after about the year 500, we find them casting horoscopes—that is, charts of the signs of the zodiac and the positions of the planets at the time when a person was born so as to foretell his future. Astrology operated on the assumption that the seven heavenly bodies that moved—the sun, moon, Saturn, Jupiter, Mars, Venus, and Mercury, called "the wanderers" or "planets," from the Greek *planêtês*, which means wanderer—and the 12 constellations of the zodiac were linked to the fate of man. Astrology captured the imagination of the man on the street in a way that the elaborate calculations of the astronomers could never do. Astrologers, like magicians, were held in awe. They claimed to know the future and they could be dangerous to the established order.

However much Greek astronomy owed to Babylon, there is no doubt that it made great strides thanks to a number of brilliant scientists. At the beginning of the Hellenistic age, the accepted view was that earth did not move, and the sun, the moon, and the planets revolved around it in concentric circles. Then Heracleides, of Heraclea on the Black Sea, who was a little younger than Aristotle, discovered that Earth turned on its axis and Mercury and Venus revolved around the sun. He was followed by Aristarchus of Samos, who was born about 310 and died in 230. Aristarchus put forward an astounding theory. He suggested that the earth and the planets revolved in circles around the sun, which was far bigger than earth.

That was indeed a startling view. The sun was an important god in pagan religion. He was Helios to the Greeks, identified with Apollo, and he arose in the east each day in the splendor of dawn, and sank into the west each night. In Egyptian religion, the sun was the god Re, and the pharaohs, whose throne now belonged to the Ptolemaic kings, were sons of Re. A universe with the sun in the center would have challenged the worldview of the man in the street, and he was not ready for that. Moreover, Aristarchus had no scientific proof for his heliocentric theory. His fellow researchers, including the great Archimedes, could not make their observations of the night sky fit Aristarchus's conjecture, for Aristarchus made the planets revolve in circles around the sun, whereas their orbits are actually ellipses, and though there was still an astronomer at Seleucia-on-Tigris in the second century, named Seleucus, who continued to defend Aristarchus's heliocentric theory, it was the system put forward by Seleucus's contemporary, Hipparchus of Nicaea, that was generally accepted. In the universe according to Hipparchus, the planets went around the sun and the sun revolved around the earth. It was this organization of the universe that would be taken over and systematized by the Alexandrian astronomer and geographer Claudius Ptolemaeus in the second century C.E., and the Ptolemaic universe remained unchallenged until the Polish astronomer Nicolaus Copernicus (1473–1543) showed that the earth did revolve around the sun.

Mathematics was a field in which the Hellenistic world made great progress, but it was held back by the failure to develop numerals. Arabic numerals, as the name suggests, were developed by the Arabs. The Greeks continued to designate numbers by the letters of their alphabet. Perhaps for this reason, their greatest achievement was in geometry, and the greatest name was Euclid, whose textbook on geometry was used in schools up until the last century. Algebra was not a Hellenistic science, and many problems that today would have algebraic solutions were solved by geometry. For all that, the achievements of the Hellenistic mathematicians were remarkable. Once, when the Delians pleaded with the gods to check a plague on the island, they were told to double the size of an altar there, which was a perfect cube. Eratosthenes, the librarian of the Great Library of Alexandria under Ptolemy III, took up the problem and demonstrated how to double a cube.

Eratosthenes was a universal genius who wrote on many subjects and was known as Number Two, because he was the second greatest expert on a great number of subjects. One of his achievements was to measure the circumference of the earth using geometry. He learned that in the south of Egypt, at Syene, modern Aswan, there was a well so deep that the sun's rays reached the bottom only at high noon. Reasoning that the sun must be directly overhead the well at noon, he then measured the angle of the sun at noon in Alexandria, and once he had the correct distance between Alexandria and Syene, he had one side and two angles of a right-angled triangle. It was then an easy step to deduce what fraction of the earth's circumference the distance between Alexandria and Syene represented. Eratosthenes made his measurement in stades, and unfortunately the stade was not a standardized unit. But the most probable calculation makes his calculation of the circumference 24,662 miles or 39,688.5 km. He was remarkably close to the true circumference (24,857 miles or 40,002 km), and his feat was all the more remarkable because it must have been difficult to get an exact measurement of the distance between Syene and Alexandria. We need not be surprised to learn that Eratosthenes was the first to deduce that a ship could reach India by sailing directly west from Spain, though we had to wait for the Panama Canal before it could be done.

Archimedes of Syracuse was the greatest mathematician of them all, and the discovery for which he is best known now is specific gravity. Hiero, the king of Syracuse, had been given a golden statue and he wanted to know if the gold was pure, but did not want to harm the statue in any way. The solution came to Archimedes as he was in one of the public baths in Syracuse, and in his excitement, he leaped up and ran home naked, shouting *"heureka!"* (I have discovered it!). Archimedes had realized that he could measure the density of gold as compared to that of water, and if the statue did not have the density of gold, it was not pure gold. It did not; the gold was adulterated. Archimedes shared the common view that practical knowledge was no business of a mathematician; nonetheless he was an inventor as well as a theoretician. At the end of his life, the Romans placed his home city, Syracuse, under siege, for it had gone over to Carthage during Rome's long war with Hannibal, and Archimedes invented various mechanical devices to thwart the Roman efforts to storm the city walls. He managed to prolong the siege by three years. But Syracuse did eventually fall, and Archimedes was killed by a Roman soldier who did not recognize him.

TECHNOLOGY

"In mechanics and the application of technology, the Hellenistic age made some progress, but on the whole its achievements were disappointing." So wrote one of the foremost historians of the Hellenistic age, F. W. Walbank, in 1981, and regrettably the verdict is not far wrong.[1] The greatest advances were made in the technology of warfare, which need not surprise us, since war has always nurtured new technological advances. In naval warfare, Alexander himself introduced the new technology of sea battle. Tyre held out against him as he advanced down the coast of the Levant after defeating king Darius at the battle of Issus, and the siege of Tyre lasted for seven months. Tyre was on an island, out of reach of catapults on the mainland. Fortunately Alexander had 230 Phoenician and Greek ships that had surrendered to him after his victory at Issus, and he took 220 of them, placed his catapults on them, and bombarded Tyre from sea. A new idea was born. Hitherto when a warship attacked an enemy vessel, it tried either to ram it or board it. Now if it was equipped with catapults, it could bombard the enemy ship.

But ships had to support the weight of a catapult, and for that, larger naval craft had to be built, and bigger timbers were needed to build them—larch, fir, and cypress were preferred. In the years following Alexander's death, when Ptolemy of Egypt and Antigonos the One-Eyed fought for naval supremacy, new super warships were designed to replace or supplement the trireme, which had been the standard battleship in the classical period. First there appeared the quadrireme, then the quinquereme with its crew of 300 and 120 marines. Then Ptolemy's shipwrights produced a warship with six banks of oars, and Antigonos's son, Demetrius the Besieger of Cities, produced one with seven. A race was on for bigger warships. Demetrius would eventually build a 13, a 15, and a 16. King Philip V of Macedon built a 16 that survived the end of the Macedonian kingdom and went to Rome after Perseus, the last king of Macedon, was defeated. The victorious general, Aemilius Paullus, sailed it to Rome and up the Tiber River as a feature of his victory celebration.

Ptolemy Philopator of Egypt (221–205) built a 40, a huge ship with two bows and two sterns. In other words, she was a catamaran. She had 4,000 rowers and 400 crewmen and she could carry 3,000 soldiers. But she could barely move. All the muscle of her 4,000 rowers was not enough to make this impractical warship sail at more than a snail's pace.

Hellenistic siege warfare was transformed by the invention of artillery. In the classical period, the standard method of taking a well-fortified enemy city was to cut it off from supplies and starve it out. The new artillery appeared first in Sicily before the Hellenistic age began, for at the end of the fifth century, Carthage invaded the island and the dictator of Syracuse, Dionysius the Elder, led the resistance. In 397, he introduced his new siege equipment against the Carthaginian stronghold of Motya on the west of the island, and this siege became a model for later military commanders, including Alexander the Great at the siege of Tyre. But it was the royal engineers of the Ptolemies who devised the right formulas for calibrating machines so that they could hurl a missile of a certain weight a certain distance. This was no easy problem, but by about 275, the royal engineers at Alexandria solved it. Catapults were the artillery of Greek and Roman armies, and they were as effective as the cannon in the early modern period, and less of a danger to the artillerymen.

The great Archimedes invented the so-called Archimedean screw. It was an ingenious screw augur within a cylinder that lifted water when the augur was turned. It was used to pump bilge water out of ships, and to help drain the fields after the Nile flood. Sundials were improved, and a better water clock was invented. Heron of Alexandria invented a steam engine, and a shadowy engineer in Alexandria, Ctesibius, built a water pump, but it was the Romans who developed and used his design. Archimedes invented the compound pulley, and a windlass for hoisting heavy weights. Someone in the Phoenician cities in Syria discovered glass blowing in the last century of the Hellenistic period. Windowpanes became possible; at the Suburban Baths at Herculaneum in Italy, which were destroyed by an eruption of Mount Vesuvius in 79 c.e., one can still see the remains of a glass window that was broken by the pressure of the magma that pressed against it.

But there was no great technological breakthrough. The Hellenistic age would not have an industrial revolution. Some historians have blamed slavery, arguing that as long as labor was cheap, there was no incentive to build laborsaving devices. Another reason may have been the disdain that the aristocratic elite felt for craftsmen and engineers: They belonged to a lower class in the imagination of the philosophers. Yet an important factor that tends to be overlooked was the lack of fuel. Our modern industrial revolution was fueled first by coal, and then by oil, and the Hellenistic world had neither. Heron of Alexandria's steam engine had no future as long as the fuel that boiled the water to produce steam was wood or charcoal. Finding enough sticks and grass to heat the bakers' ovens or warm the water in the public baths was difficult enough.

Yet the Hellenistic period was a golden age for science and technology. We have to wait for the nineteenth century before we find anything comparable. In 1901, a remarkable mechanism was retrieved from a small ship wrecked about the year 76, off the island of Antikythera in Greece. On first sight, it looked like a jumble of gears encased in a wooden box. Advanced image technology has finally revealed what it was: a complete planetarium, showing the orbits of the sun, moon, and the five planets that the Greeks knew— Venus, Mars, Jupiter, Mercury, and Saturn. The instrument is a remarkably sophisticated example of clockwork and shows what Hellenistic technology was capable of producing. Yet the Antikythera Mechanism was essentially a toy. It did nothing to increase production or make life easier for the man who labored in the fields or the workshops.

MEDICINE

The doctor who laid the foundations for Greek medicine was Hippocrates of Cos, who was a contemporary of Socrates, but his influence extended into the Hellenistic period. He was an Asclepiad who practiced in Cos, where the Asclepiads were a hereditary order of physicians connected with the great temple of Asclepius on the island, which they had built in the mid-fourth century, after Hippocrates's death. Whether or not we should call the Asclepiads priests is uncertain, but they treated disease according to rational principles as laid down by Hippocrates; at Cos there were no semimagical treatments suggested to the patient by the god himself appearing in dreams. Our evidence for exactly what Hippocrates taught is unreliable—the Asclepiads themselves were a secretive order—but there is a large collection of medical writings called the *Hippocratic Corpus* that was assembled in Alexandria in the early Hellenistic period, and its contents are various: There are diagnoses, research notes on the progress of diseases, essays, and philosophic ruminations on various medical subjects. The art of healing in the Hellenistic period did not progress a great deal further than Hippocrates.

But research into the nature of the human body did make great progress, and the two great names in Hellenistic medicine were Herophilus and his younger contemporary, Erasistratus. Both lived and did research in Alexandria, though Erasistratus spent a brief period as the court physician of king Seleucus I. Egypt had an ancient medical tradition of its own, and Egyptian embalmers had a great deal of experience dissecting corpses for mummification, but how much information they gleaned about the internal organs from their dissections is nor clear. Probably not a great deal. Nor does it seem likely that the medical schools in Alexandria learned a great deal from the Egyptian doctors. But the hereditary priests in the Egyptian temples did continue their practice of medicine and there may have been some transfer of knowledge.

What separated the research of Herophilus and Erasistratus from their predecessors was that they drew their inferences from observation of the human body, and not from philosophic speculations. Royal patronage made it possible for them to dissect corpses; there was even a tradition that Herophilus dissected prisoners while they were still alive. Some accept the tradition, and others argue against it, but on the whole it seems likely that it is true. There is no doubt, however, that both men did dissect corpses, which their royal patrons provided. Herophilus recognized that the brain, and not the heart, was the center of intelligence. He studied the eye, the liver, the pancreas, the alimentary canal, the genitalia, and the female reproductive organs; he discovered, for instance, the Fallopian tubes and the ovaries. Erasistratus researched the circulation of the blood, and came close to understanding it; however, he thought that the veins carried blood and the arteries pneuma: a Greek word that can be translated as "breath," "the breath of life," or the "animating spirit." He understood the difference between sensory and motor nerves, but he thought that the nerves were hollow tubes that contained fluid. Illness he attributed to plethora—that is, too much blood—or a quantity of food too great for the digestive system to handle. Diet was the proper treatment, not harsh purges.

In the later Hellenistic period, royal patronage was withdrawn from the Alexandrian medical schools and they soon sank into mediocrity. But for a brief period, medical research in Alexandria led the Hellenistic world.

IMPACT OF SCIENTIFIC ADVANCES

It is fair to ask what difference the advances in technology, science, and medicine made to everyday life. Hellenistic architecture and engineering made urban life in the Hellenistic city a different experience from what it had been in the earlier classical period. Did the achievement of the Hellenistic astronomers, inventors, and medical researchers make a similar difference?

This much we can say: The Hellenistic age was a time when horizons were broadened. Many men and women still believed in oracles and astrology, but among the educated classes, at least, there was a new confidence in the ability of the human mind to find solutions to problems. When Hiero of Syracuse wanted to discover the purity of the gold in a golden statue that had come to him as a gift, he turned to Syracuse's most famous scientist, Archimedes, and after much thought, Archimedes discovered specific gravity and solved the problem. That is a very Hellenistic story. It belongs to an age that believed there were rational solutions to everyday problems. The same spirit animated Hellenistic medicine. Curing disease was a problem that research should be able to solve. So also in astronomy: The nature of the universe was a problem that research should be able to solve. It is not fair to ask why the ancient researchers did not evolve into modern scientists. Rather we should recognize how remarkable their progress was.

NOTE

1. Walbank, *The Hellenistic Age*, p. 190.

16

The Persistence
of Hellenistic Culture

The first generation after the death of Alexander the Great was filled with the marching and countermarching of armies, but by the start of the third century, the political structures of the new age were taking shape. It was a new world of city-states and kingdoms, though on the fringes there were still tribal structures. The third century, between the years 300 and 200, was a time when the intellectual horizons of the man on the street must have undergone a radical change. A Greek of the classical period living, let us say, in the year 450, may have heard of Babylon and of India, and he might have listened to tales told by travelers who had been to Egypt and seen the pyramids and the vast temples to be found there. In this new age, a Greek might himself immigrate to Egypt and take up residence there. Travel became easier. The Greek palate became accustomed to new foods. The researchers in the Mouseion in Alexandria produced new ideas about the nature of the universe that upset the views that classical man had held.

The atmosphere became chillier after the year 200, and the reason was Rome. The Hellenistic world had not paid a great deal of attention to Rome. They were barbarians. It is unlikely that many Greeks called the Romans barbarians to their faces, but they did so behind their backs, and the Romans were aware of it. Learning foreign languages did not greatly interest the Greeks—languages were not included in the curriculum taught in their schools—and whereas educated Romans in the Hellenistic period learned Greek, the Greeks did not learn Latin. In fact, educated Romans in the second century developed a love affair with Greek culture. But that did not save the Hellenistic world. The record of Roman imperialism in Greece was appalling. But once the civil wars were over, and the last Hellenistic monarchy was suppressed, the Hellenistic world came to terms with its new lot as the eastern provinces of the Roman empire, thankful that the wars were over at last. Under Julius Caesar's heir, Octavian, who received the title "Augustus" from the Roman senate, a new era of peace began that lasted more or less continuously for two centuries.

Everyday life cannot have changed too much. The Roman empire brought law and order, and the imperial fleet kept piracy in check. In the Hellenistic period, the propertied classes in the Greek *poleis,* who made up the citizen body, had always been apprehensive of the masses—the slaves, the metics, and most dangerous of all, citizens who were landless and poor. This was particularly true in places such as Anatolia, Syria, and Egypt, where the cities were surrounded by a native population who resented the Greek settlers. Under the Roman empire, Greek landowners felt more secure. Roman governors would not tolerate any insurgency of the masses, especially not if they were natives of Egypt or Syria.

In science, medicine, and technology, the age of brilliance that took place in the early Hellenistic period was not repeated. But there was solid progress, at least for two centuries. The physician who transmitted Greek medical science to the Middle Ages was Galen of Pergamon, who began his career as a gladiator doctor, that is, he treated the wounds that gladiators suffered in their fights. He became court physician to the emperor Marcus Aurelius[1] and spent much of his life in Rome. As an anatomist, he collected and corrected the results of earlier generations of research—he proved, for instance, that veins carry blood quite as much as arteries, which brought him closer than Erasistratus to understanding the circulation of the blood, but not close enough. His experimental research on the spinal cord was as good as anything done in the Hellenistic world. But he marks the end of the great tradition of medical research that went back to Hippocrates in the Greek classical period.

In astronomy, Galen's earlier contemporary, Claudius Ptolemaeus of Alexandria, did for Hellenistic astronomy what Galen did for Hellenistic medicine. He produced a definitive account of Hellenistic astronomy according to Hipparchus, whose work he refined with some observations of his own. He produced a geocentric theory of the universe that seemed to fit the movement of the planets that astronomers could observe in the night sky. His great work on astronomy, the *Almagest*—the title came from the Arabic translation of it—dominated astronomical thought in the Middle Ages. Ptolemy was also a geographer, and his *Geography* reproduced the achievements of the Hellenistic geographers and brought them up-to-date. It shaped the geographical imagination of medieval Europe.

Athens found a new role as a university city, where young men came to acquire some knowledge of philosophy. The Romans were no great philosophers; they liked to pick and choose from the great ideas of the past, but they did rather like Stoicism, which fit well with their ideas of Roman virtue. But thanks to her reputation as an intellectual center, Athens survived the wars the marked the end of the Hellenistic age reasonably well. Once peace returned, Roman patronage brought her a new marketplace: a great court surrounded by a colonnade, which was more in tune with Hellenistic agora design than the old agora beside it. At one end of the new Roman market, about 2 B.C.E., a donor named Andronikos of Kyrrhos built the Tower of the Winds, an octagonal building constructed of marble with a frieze showing the eight winds around the top of the outer wall. It was a weather vane and a water clock, and it must have been beautiful, fascinating, and impractical, in the tradition of Hellenistic technology. In the center of the old agora, the emperor Augustus's right-hand man, Marcus Agrippa, built a great *odeion* or music hall, a large roofed building for concerts.

The tradition begun by the Hellenistic kings of making a conspicuous donation to Athens as a mark of respect to the cultural achievement of Greece continued into the second century C.E. The Roman emperor Hadrian,[2] who admired all things Greek, gave Athens her first purpose-built library, and he finished the temple of Olympian Zeus. The Seleucid king Antiochus IV had almost completed it before he died, but then the Romans destroyed the unfinished structure. The Roman general Sulla carried off its columns to Rome and Antiochus's structure lay in ruins. It fell to Hadrian to complete it. It became a great temple belonging to the Corinthian order, which the Romans had adopted as their own.

Odd as it may seem, the educated classes in the Greek world under the Roman empire seem to have looked back on the Hellenistic period with distaste. They preferred to take their inspiration from the classical period. Sculptors imitated the style of the classical period. Part of the reason must have been the taste of the Romans, the new masters of the Greek world, who commissioned copies of classical Greek masterpieces for their houses and gardens. But the preference also affected literature. In the first century, Catullus and his friends, contemporaries of Julius Caesar in Rome, had taken Alexandrian poets as their models. A generation later, after the emperor Augustus had brought peace and stability, the Latin poet Horace looked back to the early Greek poets Sappho and Alcaeus as his models. Alexandrian literature was neglected, and for that reason its chances of survival were poor. Fortunately, the sands of Egypt have inadvertently preserved large numbers of papyri, and hence we have recovered some of these neglected authors.

But the Romans were not the only heirs of Alexander's empire. The old heartland of the Seleucid empire was lost to the Parthians. Briefly, at the start of the second century C.E., the emperor Trajan[3] moved into Mesopotamia and conquered Babylonia, but his empire was overstretched; Trajan's successor, Hadrian, abandoned the province of Mesopotamia. The persistence of Hellenistic culture in Asia under Parthian rule is another question. But in the eastern Mediterranean, the Hellenistic way of life not only persisted—it flourished. In the fifth century C.E., the Roman empire in western Europe faded out; the last Roman emperor in the west was forcibly retired in 476 C.E. But in the east, the empire continued, with its capital in Constantinople and Greek-speaking emperors who called themselves Romans. The Hellenistic world was the foundation of the Byzantine empire, and it did not come to an end until 1453 C.E.

NOTES

1. Emperor from 161 to 180 C.E.
2. Emperor from 117 to 138 C.E.
3. Emperor from 98 to 117 C.E.

Appendix: The Reigns of the Hellenistic Kings

SELEUCID KINGS

Seleucus I Nikator—312–281

Antiochus I Soter—280–261

Antiochus II Theos—261–247

Seleucus II Kallinikos—246–226

Seleucus III Keraunos—226–223

Antiochus III the Great—223–187

Seleucus IV Philopator—187–175

Antiochus IV Epiphanes—175–163

Antiochus V Eupator—163–162

Demetrius I Soter—162–150

Alexander Balas—150–145

Demetrius II Nikator—145–140

Antiochus VI Epiphanes—145–142

Antiochus VII Sidetes—138–129

Demetrius II Nikator—129–125

Cleopatra Thea—126

Cleopatra Thea and Antiochus VIII Grypos—125–121

Seleucus V—125

Antiochus VIII Grypos—125–96
Antiochus IX Kyuzikenos—115–95
Seleucus VI Epiphanes Nikator—96–95
Demetrius III Philopator—95–88
Antiochus X Eusebes—95–83
Antiochus XI Philadelphus—94
Philippus I Philadelphus—94–83
Antiochus XII Dionysos—87–84
Tigranes I of Armenia—83–69
Antiochus XIII Asiatikos—69–64
Philippus II—65–64

PTOLEMAIC KINGS

Ptolemy I Soter—305–282
Ptolemy II Philadelphus—285–246
Ptolemy III Euergetes—246–222
Ptolemy IV Philopator—221–205
Ptolemy V Epiphanes—204–180
Ptolemy VI Philometor—180–145
Ptolemy VII Neos Philopator—145
Ptolemy VIII Euergetes II—170–116
Ptolemy IX Soter II—116–80
Ptolemy X Alexander—114–88
Ptolemy XI Alexander—80
Ptolemy XII Auletes—80–51
Ptolemy XIII Dionysos—52–47
Ptolemy XIV Philopator—47–44
Cleopatra VII—51–30

ANTIGONID KINGS OF MACEDONIA

Antigonos II Gonatas—283–238
Demetrius II Aetolicus—229–221
Antigonos III Doson—221–179
Philip V—221–179
Perseus—181–168

Glossary

Academics—followers of the philosophy taught in Plato's Academy in Athens.

Achaemenids—the royal family of Persia.

agora—an open gathering place in a Greek city where people met and buying and selling took place; a marketplace.

agoranomos—the magistrate who supervised the agora.

amphora—a large earthenware container with a pointed end, used for transporting foodstuffs.

andron—the room in a Greek house reserved for men where symposiums could be held. It can be recognized by a slightly raised platform around the perimeter, intended for the couches where guests reclined to eat, and by the fact that the doorway into the room is off center.

archon—a leader or ruler. In Athens there were nine archons chosen each year by lot, one of whom was, nominally at least, the chief magistrate of the state and gave his name to the year.

Argeads—the royal family of Macedon, supposedly founded by an immigrant from Argos in Greece. With the death of Alexander the Great's son, the family became extinct.

Atargatis—The Aramaic name for the ancient goddess of the Middle East known as Ishtar, Ashtoreth, or Astarte. The Greeks called her the Syrian Goddess.

Attica—the territory belonging to the *polis* of Athens.

basileus—a hereditary king. In some states, however, the title might be given to a magistrate. For example, Athens had a *basileus* chosen each year by lot.

boule—the deliberative council of a *polis.*

bouleuterion—the council house where the boule met.

chôra—the rural territory surrounding the urban center of a *polis.* The term might also apply to areas that did not belong to any city; thus all of Egypt that did not belong to the territories of the three cities, Alexandria, Ptolemais, and Naucratis, was the *chôra.*

Delos—a small island in the center of the Cyclades archipelago, where according to mythology Apollo and his sister Artemis were born.

Delphi—the site on the slopes of Mount Parnassus where Apollo had his most famous oracle.

deme (in Greek, *demos,* plural *demoi*)—1) the common people, the commons; 2) in democracies, the citizen body; 3) in Athens, townships or villages. When Cleisthenes founded the Athenian democracy at the end of the sixth century, he distributed the demes among his newly constituted 10 tribes, which became the basis for Athenian democracy.

democracy—government where the ruling power is in the hands of the *demos,* which for practical purposes was the male citizen body. The term was loosely used in the Hellenistic period.

Dodona—site of an oracle of Zeus in the mountains of Epirus. Zeus worshipped there was known as Zeus *Naios* (the sailor?), and the Hellenistic festival founded there was known as the *Naia.*

drachma—a silver coin worth six obols. A drachma on the Athenian standard, which was widely used in the Hellenistic world, but not in Egypt, weighed about 4.3 grams.

dynasty—a royal family.

fresco—a wall painting where the paint is applied to the plaster before it is dry.

holocaust—a type of sacrifice where the victim is completely consumed by fire.

kleros (plural, *kleroi*)—a parcel of land assigned to someone. Soldiers in Egypt were assigned *kleroi.*

kleruch—a soldier assigned a parcel of land (see *kleros*) for income and support instead of a salary.

krater—a large bowl used for mixing wine with water.

liturgy—a compulsory service that a state imposed on citizens.

mina—a coin worth 100 drachmas. On the Athenian standard, it would weigh about 15 ounces or about 430 grams.

naos—the inmost part of a temple where the god's cult image was housed.

obol—one-sixth of a drachma. The smallest coin denomination.

oligarchy—government where the ruling power is in the hands of a small minority of the citizens.

orchestra—a dancing place. The term refers to the round area in front of the *skene* in a theater, where the chorus danced and sang.

Peripatetics—the followers of Aristotle's philosophy.

peristyle court—a courtyard surrounded on all sides by a portico.

polis—a city or country; a self-governing state consisting of an urban center and its *chôra*.

prytaneion—the town hall in a city-state.

Sarapeion (Latin, Serapeum)—a temple to the god Sarapis.

satrapy—a province of the Achaemenid Persian empire, ruled by a satrap who was both a civil and a military governor.

skene—a tent. It was originally a tent for the use of actors and dancers, and in front of it was the orchestra where the chorus danced and sang. In the Hellenistic theater, the *skene* was usually a permanent building, and at least by the second century there was a raised stage where the dramatic action took place.

stade (stadion)—a unit of distance; 600 Greek feet = 583 English feet, Athenian measurement. At Olympia, a *stadion* was the standard distance of the footrace, and it was about 630 English feet.

stoa—a portico; a long, narrow building with columns along the front, and occasionally along the front and the rear.

talent—6,000 drachmas, which on the Athenian standard would be about 57 pounds of silver, or slightly less than 26 kilograms. *Talent* was also used as a measure of weight.

Bibliography

Ager, Sheila. "Civic Identity in the Hellenistic World." *Greek, Roman, and Byzantine Studies* 38 (1998): 5–21.

Ault, Bradley. "Housing the Poor and Homeless in Ancient Greece." In *Ancient Greek Houses and Households*, ed. Bradley Ault and Lisa Nevett, 140–159. Philadelphia, 2005.

Ault, Bradley, and Nevett, Lisa C., eds. *Ancient Greek Houses and Households: Chronological, Regional, and Social Diversity*. Philadelphia, 2005.

Austin, M. *The Hellenistic World from Alexander to the Roman Conquest: A Selection of Ancient Sources in Translation*. Cambridge University Press, 1981.

Bagnall, Roger S. "Alexandria: Library of Dreams." *Proceedings of the American Philosophical Society* 146/4 (2002): 348–362.

Bagnall, Roger S., and Derow, Peter. *Greek Historical Documents: The Hellenistic Period*. Chico, California, 1981.

Bengston, Hermann. *History of Greece from the Beginnings to the Byzantine Era*. 4th ed., trans. Edmund F. Bloedow. Ottawa, 1988.

Bernard, P. "Ai Khanum on the Oxus: A Hellenistic City in Central Asia." *Proceedings of the British Academy* (1967): 71–95.

Berthold, Richard M. *Rhodes in the Hellenistic Age*. Ithaca, 1984.

Betz, Hans Dieter, ed. *The Greek Magical Papyri in Translation, Including the Demotic Spells* I, Chicago, 1986.

Bickerman, Elias J. *The Jews in the Greek Age*. Cambridge, MA, 1988.

Bilde, Per, Engberg-Pedersen, T., Hannestad, L., and Zahle, J, eds. *Religion and Religious Practices in the Seleucid Kingdom*. Studies in Hellenistic Civilization 1. Aarhus, 1990.

————. *Conventional Values of the Hellenistic Greeks.* Studies in Hellenistic Civilization 8. Aarhus, 1999.

————. *Aspects of Hellenistic Kingship.* Studies in Hellenistic Civilization 7. Aarhus, 1996.

Billows, Richard A. *Antigonos the One-Eyed and the Creation of the Hellenistic State.* Berkeley, 1990.

Bosworth, A. P. "Alexander the Great and the Creation of the Hellenistic Age." In *The Cambridge Companion to the Hellenistic World,* ed. Glenn R. Bugh, 9–27. Cambridge, 2006.

Bugh, Glenn R., ed. *The Cambridge Companion to the Hellenistic World.* Cambridge, 2006.

Bulloch, Anthony W., Gruen, Erich S., Long, A. A., and Stewart, Andrew F. *Hellenistic Constructs: Essays in Culture, History, and Historiography.* Berkeley, California, 1997.

Burstein, Stanley M., ed. and trans. *The Hellenistic Age from the Battle of Ipsos to the Death of Kleopatra VII.* Cambridge: 1981.

————. *The Reign of Cleopatra.* Norman, OK, 2007.

Cartledge, Paul, and Spawforth, Antony. *Hellenistic and Roman Sparta. A Tale of Two Cities.* London, 1989.

Cartledge, Paul. "Spartan Wives: Liberation or License." In *Spartan Reflections,* ed. Paul Cartledge, 106–126. London, 2001.

————. *The Spartans.* Woodstock, 2003.

Casson, Lionel. *Ships and Seamanship in the Ancient World.* Princeton, 1971.

————. *The Ancient Mariners.* 2nd ed. Princeton, 1991.

Chamoux, François. *Hellenistic Civilization.* Trans. Michel Roussel. Malden, MA, 2003.

Clarysse, Willy. "Greeks and Egyptians in the Ptolemaic Army and Administration." *Aegyptus* 65 (1985): 57–66.

Cohen, Getzel. "The Seleucid Colonies: Studies in Founding, Administration, and Organization." *Historia Einzelschriften* 30 (1978).

Dalby, Andrew. *Siren Feasts: A History of Food and Gastronomy in Greece.* London, 1996.

————. *Food in the Ancient World, from A to Z.* London, 2003.

De Souza, Philip. *Piracy in the Greco-Roman World.* Cambridge, 1999.

Eddy, Samuel K. *The King is Dead: Studies in the Near Eastern Resistance to Hellenism, 334–31 B.C.* Lincoln, Nebraska, 1961.

Edinow, Esther. *Oracles, Curses, and Risk among the Ancient Greeks.* Oxford, 2007.

El-Abbadi, Mostafa. *The Life and Fate of the Ancient Library of Alexandria.* Paris, 1990.

Erskine, Andrew, ed. *Companion to the Hellenistic World.* Malden, MA, 2003.

Evans, James Allan, ed. *Arts and Humanities through the Eras: Ancient Greece and Rome, 1200 B.C.E.–476 C.E.* New York, 2005.

Evans, James Allan. "A Social and Economic History of an Egyptian Temple in Greco-Roman Egypt. *Yale Classical Studies,* 17(1961): 143–283.

————. "Dance." In *Arts and Humanities through the Eras*, ed. James Allan Evans, 44–70. New York, 2005.

Fiedler, Manuel. "Houses at Leucas in Acarnania: A Case Study in Ancient Household Organization." In *Ancient Greek Houses and Households*, ed. Bradley Ault and Lisa Nevett, 99–118. Philadelphia, 2005.

Finley, M. I. "Technical Innovation and Economic Progress in the Ancient World." *Economic History Review,* 2nd Series, 18 (1965): 29–45. Reprinted in *The Legacy of Greece: A New Appraisal*, ed. M.I. Finley, 176–195. Oxford, 1981.

Festugière, André-Jean. *Personal Religion among the Greeks*. Berkeley, 1954.

Foley, H. P., ed. *Reflections of Women in Antiquity*. New York, 1981.

Forbes, C. A. *Neoi: A Contribution to the Study of Greek Associations*. Middletown, CT, 1933.

Fraser, P. M. *Ptolemaic Alexandria*. 2 vols. Oxford, 1971.

Furla, Kleopatra, ed. *Priene* ². Athens, 2006.

Gabrielson, Vincent. *The Naval Aristocracy of Rhodes*. Studies in Hellenistic Civilization 6. Aarhus, 1997.

Gardiner, Norman F. *Greek Athletic Sports and Festivals*. London, 1910.

Garland, Robert. *Daily Life of the Ancient Greeks*. Westport, CT, 1998.

Garnsey, Peter. *Famine and Food Supply in the Greco-Roman World*. Cambridge, 1988.

————. *Food and Society in Classical Antiquity*. Cambridge, 1999.

Gentili, Bruno. *Theatrical Performances in the Ancient World*. Amsterdam, 1979.

Grainger, John D. *The Cities of Seleukid Syria*. Oxford, 1990.

————. *Seleucus Nikator: Constructing a Hellenistic Kingdom*. London, 1990.

————. *Hellenistic Phoenicia*. Oxford, 1991.

————. *Alexander the Great's Failure: The Collapse of the Macedonian Empire*. London, 2007.

Green, Peter. "The Dog that Barked in the Night: Revisionist Thoughts on the Diffusion of Hellenism." In *The Crake Lectures, 1984*, Sackville, New Brunswick, 1–26. 1986.

————. *Alexander to Actium: The Historical Evolution of the Hellenistic Age*. Berkeley, 1990

————. *The Hellenistic Age: A Short History*. New York, 2007.

Griffith, G. T. *The Mercenaries of the Ancient World*. Cambridge, U.K., 1935.

Hadas, Moses. *Hellenistic Culture: Fusion and Diffusion*. New York, 1959. Reprint New York, 1972.

Hamilton, J. R. *Alexander the Great*. London, 1973.

Hammond, N. G. L. *The Genius of Alexander the Great*. London, 1997.

Hölbl, Günther. *A History of the Ptolemaic Empire*. Trans. Tina Saavedra. London, 2000.

Hopper, R. J. *Trade and Industry in Classical Greece*. London, 1979.

Hughes, Bettany, and Cartledge, Paul, "At Home with the Spartans," *BBC History Magazine*, December 2002, 34–36.

Jones, A.H.M. *The Greek City from Alexander to Justinian*. Oxford, 1940.

Jones, Prudence J. *Cleopatra. A Sourcebook*. Oklahoma Series in Classical Culture. Norman, OK, 2006.

Kelly-Blazeby, Clare. "Tavernas in Ancient Greece, c. 475–146 B.C.: An Archaeological Perspective." *Assemblage* 6 (*assemblage@sheffield. ac.uk*).

Kuhrt, Amélie, and Sherwin-White, Susan, eds. *Hellenism in the East: The Interaction of Greek and Non-Greek Civilizations from Syria to Central Asia after Alexander*. Berkeley, 1987.

Kyle, Donald G. *Sport and Spectacle in the Ancient World*. Malden, 2007.

Lape, Susan. *Reproducing Athens: Menander's Comedy, Democratic Culture, and the Hellenistic City*. Princeton, NJ, 2004.

Lea, Bonnie. *Palaces and Large Residences of the Hellenistic Age*. Lewiston, NY, 1998.

MacDowell, D. W., and Taddei, M. "The Greek City of Ai-Khanum." In *The Archaeology of Afghanistan from Earliest Times to the Pimurid Period*, ed. F. R. Allahin and Norman Hammond, 218–232. London, 1978.

Macurdy, Grace Harriet. *Hellenistic Queens: A Study of Woman-Power in Macedonia, Seleucid Syria, and Ptolemaic Egypt*. Baltimore, 1932.

Marsden, E. W. *Greek and Roman Artillery*. Oxford, 1968.

Merola, Marco. "Letters to the Crocodile God." *Archaeology* 60/6 (2007): 22–27.

Miller, Harvey F. "The Practical and Economic Background to the Greek Mercenary Explosion." *Greece and Rome* 31 (1984):153–160.

Mossé, Claude. "Women in the Spartan Revolutions of the Third Century B.C." In *Women's History and Ancient History*, ed. Sarah B. Pomeroy, 138–153. Chapel Hill, 1991.

Murray, Oswyn. "Hellenistic Royal Symposia." In *Aspects of Hellenistic Kingship*, ed. Bilde, Engberg-Pedersen, Hannestad, and Zahle, 15–27. 1996.

Murray, Oswyn, and Price, S., eds. *The Greek City: From Homer to Alexander*. Oxford, 1990.

Nielsen, Inge. *Hellenistic Palaces: Tradition and Renewal*. Studies in Hellenistic Civilization 5. Aarhus, 1998.

Parker, R. "New Panhellenic Festivals in Hellenistic Greece." In *Mobility and Travel in the Mediterranean from Antiquity to the Middle Ages*, ed. R. Schleier and U. Zellman, 9–22. Münster, 2004.

Parsons, E. A. *The Alexandrian Library: Glory of the Hellenic World*. London, 1952.

Pickard-Cambridge, Arthur. *The Dramatic Festivals of Athens*. 2nd ed., revised by John Gould and D. M. Lewis. Oxford, 1968.

Pollitt, J. J. *Art in the Hellenistic Age*. Cambridge, 1986.

Pomeroy, Sarah B. *Women in Hellenistic Egypt from Alexander to Cleopatra*. New York, 1984.

———. "Infanticide in Hellenistic Greece." In *Images of Women in Antiquity,* ed. Averil Cameron and Amélie Kuhrt, 207–222. London, 1983.

———. *"Technikai kai Mousikai:* The Education of Women in the Fourth Century and in the Hellenistic Period." *American Journal of History* 2 (1977): 51–68.

———. *Families in Classical and Hellenistic Greece: Representations and Realities.* Oxford, 1997.

Poole, Lynn and Poole, Gray. *A History of the Ancient Olympic Games.* London, 1965.

Rhodes, P. J. *The Greek City States: A Source Book.* Norman, OK, 1986.

Ricotti, Salza Prina, ed., *Eugenia: Meals and Recipes from Ancient Greece.* Trans. Ruth Anne Lotero. Los Angeles, 2007.

Rigsby, Kent J. *Asylia: Territorial Inviolability in the Hellenistic World.* Berkeley, 1997.

Ripay, Pauline. "The Language of Oracular Inquiry in Roman Egypt." *Phoenix* 60 (2006): 304–328.

Robsjohn-Gibbings, T. H., and Pullin, Carlton W. *Furniture of Classical Greece.* New York, 1963.

Rostovtzeff, Michael Ivanovitch. *A Large Estate in Hellenistic Egypt.* Madison, WI, 1922.

———. *A Social and Economic History of the Hellenistic World.* 3 vols. Oxford, 1941.

Rotroff, Susan I. "Material Culture." In *The Cambridge Companion to the Hellenistic World,* ed. Glenn R. Bugh, 136–159.

Samuel, Alan E. "The Shifting Sands of History: Interpretations of Ptolemaic Egypt." *Publications of the Association of Ancient Historians* 2. Lanham, 1989.

Shahbazi, A. Sh. "Iranians and Alexander." *American Journal of Ancient History* 2/1, (2003): 6–38.

Sherwin-White, Susan, and Kuhrt, Amélie. *From Samarkand to Sardis: A New Approach to the Seleucid Empire.* Berkeley, 1993.

Shimron, B. *Late Sparta: The Spartan Revolution, 243–246 B.C.* Buffalo, 1972.

Shipley, Graham. *The Greek World after Alexander, 323–30 B.C.* London, 2000.

Sicker, Martin. *The Pre-Islamic Middle East.* Westport, CT, 2000.

Sifakis, G. M. *Studies in the History of Hellenistic Drama.* London, 1967.

Tarn, W. W., and Griffith, G. T. *Hellenistic Civilization.* 3rd ed. London, 1952.

Tcherikover, Victor. *Hellenistic Civilization and the Jews.* 1959. Reprint New York, 1970.

Thompson, Dorothy J. *Memphis under the Ptolmies.* Princeton, 1988.

Toomer, G. J. *Ptolemy's Almagest.* London, 1994. Reprint Princeton, 1998.

Trümper, Monika. "Modest Housing in Late Hellenistic Delos." In *Ancient Greek Houses and Households,* ed. Bradley Ault and Lisa Nevett, 119–135. Philadelphia, 2005.

Van Bremen, Riet. "Women and Wealth." In *Images of Women in Antiquity,* ed. Averil Cameron and Amélie Kuhrt, 223–242. London, 1983.

Veyne, Paul. *Bread and Circuses: Historical Sociology and Political Pluralism.* Trans. Brian Pearce. London, 1990.

Walbank, F. W. *The Hellenistic World.* Brighton, Sussex, 1981.

Welles, C. B. *Royal Correspondence in the Hellenistic Period.* 1934. Reprint, Chicago: Ares, 1974.

———. *Alexander the Great and the Hellenistic World.* Toronto, 1970.

Westerman, William L. "Warehousing and Trapezite Banking in Antiquity." *Journal of Economic and Business History* 3 (1930–1931): 30–54.

White, K. D. *Greek and Roman Technology.* London, 1984.

Wilkins, John M., and Hill, Shaun. *Food in the Ancient World.* Oxford, 2006.

Worthington, Ian. *Alexander the Great: Man and God.* Harlow, 2004.

Wycherley, R. E. *The Stones of Athens.* Princeton, 1978.

Zaidman, Louise Bruit, and Pantel, Pauline Schmitt. *Religion in the Ancient Greek City.* Trans. Paul Cartledge. Cambridge, 1992.

WEB SOURCES

"Alexander and Alexandria." http://www.hccfl.edu/facultyinfo/kwilliams/files/aschapters1–5.pdf.

"Alexander the Great on the Web." http://www.isidore-of-seville.com/Alexanderama.html.

Attalus.org. "Greek and Roman History, 320–50 B.C." http://www.attalus.org/bc3/index.html.

Journal for the Study of the Old Testament. "On Hellenistic Palaces." http://jot.sagepub.com/cgi/reprint/22/73/116-a.

Livius.org. Features several articles on ancient history. http://www.livius.org.

Livius.org. "The Seleucid Empire." http://www.livius.org/se-sg/seleucids/seleucids.html.

Macedonia.org. "Alexander the Great." http://faq.macedonia.org/history/alexander.the.great.html.

Index

About the Author

JAMES ALLAN EVANS is Professor Emeritus in the department of Classical, Near Eastern, and Religious Studies at the University of British Columbia, Vancouver. He has published several works on ancient Greece and Rome including *The Age of Justinian: The Circumstances of Imperial Power* and *The Emperor Justinian and the Byzantine Empire* (Greenwood 2005).